For
So you
Something about
New Zealand
before coming over
Lots of Love
from Fiona

Christmas 2007

The Big Book of
KIWI
TRIVIA

The Big Book of KIWI TRIVIA

Graham Hutchins

Hodder Moa

National Library of New Zealand Cataloguing-in-Publication Data
Hutchins, Graham.
The big book of Kiwi trivia / Graham Hutchins.
ISBN-13: 978-1-86971-088-0
ISBN-10: 1-86971-088-6
1. New Zealand—Miscellanea. I. Title.
993.002—dc 22

A Hodder Moa Book
Hardback edition published in 2005 by Hachette Livre NZ Ltd
4 Whetu Place, Mairangi Bay
Auckland, New Zealand

This edition published in 2006

Cover design and illustrations by Donovan Bixley
Typeset by BookNZ
Printed by Everbest Printing Co Ltd, China

Contents

The Author.. 7

Acknowledgements 7

All Together Now — The National Anthem in Maori (Te Reo) and English................. 8

History — Old Bones and Stones 10

Population — Counting Heads.. 21

Modern Maori Society — Great Gains for the Greater Good...................... 27

Geography — You Are Here 29

Place Names — Just South of Somewhere 40

Flora & Fauna — Things That Grow in the Night 65

Famous & Infamous New Zealanders — From JHC Sidebottom to Minnie Dean 73

Religion — The Wrath of a Down Under God 81

Agriculture & Farming — From Chew Chong to Chewings Fescue 86

Fishing — Farms Without Grass 92

Trade — Thirty Jars of Pickled Oysters 94

Mining & Energy — Let There Be Light . . . and Ignimbrite...................... 99

Politics — Of 'Sufferage' and Suffering.. 102

Law & Order — Keeping Kiwis in Line... 117

Education — Tomorrow's Schools and the University of Hard Knocks..................... 125

Science & Technology — Of Atoms and Bigger Things............................ 127

Transport — Getting Around Down Under 133

Business & Finance — Business as Usual and Unusual 143

Medical Matters — Of GPs, DDT and HIV... 145

Military Matters — Gunboats up the Waikato.. 149

Disasters — Off the Beaten Track.. 155

Performing Arts — End of the Golden Wether 165

Literature — A Good Keen Man Alone.. 167

Comedy — Do Your Gumboots Lose Their Flavour (in the Woolshed Overnight)? ... 171

Films — Goodbye Pork Piecart... 175

Radio & Television — From a Shed in Newtown to 'Country Calendar'.................. 180

Music — Split Enz of the Earth... 185

Museums & Historic Places — 600 Museums and 6 Million People 193

Women's Affairs — Equality is a Many-lettered Word 195

Fashion & Clothing — Hat Pins, Steel Corsets and Bush Nighties.......................... 198

Food & Drink — Eating Out and In; Drinking In and Out 202

Sport — What New Zealanders Do When They're Not Sleeping............................... 214

Horse Racing — The Bit that Goes with Rugby and Beer.. 250

Hunting — Stalkers and Shooters 256

Social Changes — What Happens When You're Not Looking 259

Kiwi Things — From the 'Long Drop' to the 'Lost Tribe'.. 263

Kiwi Types & Stereotypes — Ankle Biters and Boguns 269

Bizarre Kiwi Behaviour & More 'Normal Stuff' — Don't Try This at Home.............. 273

The Kiwi Language — The Flightless Tongue... 277

Quotations — Caught in Two/Too Many Minds 285

Architecture — Of Beehives and Mirror-glass Canyons.. 290

Horoscopes from Hell — Outcomes and Incomes 293

Official Abbreviations — Of CAB and TAB and OSH.. 296

Fundraising — Bull Rides and Burn-outs 298

Really Important Trivia — The Highest and the Flightless 300

Bibliography.. 302

The Author

Graham Hutchins has been a writer for over 20 years with 23 books to his credit. He has written books on travel, rugby and cricket, and rock music, along with local histories and two novels. His most recent publications, both published in 2004, are *Both Sides Now: The Story of a Kiwi Friendship* and *Eight Days a Week: The Beatles Tour of New Zealand, 1964*. Much of his writing has a humorous bent and, being the possessor of a keen eye for the quirkier aspects of life, he was well positioned to write and compile *The Big Book of Kiwi Trivia*.

Acknowledgements

I wish to thank the hard-working team at Hachette Livre NZ for their support and expertise in helping to bring this book to fruition. I also wish to thank the following for providing the 'movies with a food theme' material — Jenny Hutchins, Mark Win, Paul Fuller and Jo Sutherland.

In addition, the Department of Conservation website was most useful for researching material on the National Parks as were the Wagner Society of New Zealand website for information on Chris Doig, and the Rattle Company website, on John Psathas. The Countrywide website provided some of the information on exotic cattle breeds. Other sources are listed in the Bibliography.

Graham Hutchins

ALL TOGETHER NOW

The National Anthem in Maori (Te Reo) and English

In 1940, the government of the day declared that 'God Defend New Zealand' was to be the national hymn. In 1977, it was given equal status, with 'God Save the Queen', as New Zealand's national anthem. The verses were written by Thomas Bracken in the 1870s, and the music was composed by John Joseph Woods, a schoolteacher from Lawrence in Otago.

ALL TOGETHER NOW

Aotearoa

1. E Ihowa Atua
   O nga iwi matou ra
   Ata whakarongona;
   Me aroha noa
   Kia hua ko te pai;
   Kia tau to atawhai
   Manaakitia mai
   Aotearoa

2. Ona mano tangata
   Kiri whero, kiri ma
   Iwi Maori Pakeha
   Ruapeke katoa,
   Nei ka tono ko nga he
   Mau e whakaahu ke
   Kia ora marire
   Aotearoa

3. Tona mana kia tu!
   Tona kaha kia u;
   Tona rongo hei paku
   Ki te ao katoa
   Aua rawa nga whawhai
   Nga tutu a tata mai;
   Kia tupu nui ai
   Aotearoa

4. Waiho tona takiwa
   Ko te ao marama;
   Kia whiti tona ra
   Taiawhio noa
   Ko te hae me te ngangau
   Meinga kia kore kau:
   Waiho i te rongo mau
   Aotearoa

5. Tona pai me toitu
   Tika rawa, pono pu;
   Tona noho, tana tu;
   Iwi no Ihowa.
   Kaua mona whakama;
   Kia hau te ingoa
   Kia tu hei tauira;
   Aotearoa

God Defend New Zealand

1. God of Nations at Thy feet,
   In the bonds of love we meet,
   Hear our voices, we entreat,
   God defend our free land.
   Guard Pacific's triple star
   From the shafts of strife and war,
   Make her praises heard afar.
   God defend New Zealand.

2. Men of every creed and race
   Gather here before Thy face,
   Asking Thee to bless this place,
   God defend our free land.
   From dissension, envy, hate,
   And corruption guard our State,
   Make our country good and great,
   God defend New Zealand.

3. Peace, not war, shall be our boast,
   But, should foes assail our coast,
   Make us then a mighty host,
   God defend our free land.
   Lord of battles in Thy might,
   Put our enemies to flight,
   Let our cause be just and right,
   God defend New Zealand.

4. Let our love for Thee increase,
   May Thy blessings never cease,
   Give us plenty, give us peace,
   God defend our free land,
   From dishonour and from shame
   Guard our country's spotless name,
   Crown her with immortal fame,
   God defend New Zealand.

5. May our mountains ever be
   Freedom's ramparts on the sea,
   Make us faithful unto Thee,
   God defend our free land,
   Guide her in the nations' van,
   Preaching love and truth to man,
   Working out Thy glorious plan,
   God defend New Zealand.

HISTORY

Old Bones and Stones

Before the Pakeha — archaeological evidence

By AD1000, the first of the occupations had occurred at the moa-hunter site at the mouth of the Waitaki River in North Otago.

Obsidian, a valuable stone, was being used by New Zealand populations by this time.

Large kumara and gourd gardens were established at Palliser Bay, at the southern tip of the North Island, but by 1600 they had been abandoned.

The hunting of moa and seals began in the south of the South Island and continued for 300 years.

Metasomatised argillite from D'Urville Island was used in the manufacture of adzes around AD1100.

Moa used to be hunted in what became known as the Mackenzie Country, in the central South Island.

A significant centre of stone adze-making was established at Opito on the Coromandel Peninsula, where fine-grained Tahanga basalt was found in abundance.

Kumara, originally a tropical plant, was successfully adapted to cooler New Zealand climatic conditions.

By 1200 a number of bird species like the eagle, swan and flightless goose were extinct in the southern part of New Zealand.

Bodies of individuals who had died violent deaths were buried at Palliser Bay in the thirteenth century.

Rangitoto, Auckland's youngest volcano, was formed by a series of eruptions around 1350.

By 1500, inter-tribal fighting in northern areas had led to the building of fortified pa.

Shellfish gathering was an important part of the economy and lifestyle of Maori living along the inner shores of Tauranga Harbour.

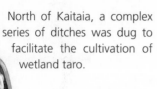

North of Kaitaia, a complex series of ditches was dug to facilitate the cultivation of wetland taro.

As the moa died out, fishing became the focal activity of populations — initially in the North but eventually in the South Island as well.

The first recorded contact between Maori and European occurred when two Dutch ships, the *Heemskerck* and the *Zeehaen*, commanded by Abel Tasman, anchored at Golden Bay, west of Nelson.

Most of New Zealand's pa were constructed between 1500 and the first half of the nineteenth century.

In the northern half of the North Island, where most pa sites were located, there were between 4000 and 6000 pa constructed. Only 100 pa sites were constructed in the entire South Island.

The People Before

Moriori

Moriori discovered the Chatham Islands nearly 1000 years ago and they named the main island Rekohu.

The Moriori abstained from warfare and killing.

Five hundred years ago Nunuku initiated a covenant of peace which allowed Moriori to duel but required them to stop as soon as blood was drawn.

In 1835, Ngati Tama and Ngati Mutunga warriors invaded the Chatham Islands, killing 300 Moriori and enslaving the rest. By 1862 the Moriori population had declined to about 100.

Over 2000 current inhabitants of the Chatham Islands are descended from the Moriori. The principal family names are Davis, Solomon, Riwai and Tamehana.

A $4-million marae was opened on Rekohu in 2005. At the centre of the five-sided meeting house is a pole which records the names of all Moriori living on the island in 1835 when the Taranaki Maori invaded.

Convicts and Missionaries

The arrival of the Europeans

Lt Roux of Marion du Fresne's expedition in 1772 wrote that Maori in the Bay of Islands and Doubtless Bay were 'greatly plagued with venereal disease'.

A severe epidemic called rewha-rewha broke out around 1790 and three-fifths of the population in the south of the North Island were wiped out.

In 1793, two Maori were captured and taken to Norfolk Island to teach the convicts there the art of processing flax.

On 25 December 1814, missionary Samuel Marsden first preached to a Maori congregation in English.

Escaped convicts from New South Wales abducted the sister of the Bay of Islands Taiamai chief Te Morenga. She was eventually released on the east coast of the North Island where she was eaten by the Ngaiterangi people. The Ngapuhi campaigns of 1818 were the upshot of these events.

The musket trade and possession of firearms intensified tribal warfare.

Significant amounts of flax harvested by Maori were exported to Australia.

In 1833, a new cult — Nakahi (The Serpent) — combining aspects of Christianity with Maori spiritual concepts, became established in Northland.

In 1835, British resident James Busby persuaded chiefs in the Bay of Islands and Hokianga to sign a Declaration of Independence, thereby declaring themselves the 'United Tribes of New Zealand'.

Dickie Barrett, a whaler with a very rudimentary knowledge of Maori, acted as interpreter between William and Arthur Wakefield and significant Maori chiefs during land deals that led to the establishment of the Port Nicholson (Wellington) settlement. Confusion reigned, with the Wakefields declaring the chiefs to be happy to sell all the land in the area, apart from certain tracts. The chiefs, by contrast, thought the muskets and other items received in the transactions were merely to cover the right to anchor the Wakefields' ship, the Tory, in the harbour.

The Way it Was

Historical titbits

Zeelandia Nova is the name for New Zealand that appeared on Dutch maps towards the end of the seventeenth century.

Staten Landt was the name Abel Tasman gave New Zealand at a time when he thought New Zealand was the western edge of a large land mass extending westward from South America — in effect a southern continent.

Captain Cook and his crew ate pickled cabbage to ward off scurvy.

Albertlanders was the name given to New Zealand settlers who settled at Port Albert on the Kaipara Harbour in the 1800s.

John Butler was the first ordained clergyman to settle in New Zealand. He arrived in the Bay of Islands in 1819.

New Zealand's first brewery was set up by Joel Polack at Kororareka (now Russell) in the Bay of Islands in 1831.

Luncheon Cove near Dusky Sound is the site of the first known European house in New Zealand.

It took the best part of eight months for the Treaty of Waitangi to be carried around New Zealand to be signed.

In 1842, the Tainui canoe was the first of the canoe traditions to be written down.

New Zealand's first hospital was built in Auckland in 1846.

Dr IE Featherston and Colonel Wakefield fought a duel with pistols in Wellington in 1847. According to accounts, Featherston fired first and missed. Wakefield then fired into the air, announcing that he could not shoot a man who had seven daughters.

The Oriental Banking Corporation set up offices in New Zealand in the 1850s, but decided to pull out just before gold was discovered, thereby missing out on the windfall.

Oil exploration began in New Zealand as early as 1860. Taranaki was the main centre of focus and eventually, in 1886, black gold was discovered there.

Public executions were carried out in New Zealand before 1862.

Before the 1870s, the crime of buggery was punishable by death.

In the early days, the New Zealand Police Force had wooden rattles rather than whistles to sound when they needed to raise the alarm.

Fool's gold, or mica dust and iron pyrites, often gave fake hope to tyros during the various gold rushes.

Gabriel's Gully goldfields produced a million ounces of gold in their first two years of operation.

Hamilton was named after John Fane Hamilton, commander of the HMS *Esk*, who was killed in skirmishes with Maori at Gate Pa.

Despite claims to the contrary, neither Maori nor early settlers used the cabbage tree's bushy crown as a substitute for cabbage, although the Maori derived food from the root.

Shagroons were Australian pastoralists who brought their sheep to Canterbury, Otago and Marlborough to graze on native New Zealand grasslands.

In 1885, there were genuine fears in New Zealand of a Russian invasion. This didn't happen but the perceived threat was taken seriously enough for Auckland men to practise a mock landing at St Heliers Bay.

The first refrigerated shipment of meat bound for Britain left New Zealand aboard the *Dunedin* in 1888.

Ballooning developed as a source of entertainment early in New Zealand's history. In 1889 a 'Professor' Baldwin ascended from Dunedin's Caledonian sports ground. In 1899 a 'Captain Lorraine' lost control of his balloon after his parachute accidentally activated on take-off in Christchurch, providing a total snarl-up. The balloon disappeared beyond the Port Hills and plummeted into the sea. The captain was drowned while attempting to swim to shore.

G and J Park were the first Pakeha sportsmen to cross Cook Strait by canoe — in 1890.

Poneke, the Wellington suburb, derived its name from the Maori version of Wellington's original name, Port Nicholson, which itself had been shortened to Port Nick.

Urukehu were light- or red-haired Maori with blue eyes and fair skin.

Robert Fitzsimmons, who moved to New Zealand as a child, was one of this country's more colourful sporting heroes. In 1891 he won the world middleweight boxing title in San Francisco and in 1901 became heavyweight champion of the world. He was also an eccentric showman and fought in the ring with a lion, a mule and a bear.

The 1898 Dog Tax Rebellion in the Hokianga occurred when local Maori refused to pay a tax on dogs imposed by the local county council.

During the Boer War, which broke out in South Africa in 1899, New Zealand committed 8500 men to the war. Over 200 New Zealanders died as a result of the conflict.

The Three Kings Islands were so notorious for shipwrecks in the early days that goats were released there to provide for survivors.

The Southland town of Lumsden was originally called Elbow.

The largest wooden building in the southern hemisphere is the Old Government Building on Lambton Quay in Wellington.

The Maori language was given a written form by missionaries and British linguists in the nineteenth century.

In the King Country in 1903 there were 173 prosecutions for the selling of sly grog. In 1896 there had been 11.

The Wellington Zoological Gardens were opened in 1906 — New Zealand's first zoo. It was New Zealand's only zoo until 1912.

In New Zealand, Labour Day was originally celebrated on the second Wednesday in October. In 1910 it was changed to the last Monday in October.

The first professional lighthouse keeper in New Zealand was a woman — Mrs M Bennett.

The Rangitikei town of Bulls was first known as Bull's Town, not because it was inundated with polled anguses, but because the surname Bull was associated with the town's founding fathers.

Prior to 1910, mixed swimming in New Zealand used to be a no-no and sunbathing was not allowed.

For the five-year period 1913–1917, the Te Kuiti courthouse recorded 38 convictions for sly-grogging. The amount received in fines was 287 pounds.

'Baby farming' was the term given to the practice of women taking unwanted babies and children into care for money.

The first airmail was carried by plane from Auckland to Dargaville in 1919.

In the Waitomo Licensing District in 1919, 2933 voters opted for National Continuance, 491 for State Purchase and Control and 2372 for National Prohibition. Thirty years later, in 1949, the figures were 9262 for National Continuance, 1306 for State Purchase and Control, and 2351 for National Prohibition.

Illegal bookmakers used to be known as 'turf commission agents'.

Following a national referendum, New Zealanders voted overwhelmingly for the establishment of Totalisator Agency

Boards. The first two TABs were set up at Feilding and Dannevirke.

Prohibition in the King Country reached the stage where the Railways Department, who had been the principal purveyors of the forbidden fruits, issued a proclamation forbidding the transport of liquor. In the face of prohibition, sly grog sales had reached the point where a train running from the Poro-o-tarao tunnel to Ongarue, carried a consignment of 60 cases of spirits for one man. As 'public carriers', the railways found (following an inquiry into their initial refusal to carry such hot property) they had no option but to carry the liquor.

The Methodist Conference of 1922 tried in vain to have mixed swimming condemned, but the tide of public opinion was turning. In due course, 1933 to be precise, even the council by-law forbidding swimmers to loiter on the beach while still in their togs was disregarded.

Mary Muller, a schoolteacher and early feminist, wrote a pamphlet called 'An appeal to the men of New Zealand', using the pseudonym 'Femina'.

'The Bridge to Nowhere', located in the Mangapurua Gorge in the upper Wanganui region, came about as a result of the Great Depression of the 1930s. Although the bridge had been built to improve access to the settlement of Mangapurua, the government closed the village soon after, and the bridge did indeed lead to nowhere.

Before World War II, the New Zealand non-Maori population lived longer than any other national group in the world.

The term 'first echelon', relates to the first group of New Zealand soldiers to serve abroad in World War II. They were mainly volunteers.

During World War II thousands of United States servicemen visited New Zealand for rest and recreation. Reports reveal there was little rest involved, although the recreation created many unwanted 'war babies'. A common complaint levelled at the Americans was that they were 'over-paid, over-sexed and over here'. New Zealand soldiers resented their intrusion and in 1943 the 'Battle of Manners Street' erupted as a result of the ill feeling. A tremendous brawl caused much damage to shop windows, although no one was killed.

During World War II, by the end of 1941, New Zealand women had knitted 95,000 scarves, 94,000 balaclavas, 98,000 mittens and 8600 pairs of socks for the war effort.

An uprising by Japanese prisoners of war at the Featherston POW camp in 1943 led to the killing of 48 Japanese soldiers.

The 40-hour week, based on the notion of eight hours' work, eight hours' play and eight hours' sleep, became generally accepted in 1943.

In the year 1949, at the Te Kuiti courthouse, there were no offences against the Licensing Laws. In the following year there were six.

The town of Te Kuiti has produced arguably New Zealand's greatest rugby player, Colin Meads, and a Prime Minister, James Brendan Bolger. According to some sources it used to make the best sausage rolls in the country.

Twenty people were never accounted for in the wake of the Tangiwai disaster.

The Wellington to Auckland night express train was derailed after flood waters from a breach in the crater lake of nearby Mt Ruapehu destroyed the Tangiwai rail bridge.

Uranium was discovered in the lower Buller Gorge in 1955.

Dry towns were not settlements immune from flooding, but those in which prohibition of alcohol had taken hold. Te Kuiti and Oamaru are examples which only became 'public places', in terms of pubs, in the 1960s. As recently as 1998, city precincts like Tawa, Mt Roskill and Mt Eden continued to be dry.

New Zealand was shocked in 1963 by the Bassett Road Machine-gun Murders that disturbed the genteel Auckland suburb of Remuera. Two sly-groggers were executed in a gangland-style shooting.

A group of fossil-hunters found evidence in an area north of Napier to suggest that dinosaurs once lived in New Zealand.

'God Defend New Zealand', as a feature of Olympic Games, was first heard at the 1972 Olympic Games in Munich when the rowing eight won gold.

During the Springbok tour of 1981, three clowns who had been among the protesters were beaten up by police. Three years later they received $30,000 in damages.

In 1982 at Waitangi, on Waitangi Day, Governor-General David Beattie was struck in the chest by a golf ball and in the back by an egg. Don Brash the leader of the National Party was hit by a clump of sod at Waitangi in 2004. In earlier years, Keith Holyoake was badly jostled and Prime Minister Helen Clark was reduced to tears.

In 1983, while protesting against the visit of the US nuclear warship *Texas*, Wellington feminists distributed a leaflet, advising women to 'cross your legs for peace'.

The first Neighbourhood Support Groups were set up in 1983. By the end of the year there were 18,000 such groups in New Zealand.

By early 1986 more than 100,000 New Zealanders were out of work.

In 1988, when AJ Hackett jumped from the Auckland Stock Exchange tower, it was the world's first bungy jump from a building.

In 1988, two members of Ahi Kaa, a Maori radical group, travelled to Libya to visit Colonel Gaddafi's regime.

In 1988, the Maori Language Act rendered Maori an official language.

In 1988, Kohanga Reo or 'Language Nests', promoting the use of the Maori language in early childhood education, commenced operation.

In 1988, 432 branches and agencies of the Post Office were closed as market forces, unleashed by Rogernomics, kicked in.

In the year 2000, poker machines ('pokies') in clubs and pubs turned over nearly $3.75 billion.

A Whale of a Time

Whaling and sealing

In 1792, the British whaling ship *William and Ann* was probably the first vessel to hunt whales off northern New Zealand.

By 1804, whaling vessels were stopping off at the Bay of Islands.

Foveaux Strait was discovered by an American sealing captain Owen F Smith in 1804.

A Maori named Moehanga, who travelled on a whaling boat called the *Ferret*, was the first Maori to visit England — in 1805.

A party of sealers died of cold and hunger in the Auckland Islands in 1807.

The first legally-upheld purchase of land in the South Island was granted to Peter Williams of the shore whaling station at Preservation Inlet.

The first on-shore whaling in New Zealand was based at Te Awaiti in Tory Channel.

The first sealing gang in New Zealand landed from the *Britannia* at Dusky Sound.

The first French whaling ship, the *Mississippi*, arrived in New Zealand waters in 1836.

In 1839, a Maori, named Bailey, became mate of the *Earl Stanhope*, a whaling vessel. However, he could not become a British whaling captain because he was not a British subject.

By the 1840s, the depletion of New Zealand's seal population had made the industry uneconomic.

The Maori chief Hongi travelled to England on the British whaling ship the *New Zealander*.

The whaleboat *Ocean*, and its commander Abraham Bristow, discovered the Auckland Islands.

Maori were well known as excellent sailors and whalers.

There was an active and profitable trade in native slave-girl prostitution to satisfy the needs of whalers and other sailors. The earning power of the girls, many of whom had been hired 'to do the washing', became an important component of the New Zealand economy at the time.

Captain Jean Langlois, a whaler, helped promote and develop the French colony at Akaroa.

Captain Grono, in the *Governor Bligh*, discovered a handful of sealers on New Zealand's West Coast who had been stranded there for three years.

When a method was discovered for making gas from whale oil, the demand for New Zealand oil increased dramatically.

William Tucker, a sealer, was one of the first people to sell preserved Maori heads (toi moko) in Sydney. Out of revenge, he was killed by Maori.

'New Zealand Tom' was an old sperm whale bull feared in New Zealand waters.

Joseph Perano was the founder of New Zealand's modern whaling industry.

Ambergris, found in whales, was used in the manufacture of perfume. A lump of ambergris weighing 636 kilograms, found in a whale in New Zealand waters, remains the world's record find.

Whaling ended in the Kaikoura region in 1907.

In 1964, New Zealander Trevor Norton harpooned the last whale killed in New Zealand waters.

In 1978, an Act of Parliament was passed protecting all marine mammals within 200 nautical miles of New Zealand.

Settling Down Under

Settlement and off-shore matters

New South Wales convict George Bruce is generally accepted as New Zealand's first European settler.

In 1839, William Rhodes transported 40 cattle from Sydney to start the South Island's first cattle station at Akaroa.

In 1839, John Balleny discovered islands south of New Zealand which he named after himself.

James McKay, assistant Native Secretary for the South Island, bought the West Coast from the Poutini Ngaitahu for 300 pounds.

In 1842, 500 Scottish settlers arrived at Auckland.

The Wairau Affray of 1843 was the first major clash between Maori and European during the settlement phase of New Zealand's history.

A clause in the Treaty of Waitangi gave Crown appointees first rights to buy land offered for sale by Maori. A system was started whereby the Crown bought land and resold it to European settlers, often at a handsome profit.

Arthur, one of Edward Gibbon Wakefield's brothers, was killed in the Wairau Affray.

A force of 700 soldiers belonging to the Royal New Zealand Fencibles was allocated to four military settlements located south of Auckland at Howick, Onehunga, Otahuhu and Panmure.

The town of Puhoi, just north of Auckland, became established in 1863 when 83 Bohemians began a settlement there.

A construction camp — at the railhead of the southern part of the North Island Main Trunk — was the beginning of the town of Te Kuiti.

A settlement of Presbyterians from Nova Scotia was established at Waipu, in Northland.

In 1871, 60 Scandinavian settlers arrived at Foxton.

Bernhardt Gudmundsen, a Norwegian, settled in New Zealand in 1872. Among his earlier adventures, before arriving in his new country, was the time when he jumped ship in the West Indies, contracted yellow fever and lost his shock of red hair. When it grew back it was jet black.

In 1876, the Bank of New Zealand opened in Levuka, Fiji.

The Wellington and Manawatu Railway Company, a private organisation, was set up to complete the line from Wellington to Manawatu. The company played a large part in the opening up of the Horowhenua area with three towns being named after company directors: Shannon, Levin and Plimmerton.

A syndicate named the 'Twelve Apostles' bought the Heretaunga Block at Hastings and established 144 residential sections.

In 1887, New Zealand annexed the Kermadec Islands.

Rotorua was established to serve as a base for the growing tourism trade at what was known as the Hot Lakes District.

Alexander von Tunzelmann became, in 1895, the first New Zealander to set foot on the Antarctic continent.

Eketahuna was originally called Mellenskov.

In 1901, New Zealand annexed the Cook Islands and Niue.

The town of Marton was established when four settlers subdivided their properties in the town.

James Clark Ross discovered the Ross Ice Shelf, McMurdo Sound and Ross Island. Ross Dependency is also named after him.

When Western Samoa gained independence it signed a Treaty of Friendship with New Zealand.

Marie Derby of Canterbury Museum was the first New Zealand woman to work in Antarctica.

Thelma Rogers, a New Zealand geophysicist, became the first woman to spend a winter in Antarctica.

With the outbreak of World War I, New Zealand military forces occupied Western Samoa, which had been under German control. In 1920, New Zealand received a League of Nations mandate to govern Western Samoa.

Featherston, in the Wairarapa, was originally named Burlings.

In 1929, New Zealand Police shot 11 Samoan supporters of the Mau Nationalist movement while the latter were demonstrating in Apia.

New Zealander PJ Twomey founded the Lepers Trust Board, to help lepers in Fiji.

Pamela Young, a Canterbury University biologist, was the first woman to reach the South Pole.

New Zealand troops occupied Fanning Island during World War II, to defend the cable station located there.

In 1953, the Resident Commissioner of Niue Island, Hector Larsen, was murdered.

In 1954, the hydro-town of Roxburgh had a population of more than 3000.

In 1957, Sir Edmund Hillary led a team of New Zealanders to the South Pole. They were the first to accomplish the feat on foot since Captain Scott in 1911–12.

The Cook Islands gained independence in free association with New Zealand in 1965.

The first New Zealand Race Relations Conciliator was Harry Dansey, in 1972.

In 1973, the New Zealand Government sent a naval frigate to Mururoa Atoll in protest at the testing of French nuclear weapons in the Pacific.

A joint New Zealand-French expedition made the first ascent of Mt Erebus in Antarctica in 1974.

Niue achieved self-government in free association with New Zealand in 1974.

New Zealand doubled its financial aid to Tonga after the latter commenced diplomatic relations with the Soviet Union in 1976. The fear of Russian influence was the motivating factor.

Go for Gold

New Zealand gold rushes

Coromandel. In 1842, gold was discovered by whalers but there was a lack of evidence of vast amounts in the area. Later, in 1852, a three-month-long gold rush failed to refute the earlier claims.

Marlborough. In 1864, gold was found in the Wakamarina River near Havelock and 6000 miners converged on the area. Before too long all the alluvial gold had been accounted for.

Nelson. In 1856, gold was found in payable quantities near Collingwood, in the Nelson district, and in 1857 there was a sudden rush to the Collingwood-Takaka district. Ten years later the gold returns were dwindling.

Otago. In 1861, the first significant gold rush in New Zealand occurred, following the discovery of gold by Gabriel Read near Tuapeka. Further discoveries were made near Cromwell on the Clutha River, at Waitahura, the Shotover Valley and on the Taieri Plains. Two years later the gold rush waned.

Thames. In 1867, gold miners from the south began arriving. Unlike in the alluvial fields of the South Island, Thames gold was located in deep quartz veins, and this proved so costly to extract that, once the small alluvial fields were exhausted, the itinerant gold rushers moved on. The days of New Zealand's gold rushes were at an end.

West Coast. In 1865 and 1866, gold was found at Okarito, Bruce Bay, the Grey River, Tiromoana and Charleston, but the boom began to decline in 1867. The West Coast fields were the most productive after the Otago fields.

POPULATION

Counting Heads

In 1840, the Maori population of New Zealand was estimated to be approximately 100,000. In the same year, 1000 English settlers arrived at Petone Beach.

In 1856, there were 48,193 Europeans living in New Zealand. At about the same time there were roughly 60,000 Maori, a dramatic drop in numbers since the arrival of European settlers.

The impact of the gold rushes in the South Island in terms of population growth can be seen by the fact that, in 1866, more than 43 per cent of migrants entering New Zealand did so through the West Coast port of Hokitika.

In 1867, the largest Maori tribal groups were listed as Ngapuhi (5804), Ngati Porou (4500) and Ngati Maru (3670).

Only 65 per cent of New Zealand's European population in 1871 were literate.

In 1873, the New Zealand Government offered free passage to migrants from Europe.

The first Chinese settlers in New Zealand came for the gold available in the West Coast goldfields.

In 1886, the average New Zealand population density reached 2.2 per square kilometre (5.6 per square mile). The highest density was recorded in Canterbury province; the lowest in Marlborough.

Pakeha had an average life expectancy of more than 60 years in the first decade of the twentieth century.

In 1908, New Zealand's population passed one million.

In 1918, a global influenza epidemic claimed approximately 5500 New Zealand European victims and 1200 Maori.

In 1925, permission to allow 1000 British immigrants per month became ratified.

By 1926, more than two-thirds of New Zealand's 1.4 million now lived in cities.

In 1944, over 800 Polish refugees settled in New Zealand.

The post-war 'baby boom' became a significant factor in New Zealand's population increase.

New Zealand's birth rate in 1971 was 36.5 per 1000 people. In 2001 it had plummeted to 15.3.

Big Smokes

Urban population figures at the 2001 Census

Urban Area	2001
Auckland	1,074,513
Wellington	339,750
Christchurch	334,107
Hamilton	166,128
Dunedin	107,088
Tauranga	95,697
Palmerston North	72,681
Hastings	59,142
Napier	54,534
Nelson	53,688
Rotorua	52,608
New Plymouth	47,763
Invercargill	46,305
Whangarei	46,047
Wanganui	39,423
Kapiti	33,669
Gisborne	31,772
Timaru	26,748
Blenheim	26,547
Masterton	19,497

Ethnicity in the City and Elsewhere

Ethnic groups in New Zealand

Selected ethnic group	1991 Census Number	1991 Census Percentage of Population [1,2]	2001 Census Number	2001 Census Percentage of Population [1,2]
New Zealand European	2,618,445	78.3	2,689,308	75.0
Maori	434,847	13.0	526,281	14.7
Samoan	85,743	2.6	114,432	3.2
Chinese	44,136	1.3	100,203	2.8
Indian	29,820	0.9	59,823	1.7
Cook Island Maori	37,233	1.1	51,141	1.4
Tongan	23,175	0.7	40,713	1.1
English	53,325	1.6	34,074	1.0
Dutch	24,732	0.7	27,396	0.8
Niuean	14,427	0.4	20,148	0.6
Korean	930	—	19,026	0.5
British	16,659	0.5	16,524	0.5
South African	2007	0.1	14,889	0.4
Scottish	14,094	0.4	12,792	0.4
Irish	7392	0.2	11,199	0.3
Filipino	4917	0.1	11,091	0.3
Japanese	2970	0.1	10,002	0.3
Fijian	5100	0.2	7041	0.2
Tokelauan	4146	0.1	6204	0.2
Sri Lankan	2406	0.1	6042	0.2
Arab	177	—	2856	0.1
Croat/Croatian	171	—	2502	0.1
Iraqi	246	—	2145	0.1

1. Includes response unidentifiable, response outside scope and not stated.
2. Calculated in terms of specified cases only.
— too small to be expressed.
Note: The number of responses is greater than the total population, as multiple responses are counted.

Welcome Aboard

Refugee numbers and nationalities settled under New Zealand's Refugee Quota System

Nationality	1991	1993	1995	1997	1999	2001
				Year[1]		
Afghan	—	—	—	—	41	46
Bosnian	—	31	21	4	—	—
Burmese	—	1	—	—	—	310
Eritrean	—	—	—	1	47	15
Ethiopian	—	—	50	72	199	54
Iranian	40	2	6	24	39	87
Iraqi	203	7	318	266	130	82
Kampuchean	70	50	3	2	—	—
Laotian	20	—	—	62	—	5
Somali	—	94	39	21	212	119
Sudanese	—	—	8	14	33	4
Vietnamese	245	219	341	23	—	—
Other	104	8	36	38	25	24
TOTAL	**682**	**412**	**822**	**527**	**726**	**746**

1. 1 July 1991–30 June 2001

Mainly North of South

Maori ethnic groups by region

Region	2001 Census Number	Percentage	Region	2001 Census Number	Percentage
NORTH ISLAND			SOUTH ISLAND		
Northland	40,734	7.7	Tasman	2778	0.5
Auckland	127,626	24.3	Nelson	3219	0.6
Waikato	72,822	13.8	Marlborough	3894	0.7
Bay of Plenty	63,654	12.1	West Coast	2547	0.5
Gisborne	19,365	3.7	Canterbury	31,632	6.0
Hawke's Bay	32,088	6.1	Otago	10,542	2.0
Taranaki	14,559	2.8	Southland	10,038	1.9
Manawatu-Wanganui	39,267	7.5	**South Island total**	**64,650**	**12.3**
Wellington	51,123	9.7	**TOTAL**	**525,888**	**100.0**
North Island total	**461,238**	**87.7**			

Mainly North of the Bombays

Asian ethnic group by region

Region NORTH ISLAND	2001 Census Number	Population	Region SOUTH ISLAND	2001 Census Number	Population
Northland	1998	0.8	Tasman	366	0.2
Auckland	151,602	63.7	Nelson	861	0.4
Waikato	12,021	5.0	Marlborough	387	0.2
Bay of Plenty	5202	2.2	West Coast	246	0.1
Gisborne	621	0.3	Canterbury	19,431	8.2
Hawke's Bay	2937	1.2	Otago	5766	2.4
Taranaki	1500	0.6	Southland	849	0.4
Manawatu-Wanganui	6564	2.8	**South Island total**	**27,906**	**11.7**
Wellington	27,819	11.7	**TOTAL**	**238,170**	**100.0**
North Island total	**210,264**	**88.3**			

Whose Canoes?

Maori tribal groupings

	Tribe	Canoe
Northern Tribes (Tai Tokerau)	Aupori Rarawa Ngati Kahu Ngapuhi Ngati Whatua	Kurahaupo and others
Tainui Tribes	Ngati Tai Ngati Paoa Ngati Maru Ngati Tamatera Ngati Whanaunga Waikato Maniapoto	Tainui
Taranaki Tribes	Ngati Tama Ngati Mutunga Ngati Maru Te Ati Awa	Tokomaru
	Taranaki	Kurahaupo

	Nga Ruahine Ngati Ruanui Nga Rauru	Aotea
Wanganui Tribes	Ngati Haua Te Ati Hau	Tainui and Arawa Aotea and Kurahaupo
Manawatu Tribes	Ngati Ruakawa	Tainui
	Ngati Apa Rangitane Muaupoko	Kurahaupo
Wellington Tribes	Te Ati Awa Ngati Toa	Tokomaru Tainui
Arawa Tribes	Arawa Ngati Tuwharetoa	Arawa
Bay of Plenty Tribes	Ngai Terangi Ngati Ranginui	Mataatua and Tainui
	Ngati Awa Tuhoe Whakatohea	Mataatua
	Ngai Tai Whanau-a-Apanui	Tainui Mataatua and Horouta
East Coast Tribes (Tai Rawhiti)	Ngai Porou Rongowhakaata	Horouta
	Te Aitanga-a-Mahaki Ngati Kahungunu	Takitimu
	Rangitane	Kurahaupo
South Island Tribes	Ngai Tama Ngati Mutunga Te Ati Awa	Tokomaru
	Rangitane Ngati Toa	Kurahaupo Tainui
	Poutini Ngai Tahu Ngati Mamoe	Takitimu and others

MODERN MAORI SOCIETY

Great Gains for the Greater Good

Maori have a higher rate of natural increase than other New Zealanders, with the Maori fertility rate of 2.5 births per woman in 2001 being 34 per cent higher that that of non-Maori women.

The Treaty of Waitangi was described by the government in 1877 as 'a simple nullity'. However, in 1987, a Court of Appeal ruling confirmed the special relationship between Maori and the Crown as an ongoing partnership.

The Waitangi Tribunal was set up under the Treaty of Waitangi Act in 1975. By 2001, the Tribunal had registered 900 Treaty claims.

Te Kohanga Reo is a whanau base where Maori language, values and customs are taught to pre-school children by their kaumatua.

Maori marae in need of financial assistance are able to apply to the Lottery Grants Board for funding.

The mission of the Maori Language Commission is 'Ma te reo, Me te reo, Mo te reo' — to promote, protect and progress the Maori language.

In 1947, 'Maori' replaced 'native' in Crown documents.

By 1971, 60 per cent of Maori lived in cities.

Witi Ihimaera's *Pounamu Pounamu* was the first collection of short stories to be published by a Maori writer.

Dame Whina Cooper led the famous land march (hikoi) in 1975.

Eva Rickard led the occupation of the Raglan golf course in 1978.

In 2003, the Court of Appeal ruled that Maori could take claims for customary ownership of the seabed and foreshore to the Maori Land Court.

Dot Co Dot Aotearoa

Ipurangi — Maori websites

Maori enterprise	Location	Core business	Website
Aotearoa Traditional Maori Performing Arts Society	Wellington	Maori performing arts	www.atmpas.org.nz
Biofarm Products Ltd	Manawatu	Organic dairy products	www.biofarm.co.nz
Compudigm International Ltd	Wellington	Geographic information systems software	www.compudigm.com
Huia Ltd	Wellington	Publishers	www.huia.co.nz
Kia Kaha Clothing	Wellington	Maori clothing designs	www.kiakaha.co.nz
Ngai Tahu Fisheries	Christchurch	Fisheries products	www.ngaitahufisheries.co.nz
Ngaru Toa Tribal Surf	Gisborne	Surf clothing	www.ngarutoa.com
Ngati Porou Forests Ltd	Ruatoria	Forestry owners	www.npwfl.co.nz
Power Beat Ltd	Hamilton	Technology research	www.powerbeat.com
Straker Interactive Ltd	Auckland	Software developers	www.straker.co.nz
Tairawhiti Pharmaceuticals	Te Araroa	Manuka oil cosmetics	www.manuka-oil.com
Taitokerau Maori Tourism Association	Northland	Tourism marketing	www.taitokerau.com
Tamaki Maori Village	Rotorua	Maori tourism	www.maoriculture.co.nz
Tawhiri Architects	Wellington	Architects and designers	www.tawhiri.co.nz
Te Haeata Productions	Auckland	Film and television	www.tehaeata.co.nz
Te Ohu Kai Moana	Wellington	Fisheries assets	www.tokm.co.nz
Te Whare Wananga O Raukawa	Otaki	Maori tertiary education	www.twor.ac.nz
Tiki Designs	Te Awamutu	Maori arts and crafts	www.tiki.co.nz
Tohu Wines Ltd	Nelson	Wine marketing	www.tohuwines.co.nz
Wakatu Incorporation	Nelson	Maori incorporation	www.wakatu.org.nz
Whale Watch	Kaikoura	Tourism marketing	www.whalewatch.co.nz

GEOGRAPHY

You Are Here

The Hen and Chicken Islands, off the Northland coast, are thus named because of the way they are aligned: like a brood of chickens behind a hen.

Although Lake Ellesmere is the fifth largest lake in New Zealand, it is never more than 3 metres deep at any point.

Levels is a farming district in South Canterbury. It is not level, but undulating.

The Auckland Islands are located nowhere near Auckland. They can be found 320 kilometres south-west of Stewart Island.

Barley is believed to be the first cereal crop cultivated by man. It has been grown in New Zealand since the early days of European settlement.

Lake Benmore is the largest man-made lake in New Zealand. The lake occupies considerable space behind Benmore dam. A smaller man-made lake — Lake Laird — lies at the base of the dam.

Much of the Waikato plains have been recovered from peat swamps.

Christchurch has more carbon monoxide in its air than either Auckland, Dunedin, Hamilton or Wellington, individually.

There are more than 200 mountains higher than 2300 metres in the South Island.

At Scott Base in Antarctica, winter temperatures drop as low as –27°C.

Lake Grassmere, in Marlborough, is the site of New Zealand's only commercial salt operation. It derives its name from Lake Grasmere in the Lake District of England — a spelling mistake led to Grassmere.

The Maori translation of pukaki — as in Lake Pukaki — is 'bunched up neck'.

Industry is the largest consumer of electricity in New Zealand, accounting for 45 per cent of supplies in 1997.

In February 1998, all major underground electric cables feeding the Central Business District of Auckland failed because of extremely hot weather. The subsequent blackout lasted for two months.

New Zealand has over 8000 kilometres of coastline.

Anniversary Day for the Chatham Islands is 28 November.

Dunedin is known as the 'Edinburgh of the South'.

Napier is known as the 'Art Deco capital of the world'. It owes its distinctive architecture to the 1931 earthquake. When the city was rebuilt it was in the art-deco style of the day.

The line of latitude midway between the equator and South Pole — 45 degrees south — is marked on the roadside of State Highway 1 near Hilderthorpe, north of Oamaru.

New Zealand is 26.9 million hectares in area. It is similar in size to Japan and the British Isles.

The Chatham Islands are 850 kilometres to the east of Lyttelton.

Dating from 1842, the administrative boundaries of New Zealand, including the minor islands, extend from 33 degrees to 53 degrees south (latitude) and from 162 degrees east to 173 degrees west (longitude).

The Ross Dependency in the Antarctic has been under New Zealand's jurisdiction since 1923.

Its land area is estimated to be 414,000 square kilometres.

The total area of New Zealand is 268,103 square kilometres.

Artificial harbours have been built at Gisborne and Napier.

Less than one-quarter of New Zealand lies below 200 metres.

Less than one-quarter of New Zealand's North Island runs in a south-west direction from East Cape to Turakirae Head — generally parallel to the coast.

The mountain systems of the North Island are: Raukumara, Huiarau, Ruahine, Tararua, Rimutaka, Ahimanawa, Kaweka, Kaimanawa, Hauhangaroa, Rangitoto and Moehau. Mounts Ruapehu, Ngauruhoe, Tongariro and Egmont/Taranaki stand alone.

Mt Egmont/Taranaki is the only area on the west coast of the North Island that reaches above 1200 metres.

The mountain ranges of the South Island are the Southern Alps, Victoria, Brunner, Lyell, Tasman Mountains, Paparoa, St Arnaud, Richmond, Spenser Mountains, Kaikoura, Seaward Kaikoura, and a series of ranges dominating the mountainous Fiordland and north-western Southland regions.

New Zealand has at least 223 named mountain peaks of 2300 metres or more in altitude.

The largest glacier in New Zealand is the Tasman Glacier, being 29 kilometres long.

Other glaciers that flow, albeit slowly,

eastward are the Murchison, the Mueller, the Godley and the Hooker.

The two largest westward-flowing glaciers are the Fox and the Franz Josef.

On the slopes of Mt Ruapehu in the North Island there are seven relatively small glaciers.

Of New Zealand rivers, the Waikato and Rangitaiki in the North Island, and the Waitaki, Cobb, Clutha and Waipouri in the South Island are utilised for major hydro-electric schemes.

Cook Strait is defined geographically as: Northern limit, a line between the northern point of Stephens Island and Kapiti Island; Southern Limit, a line between Cape Palliser and Cape Campbell.

Lake Benmore, New Zealand's largest man-made lake, covers 75 square kilometres in area, and is made up of two arms, the main arm being 30 kilometres in length and the Ahuriri Arm, 18 kilometres in length.

New Zealand's deepest lake is Lake Hauroko, with a maximum depth of 462 metres. Of the other South Island lakes, Lake Hawea is 392 metres deep at its deepest point and Lake Wakatipu, 378 metres.

Lake Taupo in the North Island, sometimes considered New Zealand's deepest lake, has a maximum depth of 159 metres and is nowhere near as deep as Lake Waikaremoana, another North Island lake, which boasts a maximum depth of 256 metres.

Compared with some other areas of the Pacific margins, like Japan, Chile and the Philippines, New Zealand experiences only moderate earthquake activity.

The highest daily rainfall on record in New Zealand is 582 millimetres which fell at Rapid Creek in the Hokitika Catchment area, where the mean rainfall exceeds 6000 millimetres.

In the South Island, July and August are the least windy months.

Thunderstorms in New Zealand are not numerous.

Hail is most commonly experienced in the south-west of New Zealand.

Humidity in New Zealand is usually between 70 and 80 per cent in coastal areas and 10 per cent lower inland.

Low humidity, from 30 per cent down to five per cent, sometimes occurs in the lee of the Southern Alps.

Petone, a suburb of Wellington, was originally named Britannia.

Te Kuiti is known as the shearing capital of New Zealand.

Auckland has two harbour bridges — the obvious one and a modest structure that crosses the upper reaches of the Waitemata Harbour near Hobsonville.

Golden Bay was initially called Murderer's Bay by Abel Tasman, when four of his men were killed by Maori. It was later called Coal Bay when coal was discovered at Takaka, but became Golden Bay in 1857 when gold was discovered nearby.

Approximately 1300 people live on Great Barrier Island.

Greymouth's keening wind is known as the 'Barber'.

'Gentle Annie' is the name of: a hill on the Napier-Taihape Road; another hill west of Gisborne; a road on the eastern side of the Whanganui River; and a creek that flows into the Kawarau River in Otago.

Taihape is the 'Gumboot capital of the world' and holds an annual gumboot-throwing contest.

The Taieri River, in Otago, is the fourth longest in New Zealand.

Tainui is a suburb of Dunedin.

The Sutherland Falls form the source of the Arthur River.

Kaipara Harbour is New Zealand's largest in terms of area. It is 65 kilometres long but is comparatively shallow.

The highest temperature recorded in the North Island was 39.2°C at Ruatoria on 7 February 1973. The highest in the South Island was 42.4°C at Rangiora and Jordan, Marlborough on 7 February 1973.

The lowest temperature recorded in the North Island was –13.6°C at Chateau Tongariro on 7 July 1937. The lowest in the South Island was –21.6°C at Ophir on 3 July 1995.

The highest annual sunshine hours recorded for the North Island was 2588 at Napier in 1994. The highest for the South Island was 2711 at Nelson in 1931.

The highest rainfall total in New Zealand was recorded at Waterfall, Cropp River (Hokitika Catchment), and amounted to 18,442 millimetres over a 365-day period.

This was between 29 October 1997 and 29 October 1998.

The highest rainfall recorded in New Zealand in one hour was 109 millimetres, dumped on Leigh on 30 May 2001.

The lowest rainfall in New Zealand over a 12-month period was 167 millimetres, at Alexandra from November 1963 to October 1964.

The strongest wind gust in New Zealand was recorded at Hawkins Hill, Wellington (248 km per hour), on 6 November 1959 and 4 July 1962, and at Mt John, Canterbury in the South Island (250 km per hour), on 18 April 1970.

The Met Service was established in New Zealand in 1992 as a state-owned enterprise. It provides approximately 1.6 million weather forecasts a year.

The Met Service's information is gathered from 110 weather sites around New Zealand and outlying islands. Information is also collected from ships in the Tasman Sea and the South-west Pacific and a network of drifting weather buoys.

Met Service atmospheric data is provided by weather balloons released from eight locations, including Raoul Island and the Chatham Islands, and from weather data systems on commercial airliners. They also have recourse to their four weather surveillance radar systems and information from Japanese and US satellites.

A hole in the ozone layer over New Zealand reached a maximum size in 2001 of 26 million square kilometres.

The highest point in New Zealand is

Aoraki/Mt Cook at 3754 metres. The lowest point is the bottom of Lake Hauroko — 306 metres below sea level.

The New Zealand river with the greatest flow is the Clutha — 650 cubic metres per second.

New Zealand's deepest cave is the Nettlebed, Mt Arthur, which is 889 metres deep.

The New Zealand town located the furthest from the sea is Cromwell, Central Otago, (approximately 120 km).

The North Island is 113,729 square kilometres in size; the South Island, 150,437.

Cook Strait, at its narrowest point, is 20 kilometres wide.

There are 360 glaciers in the Southern Alps.

The oldest New Zealand rocks are found in Nelson, Westland and Fiordland and are associated with the Palaeozoic era (about 570 million years ago).

Nearly three-quarters of New Zealand is covered by sedimentary rock, the most common being sandstone, mudstone, greywacke, conglomerate and limestone.

Fifty per cent of New Zealand's land is steep, 20 per cent moderately hilly and 30 per cent is rolling or flat.

The fiords of Westland were formed by glacial action.

New Zealand experiences many earthquakes because it lies on the boundary between two of the earth's large tectonic plates, the Pacific Plate and the Australian Plate.

The city of Wellington has an estimated 12 per cent probability of experiencing a 7.5-magnitude earthquake within the next 30 years.

About one per cent of the 16,000 earthquakes recorded in New Zealand each year are big or shallow enough to be felt by humans.

In New Zealand in the last 150 years volcanoes have killed more people than earthquakes.

Mt Sibbald in the Southern Alps is one metre higher than Mt Ruapehu.

Matahina hydroelectric power station, in the Bay of Plenty, boasts the largest earth dam in the North Island.

The Highest

New Zealand mountains

Mountain or peak	Height (metres)
NORTH ISLAND	
Ruapehu	2797
Egmont/Taranaki	2518
Ngauruhoe	2290
Tongariro	1968
SOUTH ISLAND	
Kaikoura Ranges	
Tapuaenuku	2885
Alarm	2877
Southern Alps	
Cook	3754
Tasman	3497
Dampier	3440
Silberhorn	3279
Lendenfeld	3201
Mt Hicks (St David's Dome)	3183
Torres	3163
Teichelmann	3160
Sefton	3157
Malte Brun	3155
Haast	3138
Elie de Beaumont	3117
Douglas Peak	3085
La Perouse	3079
Haidinger	3066
Minarets	3055
Aspiring	3027
Glacier Peak	3007
Hamilton	2996
De la Beche	2992
Darwin	2961
Chudleigh	2952
Low	2942
Haeckel	2941
Aiguilles Rouges	2911
Annan	2911
Nazomi	2911
Goldsmith	2905
Walter	2903
Conway Peak	2901
Bristol Top	2898
Grey	2893
D'Archiac	2865
Green	2850
Hutton	2834
Ronald Adair	2827
Hochstetter Dome	2822
Barnicoat	2819
Earnslaw	2819
Nathan	2804
Sibbald	2798
Arrowsmith	2795
Spenser	2794
The Footstool	2765
Rudolf	2755
The Dwarf	2751
Darran Range	
Tutoko	2756

The Longest

New Zealand rivers

River	Length (kilometres)
NORTH ISLAND	
Flowing into the Pacific Ocean	
Rangitaiki	193
Waihou (or Thames)	175
Mohaka (from source, Taharua River)	172
Ngaruroro	154
Wairoa (from source, Hangaroa River)	137
Waipoa (from source, Mata River)	121
Waiapu (from source, Waipapa Stream)	113
Tukituki	113
Whakatane	105
Piako	90
Flowing into Cook Strait	
Ruamahanga	124
Hutt	56
Flowing into the Tasman Sea	
Waikato (from source, Upper Waikato River)	425
Whanganui	290

Rangitikei	241	Waimakariri	161
Manawatu	182	Rakaia	145
Whangaehu	161	Hurunui	138
Mokau	158	Rangitata (from source Clyde	
Patea	143	River)	121
Turakina	137	Ashley	97
Wairoa (from source, Waiotu		Selwyn	95
Stream)	132	Ashburton	90
Waitotara	108	Opihi	80
Waitara	98	Shag	72
Hokianga (from source, Waihou		Waipara	64
River)	72	Waihao	64
Otaki	48	Kakanui	64
		Pareora	56
SOUTH ISLAND		Conway	48
Flowing into Cook Strait			
Wairau	169	*Flowing into Foveaux Strait*	
Awatere	126	Mataura	240
Pelorus	64	Waiau (from source, Clinton River)	217
		Oreti	203
		Aparima (Jacobs River)	113
Flowing into the Pacific Ocean			
Clutha (from source, Makarora		*Flowing into the Tasman Sea*	
River)	322	Buller (from source, Travers River)	177
Taieri	288	Grey	121
Clarence	209	Motueka	108
Waitaki (from source, Hopkins		Taramakau	80
River)	209	Karamea	80
Wauau-uha (or Waiau)	169	Hollyford	76
		Aorere (from source, Spee River)	72
		Takaka (from source, Cobb River)	72
		Arawhata	68
		Cascade	64
		Haast	64
		Hokitika	64
		Wanganui	56
		Arahura	56
		Mokihinui	56
		Whataroa	51
		Waimea (from source, Wai-iti River)	48
		Waitaha	40
		Karangarua	37
		Heaphy	35
		Cook	32
		Waiho (from source, Callery River)	32

The Largest

New Zealand lakes

	Length in kilometres	Greatest breadth in kilometres	Area in square kilometres
North Island — Natural			
Taupo	40.2	27.4	606
Rotorua	12.0	9.7	80
Wairarapa	19.3	6.4	80
Waikaremoana	19.3	9.7	54
Tarawera	11.2	8.9	36
Rotoiti	16.1	4.8	34
Rotoaira	4.8	2.8	16
Rotoma	5.2	3.6	12
Okataina	6.4	4.8	10
Rotomahana	6.4	2.8	9
Rotoehu	4.8	3.2	8
Rerewhakaaitu	4.0	2.8	8
Rotokakahi	4.0	1.6	5
Okareka	2.4	2.0	3
Tikitapu	1.6	1.2	1
North Island — Artificial			
Ohakuri	33.8	0.4	13
Arapuni	16.1	0.8	9
Karapiro	24.1	0.4	8
Whakamaru	21.7	0.8	7
Maraetai	7.2	0.8	5
Moawhango	—	—	4
Matahina	—	—	3
Otamangakau	—	—	2
Atiamuri	6.4	0.4	2
Waipapa	9.7	0.4	2
Whakamarino	0.8	0.4	1
South Island — Natural			
Te Anau	61.2	9.7	344
Wakatipu	77.2	4.8	293
Wanaka	45.1	4.8	193
Ellesmere	22.5	12.9	181
Pukaki	15.3	8.0	169
Manapouri	28.9	8.0	142
Hawea	30.6	8.0	141
Tekapo	17.7	5.6	88
Hauroko	35.4	2.4	71

Ohau	17.7	4.8	61
Poteriteri	28.9	2.4	47
Brunner	8.9	8.9	39
Coleridge	17.7	3.2	36
Monowai	19.3	1.6	31
Rotoroa	14.5	3.2	23
Kaniere	9.7	2.0	16
Sumner	9.7	2.4	14
Rotoiti	8.9	2.8	10
Waihola	6.4	2.0	8
South Island — Artificial			
Benmore — Ahuriri Arm	18.5 ⎱	4.4	75
— Main Arm	29.8 ⎰		
Aviemore	10.8	4.1	29
Mahinerangi	14.5	1.6	21
Waitaki	4.8	0.8	6
Roxburgh	32.2	0.4	6
Cobb	4.8	0.4	2

The Deepest and Longest

New Zealand caves

DEEPEST

Name	Area	Depth in metres
Nettlebed Cave	Mt Arthur	889
Ellis Basin system	Mt Arthur	775
Bulmer Cavern	Mt Owen	749
HH Cave	Mt Arthur	721
Bohemia Cave	Mt Owen	713
Incognito/Falcon	Mt Arthur	540
Viceroy Shaft	Mt Owen	440
Twin Traverse	Mt Arthur	400
Greenlink-Middle Earth	Takaka Hill	394
Windrift	Mt Arthur	362
Legless	Takaka Hill	362
Harwood Hole	Takaka Hill	357
Gorgoroth	Mt Arthur	346
Rotapot	Mt Owen	341
Blackbird Hole	Mt Arthur	315

LONGEST

Name	Area	Surveyed length (metres)
Bulmer Cavern	Mt Owen	50,125
Ellis Basin Cave System	Mt Arthur	28,730
Nettlebed Cave	Mt Arthur	24,252
Megamania	Buller	14,800
Honeycomb Hill Cave	Oparara	13,712
Gardner's Gut	Waitomo	12,197
Bohemia Cave	Mt Owen	9300
Mangawhitikau system	Waitomo	8054
The Metro/Te Ananui	Charleston	8000
Aurora-Te Ana-au	Te Anau	6400
Mangaone Cave	Gisborne	6300
Moonsilver Cave	Upper Takaka	5900
Waitomo Headwaters system	Waitomo	5618
Millars Waterfall	Waitomo	5150
Xanadu system	Punakaiki	5010

Away from it All

National parks of New Zealand

Name	Area in hectares
Fiordland	1,251,924
Kahurangi	452,002
Mount Aspiring	355,543
Te Urewera	212,672
Rakiura, Stewart Island	157,000
Westland Tai Poutini	127,541
Arthurs Pass	114,500
Nelson Lakes	102,000
Tongariro	79,598
Whanganui	74,231
Aoraki/Mount Cook	70,696
Egmont/Taranaki	33,534
Paparoa	30,000
Abel Tasman	22,530

Islands in the Sun — and Rain

New Zealand islands

Alderman Islands, 20 kilometres east of Pauanui, Coromandel

Auckland Islands, 320 kilometres south of Stewart Island

Beehive Island, Hauraki Gulf

Bounty Islands, 788 kilometres east of Stewart Island

Bream Islands, Hauraki Gulf

Browns Island, Hauraki Gulf

Campbell Island, 600 kilometres south-east of Stewart Island

Casnel Island, Hauraki Gulf

Chatham Islands, 800 kilometres east of Christchurch

Cuvier Island, Hauraki Gulf

D'Urville Island, in the Marlborough Sounds

Goat Island, Hauraki Gulf

Great Barrier Island, 20 kilometres north of Coromandel Peninsula

Hen and Chicken Islands, 25 kilometres east of Northland

Kapiti Island, 6 kilometres west of Waikanae

Kawau Island, Hauraki Gulf

Kermadec Island, 1000 kilometres north-east of Auckland

Little Barrier Island, Hauraki Gulf

Mana Island, at the entrance to Porirua Harbour

Mayor Island, 38 kilometres north of Mt Maunganui

Mercury Islands, 20 kilometres north-east of Opito Bay, Coromandel

Mokohinau Islands, Hauraki Gulf

Mokoia Island, located on Lake Rotorua

Motuihe Island, Hauraki Gulf

Motuora Island, Hauraki Gulf

Motutapu Island, Hauraki Gulf

Motutara Island, Hauraki Gulf

Poor Knights Islands, Hauraki Gulf

Rakino Island, Hauraki Gulf

Rangitoto Island, Hauraki Gulf

Saddle Island, Hauraki Gulf

Somes Island, located in Wellington Harbour

Stephens Island, at the western end of Cook Strait

Stewart Island, 30 kilometres across Foveaux Strait

Tiritiri Island, Hauraki Gulf

Waiheke Island, Hauraki Gulf

PLACE NAMES

Just South of Somewhere

Otago is a bastardisation of the Maori place name Otakau.

The Howick-Pakuranga area of Auckland became known as 'Chowick' when many wealthy Asian immigrants settled there.

Mechanics Bay, located east of downtown Auckland, derived its name from the fact that many mechanics (workmen and artisans) lived there in the early days. In recent years it has been identified as receiving just about the highest rainfall in New Zealand.

Yncyca Bay is located in the Marlborough Sounds. It is a North American Indian name meaning 'my home'.

There are at least two Big Bays in New Zealand — one on the Awhitu Peninsula and the other in South Westland.

Hoon Hay, the Christchurch suburb, is not a 'hoon' nursery, although it does produce a few undisciplined young men.

Castlepoint is on the Wairarapa coast. Castlecliff is near Wanganui. Both are open ocean beaches.

There is a Wimbledon in Wairarapa. They play tennis there too.

It is not true that Farewell Spit was originally called Expectoration Point.

Gwavas is a place in Hawke's Bay. Guavas are a kind of fruit.

Lake Humuhumu is located near the Kaipara Harbour.

The Remarkables is perhaps the most remarkable name for a New Zealand mountain range.

Aka Aka is located near Port Waikato.

Galatea is not a Maori name.

There are two 'Tokanui's in New Zealand, one in the North Island — in South Auckland — and the other located in the South Island, south of Gore.

Hihi is near Coopers Beach in North Auckland.

One Tree Hill is a suburb of Auckland. One Tree Point is located in North Auckland.

There are two 'Lake Rotoroa's, one near Kaitaia, the other in the Nelson Province.

There are two 'Lake Rotorua's, one adjacent to the city of Rotorua, the other near Kaikoura.

Inchclutha is not the shortest river in New Zealand, but a settlement in Otago.

Coutts Island is an inland suburb of Christchurch.

Bombay Street is in Dunedin.

Barbadoes, Madras, Colombo and Montreal are Christchurch street names.

Moa and Peacock are also Christchurch street names.

Hapuku is the Maori name for groper. It is also a river and a settlement located north of Kaikoura.

From Ugly River to the Groynes

Distinctive New Zealand place names

A' Deanes Bush
All Day Bay
Ant Stream
Asbestos Track
Attempt Hill
Awe Burn
Bald Hill
Ballroom Cave
Barcoo Bush
Bare Hill
Barometer
Beans Burn
Beautiful Valley
Billy Goat Track
Black Gully
Black Umbrella
Blackball
Blackhead
Blind River

Blowhard Track
Blue Grey River
Blueskin Bay
Boddytown
Boggyburn
Breast Creek
Brighams Leap
Brod Bay
Brown Grey River
Bunnythorpe
Cannibal Bay
Cape Foulwind
Cape Turnagain
Cheddar Valley
Cherry Farm
Christmas Creek
Cleland Zig Zag
Cleopatra's Pool
Climax Peak

Colonial Knob
Coonoor
Craters of the Moon
Crooked Arm
Curio Bay
Dagg Sound
Deadman's Point
Deception River
Devils Elbow
Dip Creek
Doctor Creek
Doubtful Sound
Doubtless Bay
Drybread
Dubious Stream
Dumb-bell Lake
Fast Burn
Fern Burn
Fighting Bay

First Arm
Fish River
Five Forks
Five Rivers
Flag Swamp
Flat Island
Fortification
Four Peaks
Fruitlands
Furket Pass
Gapes Valley
Garden of Allah
Gates of Haast
Glenomaru
Glentui
Glinks Gully
Glorit
Gold Arm
Granity
Gropers Bush
Gummies Bush
Gumtown
Halfway Bay
Halfway Bluff
Hamilton Rapids
Hanging Rock Bridge
Happy Valley Saddle
Headlong Peak
Hedgehope
Hell's Gate
Helmet Hill
Hicks Bay
Hidden Lake
High Burn
Honeycomb Rock
Hook
Hope
Hummock
Hump Burn
Hut Burn
Inchbonnie
Invincible Creek
Isolated Saddle
Jam Stream
Jerusalem
Klondyke Corner

Knobby Creek
Knobs Flat
Lady Barkly
Lady Lake
Lake Humuhumu
Lake Iceberg
Lake Luna
Lake Rasselas
Lake Stream
Lake Teardrop
Lake Unknown
Lake Widgeon
Lake Wisely
Larrikin's Creek
Little Bay
Lottery River
Maimai
Malaspina Reach
Mangles Valley
Martyr Saddle
Maymorn
Measly Beach
Meeanee
Merrijigs
Mesopotamia
Mid Dome
Minarets
Mistake Creek
Moneymore
Mons Sex Millia
Moonlight
Moonshine
Morton Mains
Mounds of Misery
Mount Brazenose
Mount Crowfoot
Mount Hercules
Mount Hopeless
Mount Longsight
Mount Misery
Mount Patriarch
Mount Pisgah
Mount Pleasant
Mount Pollux
Mount Sebastopol
Mount Soaker

Mount Solitary
Mount Technical
Mount Tinline
Muttontown
Muzzle Stream
Myth Tarn
Nardoo Creek
Nigger Stream
Nightcaps
Nine Mile
Nitz Creek
North Rough Ridge
Notown
Nuggety Creek
Obelisk
Oeo
Oio
Okiwi
Omega
Opua River
Organ Range
Orinoco
Otaki Forks
Otoko Walk
Ox Burn
Pancake Rocks
Paradise
Pea Viner Corner
Peebles
Peep-O-Day
Penk River
Pepepe
Perpendicular Point
Phantom River
Piano Flat
Pleasant Point
Pleckville
Pokopoko Stream
Polnoon Burn
Princess Burn
Pudding Hill Creek
Pukemoremore
Pupu Springs
Ragged Point
Raggedy Range
Rainbow Island

Rainy River
Ram Rock
Ramcliff
Rankle Burn
Rappahannock Saddle
Rings Beach
Round Hill
Rum River
Rumbling Burn
Rununder Point
Sandy Knolls
Scour Stream
Secretary Island
Separation Point
Sergeants Hill
Shirkers Bush
Shy Lake
Siberia Saddle
Skippers
Slope Point
Smite River
Snag Burn
Speargrass Flat
Spectacle Lake
Split Apple Rock
Spotts Creek
Spray River
Spy Glass Point
Spylaw Burn

Steaming Cliffs
Steep Head
Stitts Bluff
Stump Bay
Styx River
Supper Cove
Swampy Summit
Swannanoa
Sweetwater
Swift River
Tadmor
Taihoa
Tailrace Tunnel
Tanatana
Taniwha Springs
Tara Tama Hill
Taylors Mistake
Te Popo
Te Pu
Teschemakers
The Chasm
The Crater
The Groynes
The Haystack
The Kaik
The Punchbowl
The Remarkables
The Sluice Box Gorge
The Stopper

The Twins
Three O'clock Stream
Tomogalak Stream
Tophouse
Toreador Peak
Transit River
Tryphena
Tuna
Ugly River
Upcot Saddle
Vinegar Hill
Wash Creek
Washdyke
Washpool Stream
Wayby
Wednesday Peak
Welcome Bay
Wet Jacket Arm
Whare Flat
Whistler River
Wilberforce River
Windwhistle
Windy Point
Wisp Hill
Woody Head
Woolshed Creek
Zora Canyon

Call Me Roaring Meg

New Zealand place names featuring Christian names

Albert Burn
Mount Albert
Lake Alice
Angus Burn
Saint Anne Point
Gentle Annie Hill
Arnold River
Ashley
Athol
Avalon

Saint Bernard
The Roaring Billy
Mount Bruce
Cass
Port Charles
Queen Charlotte Sound
Charlton
Saint Clair
Clifton
Clive

Clyde
Port Craig
Mount Saint Cuthbert
Deborah
Donald Creek
Lake Dora
Dorie
Dorothy Falls
Douglas
Edith River

Edward Stream
Elizabeth River
Point Elizabeth Walk
Elsdon
Lake Emily
Lake Emma
Lake Fergus
Flora Saddle
Florence Stream
Frances River
Frieda Creek
Gabriels Gully
Garry River
George River
Geraldine
Gordon
Grahams Beach
Greta River
Hannahs Clearing
Hector River
Helena Bay
Henry Creek
Herbert
Hilda Falls
Howard
Huia
Ida Valley
Irene River
Iris Burn
Mount Isabel
Jacks Bay
Red Jacks Creek
Jacobs River
Saint James Range
Jane Peak
Jerry River
Joe River
John O'Groats River
Mount John Observatory
Julia Creek
Lake Katherine
Loch Katrine
Kellys Bay

Kelvin Heights
Kerrytown
Saint Kilda
Kimberley
Kyle
Larrys Creek
Lawrence
Leigh
Saint Leonards
Leslie Hills
Lewis Pass
Lake Lois
Lora Gorge
Lyall Burn
Lyell
Grey Lynn
Mabel Bush
Loch Maree
Martha Gold Mine
Martins Bay
Mary Burn
Saint Marys Range
Maud Creek
Mauriceville
Maxwell
Lake Mike
Nancy River
Neils Beach
Nelson
Nicholas Saddle
Mount Nicholas Station
Lake Nigel
Nina River
Lake Norma
Oona Burn
Owen Forest
Percival River
Percy Saddle
Perry Saddle
Phillips Saddle
Phoebe
Roaring Meg
Robert Creek

Mount Robert Skifield
Rock Burn
Rocky Gully
Rodger Inlet
Cape Rodney
Lake Ronald
Ross
Mount Ross Station
Rowan
Roys Bay
Ruas Track
Ruby Bay
Russell
Scott Point
Scotts Knob
Selwyn Huts
Shannon
Shelly Beach
Shirley
St Patricks
Stanley River
Staveley
Steven Burn
Stewart Falls
Stirling
Mount Stuart
Lake Sylvester
Sylvia Falls
Thomas Bluff
Tim Burn
Tom Bowling Bay
Mount Una
Mount Uriah
Lake Victor
Lake Victoria
Lake Vincent
Virginia Road
The Warren
Warwick River
Mount William
Mount William Walk
Wilsons Crossing

From Hog Burn to the Pigroot

Place names featuring names of animals, birds and amphibians

Alligator Head
Bull Creek
Bullock Creek
Bulls
Cat Creek
Cattle Creek
Dead Horse Pinch
Duck Creek
Elephant Hill
Fantail Falls
Fox Glacier
Frog Flat Junction
Goat Island

Goose Bay
Grebe River
Hawks Crag
Hen and Chicken Islands
Hog Burn
Kaka Point
Kakapo River
Kangaroo Lake
Kea Pass
Kiwi Burn
Moa Flat
Mole Saddle
Monkey Puzzle Gorge

Monkey Island Beach
Penguin Bay
Pigroot Creek
Rabbit Island
Roaring Lion River
Seal Rocks
Shag Point
Sheepwash Creek
Lake Swan
Weka Pass
Wether Burn
Woodpecker Bay

From Foot Arm to Toko Mouth

Place names featuring body parts

Devils Backbone
Devils Elbow
Elbow Creek
Five Fingers Point

Foot Arm
Knuckle Hill
Old Mans Head
The Thumbs

Toetoes Bay
Toko Mouth
Tooth Peak
Two Thumb Bay

Glenhope and Glory

Place names — the glens

Glen Afton
Glen Eden
Glen Innes
Glen Massey
Glen Murray
Glen Oroua
Glenavy
Glenbervie
Glenbrook
Glenburnie

Glencairn
Glencoe
Glendhu
Glenduan
Glenfield
Glengarry
Glenham
Glenhope
Glenledi
Glenleith

Glenomaru
Glenorchy
Glenpark
Glenrae
Glenroy
Glenside
Glentanner
Glentui
Glentunnel
Glenure

From Hicksville to Bulls

Distinctive towns, cities and districts

Akaroa was settled in 1840 by French colonists who were sponsored by the Nanto-Bordelaise Company in France.

Alexandra was named after Princess Alexandra of Denmark who married Britain's Prince of Wales in 1863.

Arapuni, in the Waikato, houses staff who work at the Arapuni hydroelectric power station. The station began producing power in 1929, but after water seepage occurred in 1930 the station was closed for two years while cracks in the dam were sealed.

Arrowtown, located on the Arrow River, owes its existence to the discovery of gold nearby.

The township of Arthurs Pass, named after explorer Arthur Dudley Dobson, is located five kilometres south of the actual pass through the Southern Alps.

Ashburton was originally known as Turton.

Auckland's climate is almost subtropical, but is categorised as warm temperate.

Balclutha's first settler was James McNeil, in 1852.

Blenheim was known as 'The Beaver' for some years, because the first survey team in the area had been trapped in a flood and forced to retreat to the highest bunks in their huts until the water receded.

Bluff was originally named Campbelltown after the family name of the wife of Governor Sir Thomas Gore Browne.

Bulls, because of its dairying aspect, is known as 'the only place in the world where you can get milk from Bulls'.

Burnham, a farming area near Christchurch, was the site of the ill-fated Burnham Industrial School for Boys, in which flogging was an integral part of the rehabilitation process. It is also the site where overseas scientists observed the transit of Venus in 1874.

Cambridge used to be the site of Horotiu Pa, a Maori tribal stronghold.

Carterton was named after a supporter of the Wairarapa Small Farmers Association.

The Catlins district was named, none too accurately, after Captain Edward Cattlin.

Christchurch has the lowest annual rainfall of New Zealand's four main centres.

Clyde was known as The Dunstan in the 1860s.

Collingwood was once considered to be a suitable national capital because of its central location at the top of the South Island.

Coromandel derived its name as long ago as 1820, when the HMS *Coromandel* sailed into the harbour to uplift kauri spars for the British Navy.

Cromwell lost its town centre when the Clyde Dam was built.

Curio Bay in Southland is well known for its fossilised forest which dates back 160 million years.

The name Dannevirke means 'Danes' work'. The area was settled by Danish immigrants.

Dargaville was founded in 1872 by Joseph McMullen Dargaville, an Irishman.

Dunedin was designed for settlers from the Free Church of Scotland, which had broken away from the traditional Church of Scotland in 1843.

Edendale in Southland was the site of one of New Zealand's first dairy factories.

Edgecumbe was badly affected by an earthquake in 1987.

Eiffelton is a mid-Canterbury farming district which owes its name to the tall chimney built on a brick kiln, known locally as the Eiffel Tower.

Eketahuna was the fictional setting of a humorous newspaper column written by Gordon McLauchlan.

Eltham is located on the Waingongoro River.

The town of Feilding was planned in England, based on the city of Manchester.

Foxton was once the port serving the Manawatu district, but because of heavy silting, port operations ceased in 1942.

Geraldine in South Canterbury was originally named FitzGerald.

Gisborne is physically the most isolated centre of population in New Zealand, being surrounded by mountain ranges on three sides and served by a shallow port.

Gore Bay in North Canterbury was named after Second Lieutenant Gore, a member of Captain Cook's *Endeavour* crew.

Gore in Southland is not named after the by-products of sheep-slaughtering, but after Sir Thomas Gore Browne, an early Governor of New Zealand.

Greymouth, like several other Westland locations, lacks a natural harbour.

Greytown is the oldest town in Wairarapa, with the first settlers arriving in 1854.

Hamilton is New Zealand's largest inland city.

Hanmer Springs used to be well known as the place where alcoholics went to receive treatment.

Hastings was first subdivided in 1870 by pioneer Francis Hicks. For a time it was known as Hicksville.

Havelock, in the Marlborough Sounds, was named after the British General, Sir Henry Havelock, a hero of the Indian Mutiny.

Havelock North, in Hawke's Bay, is also named after Sir Henry Havelock.

Hawera became an independent republic during the drawn-out resistance of Te Whiti at Parihaka Pa.

The first Europeans to settle in Helensville were Novia Scotians.

The Hokianga district's name is an abbreviation of Te Hokianga-a-Kupe, meaning 'the return of Kupe'.

Hokitika was the capital of Westland in the early days.

Huntly is named after a town in Aberdeenshire, Scotland.

Inangahua gets it name from inanga, the Maori word for whitebait.

Inglewood was originally a timber town.

Invercargill used to be the fifth largest city in New Zealand, until surpassed by Hamilton, New Plymouth, Palmerston North, Tauranga and Rotorua.

Kaiapoi, north of Christchurch, is located on the banks of the Kaiapoi River.

Kaikohe was a US Army hospital base and a US Air Force bomber base during World War II.

Kaikoura is well known for crayfish, seals and sperm whales.

Kaitaia is the northernmost borough in New Zealand.

Kaitangata was once a coal-mining town but its last mine closed in 1970 for economic reasons.

Karamea was badly damaged in the Murchison earthquake of 1929.

Karangahake once had a population of over 2000 in days when the goldfields were operating.

Karitane in Otago has given its name to the hospitals and nurses of the same name after the setting up of the Royal New Zealand Society for the Health of Women and Children (The Plunket Society).

Kawerau is one of the few 'company' towns in New Zealand, having been built by the Tasman Pulp and Paper Co. Ltd.

Kawhia is the last resting place of the Tainui canoe.

Kerikeri is the site of Kemp House, the oldest surviving building in New Zealand.

Kihikihi was once the headquarters of the Ngati Maniapoto tribe.

Kinleith was named after the Kinleith Paper Mills in Scotland.

Kumara, a township in Westland, had 80 pubs and over 4000 inhabitants in the 1870s.

Lawrence was known as The Junction and Tuapeka, before it acquired its current name in 1866.

The headquarters of the New Zealand Scouting Movement are located near Levin.

Little Wanganui, a settlement in coastal Buller, is thus named to distinguish it from Wanganui in the North Island, which is much bigger.

Lowburn is located very close to the 45th parallel of latitude, placing it midway between the equator and the South Pole.

Lower Hutt was simply called The Hutt in its early years.

Lyttelton is 12 kilometres by road from the centre of Christchurch.

Makara, near Wellington, is the site of New Zealand's main international radio receiving station.

Maketu, in the Bay of Plenty, was the arrival point of the migration canoe, Arawa.

The settlement of Manapouri is located on Surprise Bay.

Manukau City was formed in 1965.

The town centre of Martinborough was planned in the shape of a Union Jack.

Marton is named after Captain Cook's birthplace in England. Originally it was known as Tutaenui, which translated as 'dung heap'.

Masterton, because of the Rimutaka rail tunnel, operates as a dormitory town for a number of Wellingtonians.

Matamata was founded by Josiah Clifton Firth.

Mataura is located on the Mataura River, the second longest river in the South Island.

Milton was originally called Mill Town, being developed around flour and oat mills.

Morrinsville was named after its first European settlers, Thomas and Samuel Morrin.

Mosgiel was originally known as Mossgiel.

Motueka and its surrounding district grow almost all New Zealand's tobacco and hops.

Mount Maunganui became an Independent Town District in 1937.

Napier is known as the art-deco capital of New Zealand.

Naseby, in Central Otago, is the national centre for the winter sport known as curling.

National Park was once known as Waimarino.

In 1858, Queen Victoria ordained that Nelson become a bishop's see and it was constituted as a city by letters patent, although it had a population of little more than 3000.

New Plymouth is a centre of the petrochemical industry.

Ngaruawahia was formerly called Newcastle because of nearby coal deposits.

Oamaru was the home town of writer Janet Frame.

Oban is the main township on Stewart Island.

Ohakune was originally settled to act as a base for construction of the North Island Main Trunk railway line.

Opotiki became a borough in 1911.

Otorohanga is the nearest town to the world-famous Waitomo Caves.

The name Paekakariki, when translated into English, means 'perch of the parakeet'.

Paeroa was originally a river port with steamships plying the Ohinemuri and Waihou Rivers to reach the Hauraki Gulf.

Pahiatua means 'resting place of the Gods'.

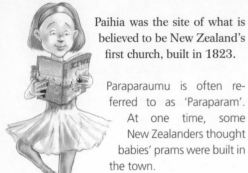

Paihia was the site of what is believed to be New Zealand's first church, built in 1823.

Paraparaumu is often referred to as 'Paraparam'. At one time, some New Zealanders thought babies' prams were built in the town.

Patea lost its major source of employment — the Patea freezing works — in the early 1980s.

Picton was the first capital of the Marlborough province and at one time was under consideration to be the nation's capital.

Porirua became a city in 1965.

Port Chalmers is the site of Dunedin's deep-water container port.

Port Gore in the Marlborough Sounds was named after Vice Admiral Sir John Gore of the British Navy.

Puhoi was settled in 1863 by a group of immigrants from the German-speaking district of Staab in Bohemia.

Putaruru is the home of country-and-western singer Patsy Riggir.

Queenstown's first settler was William Rees who moved in with his sheep in 1860.

Raetihi was relatively isolated in the early days.

Raglan's first settlers were missionaries. Today it is the home of blues musician Midge Marsden.

Rangiora was founded in the 1850s.

Raurimu is the location of the world-famous Raurimu railway spiral.

Rawene is located on the southern side of Hokianga Harbour.

Richmond, in Nelson, was named after Richmond-on-Thames in Surrey, England.

Riverton is the oldest European settlement in Southland.

Ross used to be the end of the line for the West Coast railway.

Rotorua did not become a European settlement until the 1870s.

Roxburgh is noted for its hydroelectric power station which, when it was commissioned in 1956, was the largest station in New Zealand.

Ruatahuna is located in the heart of Urewera country, the home base of the Tuhoe people.

Russell was originally known as Kororareka.

Six Mile is a small settlement close to the mouth of Six Mile Creek near Murchison.

In Stratford some of the streets are named after Shakespearian characters.

Taihape was settled when Canterbury pioneers ventured north to take up land and work as sawmillers.

Tapanui is associated with the Tapanui flu, a debilitating medical condition.

Taumarunui is located on the upper reaches of the Whanganui River.

Taupiri takes its name from the sacred Taupiri Mountain.

Taupo was sparsely settled until World War II.

Tauranga houses a lot of retired people.

Te Anau, the town, is located on the eastern boundary of Fiordland National Park.

Te Aroha was a river port in the early days, when the Waihou River was navigable as far as the town.

Te Awamutu boasts one of the oldest churches in New Zealand — St John's Anglican Church, which was founded in 1854.

Te Kauwhata used to be on the main Auckland to Hamilton highway.

Te Kuiti was established to facilitate the construction of the Waiteti Viaduct.

Te Puke is the 'kiwifuit capital of the world'.

Temuka was first settled in 1853.

Thames used to have a population greater than that of Auckland, because of the discovery of gold.

Timaru is located on the shore of Caroline Bay.

Tokomaru Bay was the scene of fighting during the Hauhau uprising.

Tokoroa, in its earlier days, was known as something of a frontier town because of the large number of single men living there.

Tuakau was founded as a flax processing centre.

Turangi was constructed almost exclusively to house workers on the Tongariro hydroelectric power project.

Twizel derived its name from the Twizel Bridge built over the River Tweed in England.

Upper Hutt became a city in its own right in 1966.

Waihi endured serious industrial unrest in 1912 when the miners' strike closed the mines for six months.

Waikouaiti, in Otago, was one of the first settlements in the South Island.

Waipawa became a borough in 1908.

Waipukurau is located 8 kilometres south-west of Waipawa.

Wairoa, in Hawke's Bay, was originally called Clyde, but was changed back to the old Maori name Te Wairoa to avoid confusion with Clyde, Central Otago.

Waitara used to have a large meat works.

Wanaka is a burgeoning tourist resort.

Wanganui was declared a city in 1924 and at the 1926 Census was found to be the largest provincial city in New Zealand.

Wellington suffered severe earthquake damage in 1848 and many Wellingtonians left the area, never to return.

Westport is located at the mouth of the Buller River.

Whakatane's first permanent European settler was Philip Tapsell who built a store in the town in 1830.

Whangarei's population increased from 23,000 to 31,000 between 1961 and 1966.

Winton is one of New Zealand's most affluent towns of its size.

Woodville was originally called 'The Junction'.

Some More Ghostly than Most

A selection of New Zealand ghost towns

Sweetwater — A mill town in Northland.

Depthford — Established in Northland in 1827 as a shipbuilding settlement.

Babylon — A gum-diggers' town north of Dargaville.

Redhill — Another gum-diggers' town near Dargaville.

Driving Creek — New Zealand's first gold-mining town near Coromandel.

Punga Flat — A gold-mining town located near Thames.

Te Wairoa — Resort town near Lake Tarawera that became known as the 'Buried Village' after Mount Tarawera erupted in 1886.

Carson City and Angel's Rest — Construction workers' towns on the North Island Main Trunk line, located west of Lake Taupo.

Ngaroma — A mill town located in South Waikato.

The Summit and Cross Creek — Railway settlements that died when the Rimutaka Incline closed in 1955.

Dogtown and Bald Hill — Gold-mining settlements on the West Coast of the South Island.

Balloon and Butcher Town — Gold-mining settlements near Motueka.

Dillmanston Larrikins and Cousin Jack — Gold-mining towns on the West Coast.

No Town and Lagoon Town — Gold-mining towns on the West Coast.

Drybread — Gold-mining town in Central Otago.

Mullocky Gully — Gold-mining town near Dunedin.

Shag Point — Coal-mining town in North Otago.

Marshland — Flax-milling town located in Marlborough.

Barrhill — A town based on a social experiment, which was built on the banks of the Rakaia River in the 1870s. John Cathcart Wason created a medieval village down-under, which faded away when the proposed railway line to Methven bypassed the town.

Namesakes

Names appearing in more than one place

Bluff: A town 27 kilometres south of Invercargill.
A knoll at the southern end of Bluff Peninsula.
The Bluff: A knoll on Ninety Mile Beach, Northland.
Bluff Hill: A residential area of Napier.

Brunner: A locality east of Greymouth.
A lake in Westland.
A range of mountains named after Thomas Brunner.

Cass: A farming settlement in inland Canterbury.
An inlet in Lyttelton Harbour.
A river in Canterbury.
A peak in the Port Hills of Christchurch.

Catlins: A district in South Otago.
A forest park in Southland, established in 1975.
A river in South Otago.

Douglas: A glacier in the Southern Alps.
A river in South Westland.
A farming settlement in Taranaki.
A pass in South Westland.
A range in Golden Bay.
A locality in South Canterbury.

Esk: A river in Hawke's Bay.
A river in North Canterbury.
A burn that flows into Lake Te Anau.
A valley in South Canterbury.

Gentle Annie: A hill on the Napier-Taihape Road.
A hill west of Gisborne.
A road on the eastern side of the Whanganui River.
A creek flowing into the Kawerau River.

Halfmoon Bay: The site of Oban, the main settlement on Stewart Island.
A suburb of Manukau City.

Hikurangi: A mountain on the East Coast.
A district near Whangarei.

Kaikoura: Twin mountain ranges in the north of the South Island.
A town on the coastal side of the Seaward Kaikouras.
A bay on which Kaikoura is located.
A peninsula in the same area.
Another bay in the Marlborough Sounds.
An island off the west coast of Great Barrier Island.

Kaingaroa: A forest extending north-eastwards from Lake Taupo.

A settlement within the forest.

A harbour on the northern side of the Chatham Islands.

A settlement within that harbour.

A town near Kaitaia, Northland.

Maori: Maori Head and Maori Hill in Dunedin.

Maori Gully, South of Greymouth.

Maori Gully and Maori Creek in Buller.

Maori Beach on Stewart Island.

Maori Pa Beach in Tasman Bay.

Maori Point in Buller and Central Otago.

Maori Bay in the Marlborough Sounds.

Maori Lakes near Ashburton.

Maoribank, a suburb of Upper Hutt.

Maraetai: A hydroelectric dam and a settlement on the Waikato River.

A beach in East Auckland.

Murchison: A coastal suburb on the Firth of Thames near Auckland.

A town in Nelson Province.

A glacier on the eastern side of the Southern Alps.

A river emerging from the Murchison Glacier.

A range of mountains that straddles the border between Southland and Fiordland.

Oamaru: The main town and port of North Otago.

A bay on Arapawa Island at the entrance to Queen Charlotte Sound.

Another bay on the Coromandel Peninsula.

Paradise: A settlement on the shores of Diamond Lake near Lake Wakatipu.

A bay in Pelorus Sound.

Hot springs in the Ngongotaha Valley near Rotorua.

Pelorus: A settlement on the shores of Diamond Lake near Lake Wakatipu.

A river that runs into the head of Pelorus Sound.

A district (Pelorus Bridge), near Havelock in Marlborough.

Raglan: A town on the west coast of the North Island.

A harbour on which the town is located.

A mountain range in Marlborough Country.

Sumner: A lake near the Lake Sumner Forest Park.

A seaside suburb of Christchurch.

Taieri: A river in Otago.

A plain which serves as the lower basin of the river.

A settlement (Taieri Mouth), at the Taieri River mouth.

A beach three kilometres further south.

An island off the river mouth.

Tarawera: A large lake in the North Island.

A mountain standing between Lakes Tarawera and Rotomahana.

A river flowing from Lake Tarawera into the Bay of Plenty near Matata.

A settlement south-east of Taupo.

Tasman:	A mountain in the Southern Alps (the second highest in New Zealand).
	A large bay on the north coast of the South Island.
	A range of mountains beyond Golden Bay.
	A glacier in the Southern Alps, the largest in New Zealand.
	A river running from Tasman Glacier into Lake Pukaki.
	A beach near Otaki on the Horowhenua coast.
Taupo:	The largest lake in New Zealand.
	A city located on the lake.
	A bay on Northland's east coast near Whangaroa Harbour.
Tokomaru:	A bay on the east coast of the North Island.
	A township on this bay.
	A township on the banks of the Manawatu River.
	Localities (Tokomaru West and Tokomaru East) north of Wanganui.
Totara:	A locality on the Coromandel Peninsula.
	A locality in North Otago.
	A locality on the Grey River near Reefton (Totara Flat).
	A locality near Kaeo in Northland (Totara North).
	A headland on Hokianga Harbour (Totara Point).
	A river in Buller.
	A locality on the Totara River.
	A creek and valley in South Canterbury.
Waihi:	A town near the Coromandel Ranges.
	A beach community (Waihi Beach), 17 kilometres from the town.
	A village in Waihi Bay at the southern end of Lake Taupo.
	A beach near Hawera.
	A river in Central Canterbury.
	An estuary south of the entrance to Tauranga Harbour.
	A point near the entrance to Queen Charlotte Sound in Marlborough.
Waihou:	A river that flows into the Firth of Thames.
	A township south-west of Te Aroha.
	A river that flows into the Hokianga Harbour, in Northland.
Wairoa:	A town in northern Hawke's Bay.
	A river in northern Hawke's Bay.
	A river, sometimes known as the Northern Wairoa, that flows into Kaipara Harbour.
	A river flowing into Tasman Bay in Nelson.
	A river flowing into Tauranga harbour from the Kaimai Range.
	A river flowing into the Hauraki Gulf from the Hunua Ranges.
	A bay in the Bay of Islands.
Waitangi:	A national historic reserve.
	A river in Northland.
	The main town on the Chatham Islands.

From Papatoetoe to Young Nick's Head

Special New Zealand places

Abbotsford, a suburb of Dunedin, suffered a devastating landslide in 1979 which destroyed 69 houses.

Abel Tasman National Park is New Zealand's smallest National Park.

The first European to climb Mount Albert in Auckland was Samuel Marsden the missionary.

Anakiwa is the location of the Outward Bound School.

The Antipodes Islands are located south-east of Stewart Island.

Arawata is the name of a river that originates in the Southern Alps. Poet Denis Glover adopted the name for his character Arawata Bill, which was based on the life of gold prospector William O'Leary.

Mount Aspiring, which is 3036 metres high, is the loftiest New Zealand mountain outside Mount Cook National Park.

Lake Aviemore, in the South Island, is the second largest man-made lake in New Zealand. It is 29 square kilometres in area.

Banks Peninsula, near Christchurch, was originally deemed, by Captain James Cook, to be an island.

Barrett Reef near Wellington has claimed both the trans-Tasman passenger ship *Wanganella* in 1947 and the inter-island ferry *Wahine* in 1968.

Bastion Point in Auckland became a symbol for Maori land grievances.

Bounty Islands near Stewart Island were discovered and named by Captain William Bligh in HMS *Bounty*.

Lake Brunner is the largest lake in Westland.

Campbell Island is the southernmost of New Zealand's islands. It is 114 square kilometres in size. The Campbell Plateau is an underwater formation that reaches 600 kilometres from Stewart Island in a southerly direction.

The Canterbury Plains represent the largest stretch of flat land in New Zealand.

Canterbury University was established in 1873. One of its most famous students was Ernest Rutherford who graduated with an MA with double first-class honours in 1894.

Cardigan Bay is not a bay, but New Zealand's most famous and successful racehorse, being the first in the world to earn a million dollars.

Chateau Tongariro is often referred to as 'The Chateau'.

Almost a quarter of the main island in the Chatham Islands group is covered by lagoons.

Christchurch is known as the most English of the New Zealand cities.

Construction of Christchurch Cathedral was started in 1864 and completed in 1901.

PLACE NAMES

The Cobb River originates from Lake Cobb in the Tasman Mountains near Mount Cobb. It flows through Cobb Valley during the first part of its journey.

Lake Coleridge was formed when the Lake Coleridge hydroelectric power station was constructed. The latter was the first of the large hydroelectric stations to be built by the government.

Mount Cook was first climbed in 1894 by George Graham, Thomas Fyfe and Jack Clarke.

Mount Cook National Park contains 19 peaks higher than 3000 metres and five large glaciers. One of the glaciers, the Tasman Glacier, is one of the largest located outside the polar regions.

Mount Cook is also a suburb of Wellington.

Cook Strait is regarded as one of the most dangerous stretches of water in the world. Abel Tasman originally categorised the strait as a bight and called it Zeehaens Bocht.

Coppermine Island is one of the Hen and Chicken Islands.

The Craigieburn Forest Park features a skating rink on the park boundary.

Deep Cove in Fiordland was notable for the fact that the ship the *Wanganella* was berthed there, to provide accommodation for workers working on the tunnel that became an integral part of the Manapouri hydroelectric power scheme.

The first Europeans to visit Doubtful Sound were believed to be Spaniards, led by Don Felipe Bauza on the *Descubienta* in 1793.

Doubtless Bay, in Northland, was named by Captain James Cook because he did not doubt it was a bay, although he did not land there.

Dusky Sound is the largest fiord in New Zealand. It is also where the first ship was built in New Zealand.

East Cape is the easternmost point of the North Island.

Mount Eden represents the southern boundary of the land purchased by William Hobson on which the city of Auckland was built.

Lake Ellesmere, in Canterbury, is the fifth largest lake in New Zealand, but it is never more than three metres deep.

Erewhon, the high-country sheep station, got its name from Samuel Butler's novel of the same name.

Fantham's Peak is the large rocky 'bump' on the southern side of Mt Taranaki/Egmont. It is named after Fanny Fantham, the first woman to climb the mountain.

Farewell Spit, in Golden Bay, extends from Cape Farewell for 24 kilometres.

Ferrymead is the Christchurch suburb where the Heathcote and the Avon Rivers meet.

Fiordland National Park is New Zealand's largest national park and one of the most extensive in the world.

Cape Foulwind, on the west coast of the South Island, was not named because of some nineteenth-century on-board bilious attack.

Cape Reinga overlooks the meeting of the Tasman Sea and the Pacific Ocean at the end of the Northland peninsula.

Deans Bush in the Christchurch suburb of Riccarton, was presented to the city by John and William Deans.

In 1963, John Van Leeuwan of the Oreti Surf Life Saving Club swam Foveaux Strait, despite its freezing waters.

Fox Glacier was named after Premier Sir William Fox.

Franz Josef Glacier was named after the Austro-Hungarian Emperor Franz Josef.

Gabriels Gully was named after Gabriel Read who discovered gold in the gully, thereby instigating the Otago gold rush in 1861.

Gate Pa, now a suburb of Tauranga, was the site of a ferocious battle between British troops and the Ngai-te-Rangi. The battle featured the heaviest shelling of a

pa by the British during the land wars, and a death toll of 111 soldiers.

Great Barrier Island is the largest island off the coast of the North Island, being 285 square kilometres in area.

Hanging Rock, located on the Opihi River in South Canterbury, is well known for its ancient Maori rock drawings.

Hanmer Forest Park contains one of the oldest exotic forests in the country. Some of the species are larch, poplar, sycamore, rowan, birch, pines and firs.

The Haparapara River in the North Island contains no introduced fish.

Hauraki Gulf Maritime Park includes more than 40 islands.

The Hauraki Plains were originally known as the Piako Swamp.

Hawke's Bay, the region, was named after Sir Edward Hawke, First Lord of the Admiralty.

Hawke Bay was named after the same gentleman, and relates specifically to the bay that curves from the Mahia Peninsula to Cape Kidnappers.

The Heaphy Track, in the north-west of the South Island, follows the Heaphy River for 10 kilometres of its 70-kilometre extent.

The flora and fauna of the Hen and Chicken Islands have been protected since 1925.

Dalmation and Lebanese settlers provided the impetus for the Henderson Valley's vineyards.

Mount Hikurangi on the east coast of the North Island, is the first place in New Zealand to receive the rays of the dawning sun.

The Hokitika Saddle crosses the main divide of the South Island between Mount Ambrose and Mount Elliot.

The Hokonui Hills in Southland were the home of illicit whisky stills in days gone by.

The Homer Tunnel in Fiordland was opened for road traffic in 1953.

Jerusalem, on the Whanganui River, is notable for the number of religious groups who made it their base. In 1885, Mother Mary Aubert established her Daughters of our Lady of Compassion community, and in the 1960s, poet James K Baxter set up a commune there.

Judges Bay in Auckland used to be known as Judicial Bay.

The Kaikouras in the South Island are twin mountain ranges — the Seaward Kaikouras and the Inland Kaikouras — that run parallel to each other for a considerable distance. Captain James Cook called them the 'Snowy Mountains' but the name eventually lost currency.

The Kaimai Rail tunnel is the longest rail tunnel in New Zealand, at nine kilometres in length.

A considerable area of the Kaimai-Mamaku Forest Park is virgin native forest.

The Kaimanawa Forest Park is one of the few areas in New Zealand where sika deer are found.

The Kaipara River flows into the southern reaches of the Kaipara Harbour.

Kapiti Island, which is very steep, has been a bird sanctuary for more than 90 years.

Karioi district near Ohakune features a small thermal lake named Rotokuru.

Katikati, in the Bay of Plenty, was founded by George Vesey Stewart in 1875, with the view of creating an entire settlement of Ulstermen.

Kawarau Falls are located near the outlet of Lake Wakatipu at the Kawarau River. The location is the site of an unsuccessful attempt to harvest the large quantities of gold believed to be in the Kawarau River bed. An extensive and expensive dam was built across the river in an attempt to lower the water level, but when the river maintained its level because of water from streams and tributaries, investors lost heavily.

Kawau Island's first European owner was J Taylor who bought the island from Maori in 1837. Sir George Grey purchased it in 1862.

Kaweka Forest Park in Hawke's Bay has suffered severely from erosion.

Kawhia Harbour, on the west coast of the North Island, is a drowned river valley.

Cape Kidnappers is world famous for its gannet colony.

The Maori name for the King Country region is Rohe Potae which means 'the edge of the hat'.

Because of its ruggedness and the presence of hostile Maori, the King Country was not surveyed until the 1880s.

A colony of North Island saddlebacks was established on Lady Alice Island in the Hen and Chicken Islands in the 1960s to ensure the birds' survival.

Lake Chalice in the Mount Richmond Forest Park was formed when a landslide blocked the Upper Goulter River 2000 years ago.

Two small lakes, Lake Marion and Morris Tarn, located in Lake Sumner Forest Park, are free from exotic fish.

Lake Waikaremoana is located 614 metres above sea level. It is the highest lake in the North Island. Lake Wairarapa is 8 metres above sea level.

Lake Tekapo in the South Island is New Zealand's highest lake (713 metres above sea level).

Lake Wakatipu, at 77.2 kilometres long, is New Zealand's longest lake.

Larnach Castle is built from, among other materials, Italian marble, Aberdeen stone, Venetian glass and exotic timber.

Lewis Pass in the Southern Alps used to be the principal route for Maori travelling to the West Coast to uplift greenstone.

The only residents on Little Barrier Island are the park ranger and his family.

Lower Moutere, a farming area in Nelson province, is home to an ongoing pacifist commune which was established in the 1940s.

Macetown is a derelict former gold-mining settlement in Central Otago. The three Mace brothers, all well-known Otago cricketers, were among the first Macetown dwellers. As a consequence, the settlement became known as 'The Maces' Town', a name that evolved into Macetown.

Mahia Peninsula, south of Gisborne, is 20 kilometres long.

Malte Brun, a mountain in the Southern Alps, was named after French geographer, Victor Adolphe Malte-Brun.

Mana Island, south of Kapiti Island off the west coast of the North Island, is the site of New Zealand's first sheep station.

Lake Manapouri is New Zealand's second deepest lake with a maximum depth of 440 metres.

The Manawatu region was covered with dense virgin bush until the 1870s, and the Manawatu River was the only means of traversing the area.

Marble Mountain, located near Takaka, produced hard limestone that has been used in the construction of significant New Zealand buildings, including Parliament House.

Marlborough became a separate province in 1859.

The Marlborough Sounds have two principal arms: Pelorus Sound and Queen Charlotte Sound.

Marsden Point, near Whangarei, was named after the Reverend Samuel Marsden.

Maungapohatu is located in the Urewera Country, home of the Tuhoe. It is regarded as their heartland and was once the headquarters of the religious sect led by Rua Kenana.

Mayor Island used to be a source of obsidian, a hard rock used by Maori for shaping into implements and weapons.

Meremere Power Station, on the Waikato River, was mothballed in 1992.

Mercury Bay was where Captain James Cook took possession of New Zealand for the British Crown.

Milford Sound is the northernmost of the Fiordland fiords and is 15 kilometres in length.

The Milford Track is 55 kilometres long, extending from Lake Te Anau to Milford Sound. It has been described as the finest walk in the world.

Mitre Peak is not a single isolated peak, but one of five similar peaks.

Mokoia Island, in Lake Rotorua, has a hot spring called Hinemoa's Pool.

Molesworth Station, in Marlborough, covers 1800 square kilometres and is the largest land-holding in New Zealand. It was taken over by the government in the 1930s, after overstocking caused soil erosion and forced farmers off the property.

Mount Bruce, a native bird reserve in the Wairarapa, has been privy to experiments to re-establish rare New Zealand birds like the kakapo, takahe and black stilt.

Mount Hicks in the Southern Alps is also known as St David's Dome.

Mount Ruapehu is an active volcano. It has seven small glaciers on its flanks.

Mount Tasman is the second highest mountain in New Zealand.

The Murchison Mountains form the border between Southland and Fiordland.

Murihiku, the Maori name for Southland, means 'last joint of the tail'.

Musick Point, near Howick, Auckland, is named after Edwin C Musick, the American pilot who pioneered the commercial air link between the USA and New Zealand.

The National War Memorial in Wellington is made up of a carillon and a hall of memories. The carillon has 44 bells that range from one weighing 4 kilograms to one weighing 5 tonnes.

The source of the Buller River is Lake Rotoroa in the Nelson Lakes National Park.

Ngamotu Beach in New Plymouth is the site of the first European settlement in Taranaki.

The Waikato and Waipa Rivers meet at Ngaruawahia.

Nightcaps, a coal-mining Southland town, is named after the conical hills to the north of the town.

Ninety Mile Beach is in reality closer to 60 miles long (96 km).

The Northland peninsula is 80 kilometres across at its widest point.

North Cape is not quite the northernmost point of New Zealand. This honour belongs to Surville Cliffs, 3 kilometres to the north-west of North Cape.

North Head, in Devonport, Auckland, was fitted with gun emplacements in response to the Russian Scare of 1885.

Nelson Forest Park is New Zealand's largest forest park, covering 377,000 hectares.

Ohinemutu, on the shores of Lake Rotorua, is the traditional home of the Ngati Arawa people.

Oihi Bay in Northland is the burial site of Thomas King, believed to be the first European born in New Zealand. He lived only three years.

Orakau Pa, near Kihikihi, is the site of New Zealand's most famous battle when 1500 British and colonial soldiers attacked 300 Maori led by Rewi Maniapoto, in 1864. Such was the courage and tenacity of the defenders that they were offered the chance to surrender, to which Rewi Maniapoto made the legendary reply: 'Kaore e mau te rongo, ake, ake!' ('We will never surrender').

Central Otago, in the lee of the Southern Alps, has one of the driest climates in New Zealand, and the surfeit of summer sunshine helps to make it a highly profitable fruit-growing area.

Papawai Marae, near Greytown, was the

setting for a strong nationwide Maori movement called Kotahitanga, designed to achieve self-government. In 1897, Te Wai Pounamu, a large meeting house there, was declared a Maori 'Parliament'.

Paradise, on the shores of Lake Diamond near Lake Wakatipu, derived its name either from the many paradise shelducks in the area, or from its pristine position and natural beauty.

Parihaka was the centre of the Maori pacifist movement led by Te Whiti and Tohu.

The parliamentary Beehive cost $18.8 million to build and was completed in 1982.

Perano Head, in the Marlborough Sounds, is the nearest point of the South Island to the North Island. It is the site of New Zealand's last whaling station.

Petone, a Wellington suburb, was the first site of the New Zealand Company settlement Britannia (Wellington). However, during the first winter, flooding from the Hutt River forced the settlers to move to higher ground. That higher ground became the present location of Wellington.

The only game animals found in Pirongia Forest Park are wild goats.

Pirongia Mountain saw what was effectively the last act of the New Zealand land wars, when, in 1881, the second Maori king Te Wherowhero and his warriors came down from the mountain and the king laid his guns at the feet of the government agent, Major Gilbert Mair.

The Polar Range in South Canterbury is named after four of the five explorers who died on Captain Robert Falcon Scott's South Pole venture: Mount Oates, Mount Wilson, Mount Scott and Mount Bowers. The fifth member of the party, Evans, missed out.

Porirua Harbour, north of Wellington, can only accommodate small pleasure craft.

Poverty Bay was named by Captain James Cook after an unsuccessful attempt to take on food and supplies to replenish his ship.

Preservation Inlet in Fiordland was the site of an attempted settlement in the late nineteenth century which came to nothing because of its remoteness and high rainfall.

Rangihoua Bay in the Bay of Islands is where the first wheat crop in New Zealand was grown by the Ngapuhi chief, Ruatara.

The Rangitaiki River is the fourth longest river in the North Island, after the Waikato, Whanganui and Rangitikei Rivers.

Ship Cove in Queen Charlotte Sound is the site where Captain James Cook visited five times during the course of three voyages in the 1770s.

The Shotover River in the South Island is called Tummel Burn near its source.

Six Mile is a settlement located close to the Six Mile Creek, which in turn is six miles from Murchison.

Skippers is a region in Central Otago associated with the gold rush. It is named after a sea skipper and gold miner named Captain Gay who initially discovered gold in the area.

Spirits Bay in Northland gets it name from the Maori belief that spirits of the dead depart from Cape Reinga, located at the end of the bay.

Taranaki had the highest proportion of Wesleyan Methodists in the 1870s.

Lake Tarawera is said to have emptied during the 1886 eruption, and refilled over a larger area immediately after the eruption.

Te Porere near Taumarunui was the setting in 1869 of the last major battle of the wars between Maori and Pakeha.

Tiwai Point, near Bluff, is the site of New Zealand's only aluminium smelter.

Tongariro National Park was the first of New Zealand's national parks, having been donated to the country in 1887.

Turangawaewae at Ngaruawahia in Waikato is the headquarters of the Maori King Movement.

Victoria Forest Park in North Westland was gazetted as recently as 1986.

The last shot of the Maori-Pakeha wars was said to have been fired in the Lake Waikaremoana region by Private Nikora Te Tehi.

That proportion of the Waikato River located south of Lake Taupo is also known as the Tongariro River.

Waipoua Forest in Northland contains the last stands of the original kauri forests.

Wairakei is located on an active volcanic fault that extends from Mount Ruapehu to White Island in the Bay of Plenty.

Wairarapa was the first New Zealand region where sheep farming was undertaken.

Waitangi translates as 'noisy or weeping water'.

The Waitomo Caves are made up of three limestone caves: Waitomo, Ruakuri and Aranui.

Lake Wakatipu is fed by the Dart, Rees, Greenstone and Lochy Rivers.

Lake Wanaka is 45 kilometres long and only about 5 kilometres wide.

The first European known to have spent time in the Whanganui river region was Joe Rowe, a dealer in preserved Maori heads, in 1831. Rowe's own head was later cut off and preserved by Maori.

Westland National Park contains the largest range of vegetation and wildlife in any area of New Zealand's national parks.

The National Parks of Aoraki/Mount Cook, Taranaki/Egmont and Abel Tasman are New Zealand's smallest.

Young Nick's Head was named after Nicholas Young, a 12-year-old surgeon's boy on Captain James Cook's ship the *Endeavour* in 1769.

FLORA & FAUNA

Things That Grow in the Night

Alfonsino is a slender, colourful fish found in New Zealand waters. Most catches are exported to Japan.

Ammonites are extinct snails. In 1978, a giant ammonite weighing 1225 kilograms was found at Taharoa on the west coast of the North Island.

The best-known ant in New Zealand is the white-footed house ant.

New Zealand has 32 native species of bee.

The bidi-bidi is a corruption of the Maori name, piripiri.

Thirty-two species of native bird were rendered extinct in pre-European times, including the world's largest eagle, two types of geese, a swan and a pelican.

Bush lawyers are brambles. They are also a term for those with pretensions towards a knowledge of the law.

A butterfish eats its own weight in seaweed every 14 days.

The cardinal ladybird was accidentally introduced to New Zealand at the end of the nineteenth century.

The New Zealand crab louse, known as 'the crabs', is very small and infests pubic hair, underarm hair and eyebrows.

The New Zealand dabchick, a member of the grebe family, builds large and untidy nests.

Dieffenbach's speargrass, found on the Chatham Islands, is experiencing resurgence after being ravaged by stock.

Approximately 30 species of flea are found in New Zealand.

Galloways and Belted Galloways are beef cattle breeds imported to New Zealand from Scotland in 1947. The Galloway is blue-black in colour, as is the Belted variety, although the latter has a wide, light-coloured strip around its girth.

The ghost shark is related to the elephant fish.

The godwit is the most numerous of New Zealand's migratory arctic waders, being capable of migrating to breeding grounds in Siberia and Alaska.

The great knot, a bird, occasionally visits New Zealand.

The green beetle arrived in New Zealand during World War II.

By 1911, there were over 400,000 horses in New Zealand.

The huhu grub becomes New Zealand's largest beetle.

Jack-knife prawns are found in the Bay of Plenty and further north.

The katipo spider is the only dangerously poisonous creature in New Zealand. Only the female is able to bite and its bite can be fatal. It is related to the Australian redback and the American black widow.

A giant snail called the kauri snail, or pupurangi, is found on the Hen and Chicken Islands — and nowhere else in the world.

The kea is the world's only alpine parrot.

The kiwi is the most primitive New Zealand bird, having been here for 70 million years.

The name 'kiwi' is thought to derive from the Maori name for the bird — kivi — which was also the Polynesian name for the night-calling bristle-thighed curlew.

The kiwi lays one or two eggs which are unusually large.

The kiwi is the only bird in the world with nostrils at the end of its nose.

The three kiwi species are the common or brown kiwi, the little spotted kiwi and the great spotted kiwi.

Kohekohe, a tree, is New Zealand's only representative of the mahogany family.

The kokako, a native New Zealand bird, seldom flies further than 100 metres. Normally it scrambles up trees and glides to where it wants to go.

The leather-jacket is a small fish, the sole New Zealand representative of the trigger-fish family.

There are approximately 1500 species of lichen in New Zealand.

New Zealand has one species of freshwater limpet which is found attached to stones in North Island streams.

Magpies have been known to attack people.

Mudfish, of which there are three species in New Zealand, can breathe air.

The world's rarest tree — *Pennantia Baylisiana* — grows on the Three Knights Islands.

The anal and pelvic fins of the perch are orange-red in colour.

The Perendale sheep was developed by Sir Geoffrey Peren of Massey University, using Cheviot and Romney genes.

In 1977, a Japanese fishing trawler operating off the coast of Christchurch hauled aboard an enormous, rotting sea creature which had been netted from a depth of 300 metres. Scientists speculated on what the object could be. Some suggested it could be a plesiosaur, a giant, lizard-like sea creature thought to be extinct for millions of years. Others plumped for the notion that it was simply a rotting whale or shark. Unfortunately the crew on the boat had returned the object to the sea, in fear that the rotting carcass would contaminate their conventional catch, and a deeper analysis of the 'sea monster' was not possible.

The large and necessarily soft leaves of the rangiora shrub had a practical early use, and became known as bushman's friend (toilet paper).

The right whale got its name from New Zealand whalers, because it was just right for whalers. It swam slowly and provided large quantities of whale oil.

The Chatham Islands are home to the taiko, considered the world's rarest seabird.

The thar (or tahr), a type of mountain goat, was introduced to the South Island from the Himalayas.

The tuatara is not a lizard.

Four species of turtle have been recorded as visiting New Zealand waters during summer.

Vegetable sheep is the term for a sub-alpine plant of the *Raoulia* species, found most commonly in Canterbury. Their dense nature and spreading white flowers give them the appearance of sheep.

The wrybill, a small wading bird found only in New Zealand, is unusual in having the tip of its bill curve to the right.

Of Thresher and Carpet

Sharks common to New Zealand waters

Broad-snouted seven-gill shark
Bronze whaler
Carpet shark
Great white shark, also known as the white death
and the white pointer
Hammerhead shark
Mako shark, also known as the bonito shark or blue pointer
School shark
Spotted smooth-hound
Thresher shark
Tiger shark

Cut-throats and Snipes

New Zealand eels

Common conger eel
Cut-throat eel
Garden eel
Grey moray eel
Hairy conger eel
Long-finned eel
Mosaic moray eel
Mottled moray eel
Northern conger eel
Parasitic eel
Sawtooth or thread eel
Serpent eel
Short-finned eel
Silver conger eel
Snake eel
Snipe eel
Speckled moray eel
Swollenhead conger eel
Umbrella conger eel
Yellow moray eel

Finless Wonders and Yellow Bellies

New Zealand flounder

Black flounder
Brill
Crested flounder
Finless flounder
Greenback flounder
Lemon sole
New Zealand or common sole
Sand flounder
Spotted flounder
Turbot
Witch flounder
Yellow-belly flounder

Croakers

New Zealand frogs

Indigenous
Leiopelma archeyi
Leiopelma hamiltoni
Leiopelma hochstetteri

Introduced
Litoria aurea — the green tree or golden bell frog
Litoria caerulea — the great green tree frog
Litoria ewingi — the brown or whistling tree frog
Litoria raniformis — the southern bell frog

Worth Two in the Bush

New Zealand birds — rare or endangered species

Maori name	
Black petrel	Taiko
Black robin	Miro
Black stilt	Kaki
Black-fronted tern	Tarapiroe
Blue duck	Whio
Brown teal	Pateke
Bush wren	Matuhi
Chatham Island oystercatcher	
Chatham Island pigeon	Kukupa
Codfish Island fernbird	
Cook's petrel	Titi
Fairy tern	
King shag	
Little grey kiwi	Kiwipukapuka
Little spotted kiwi	Kiwipukapuka
Magenta petrel	Chatham Island taiko
New Zealand dabchick	Weweia
New Zealand falcon	Karearea
New Zealand red-breasted dotterel	
New Zealand thrush	Piopio
Notornis	Takahe moho
Orange-fronted parakeet	
Owl parrot	Kakapo
Red-necked avocet	
Royal spoonbill	Kotuku spoonbill
Saddleback	Tieke
Shore plover	Tututatu
Southern crested grebe	Puteketeke
Stewart Island snipe	Tutukiwi
Stitchbird	Hihi
Yellow-eyed penguin	Hoiho
Yellowhead (bush canary)	Mohua

Of Greyish Underparts

Types of weka

The North Island weka, which has greyish underparts, is located mainly in Poverty Bay.

The Buff weka, found in the Chatham Islands.

The South Island weka is found from Nelson to Fiordland.

The Stewart Island weka is smaller and darker.

Quackers

New Zealand ducks

Blue duck
Brown teal
Grey duck
Grey teal
Mallard
New Zealand scaup (the black teal)
New Zealand shoveller
Paradise shelduck

Something for Tree Huggers

Native trees

Akeake
Black maire/Maire
Coastal maire
Hakeke/Hakekeke
Hangehange
Hinau
Horoeka — Lancewood
Horopito — Pepper tree
Houhere — Long-leaved lacebark
Hutu
Inanga
Kahikatea — White pine
Kaikomako
Kamahi and Tawhero/Towhai
Kanuka
Karaka
Karamu
Karo
Kauri
Keketara
Kohekohe
Kohuhu
Kotukutuku — Native fuchsia
Kowhai

Mahoe — Whiteywood
Maire tawaki
Makomako — Wineberry
Mamaku — Black tree fern
Manatu — Ribbonwood
Manawa — Mangrove
Mangeao
Manuka — Tea tree
Mapou/Mapau/Red Matipo
Matagouri — Wild Irishman
Matai — Black pine
Mingimingi
Miro — Brown pine
Monoao
Mountain neinei
Mountain ribbonwoods
Narrow-leaved lacebark
Ngaio
Nikau
Ongaonga — Tree nettle
Papauma — Broadleaf
Pate
Pohutukawa
Ponga — Silver fern
Porokaiwhiri — Pigeonwood
Poroporo
Pukatea
Puriri
Putaputaweta
Ramarama
Rangiora
Rata and Southern Rata
Rewarewa — New Zealand honeysuckle
Rimu — Red pine
Rough-leaved tree daisy
Silver pine
Streamside tree daisy
Tanekaha and Pahautea
Taraire
Tarata — Lemonwood
Taupata
Tawa
Tawapou
Tawari
Tawhai — Silver beech
Tawhairaunui — Hard beech

Tawhairaunui — Red beech
Tawhairauriki — Black beech
Ti Kouka — Cabbage tree
Ti ngahere/Ti parae — Forest cabbage
tree
Titoki
Toro
Totara
Whau
Whauwhaupaku/Puahou — Five-finger
Wheki

Of Pigweed and Stinkwood

Distinctive native flowering plants

Barbless bidibidi
Benmore gentian
Bog daisy
Coastal cutty grass
Common drapetes
Common scabweed
Crag-loving daisy
Creeping fuchsia
Creeping lily
Cudweed
Dainty daisy
Dense tutu
Dwarf cabbage tree
False buttercup
Fleshy lobelia
Golden tainui —
kumarahou/gum-diggers
soap
Haast's carrot
Hairy coprosma
Hairy forget-me-not
Hooker's daisy
Horizontal orchid
Horokaka — Maori ice

plant
Horrid Spaniard
Hupiro — stinkwood
Karo — turpentine tree
Leafless lawyer
Lesser New Zealand
eyebright
Maori musk
Matagouri — tumatakuru/
wild Irishman
Mountain cress
Mutton-bird sedge
Niggerhead
North Island edelweiss
Northern snowberry
Onion-leaved orchid
Penwiper plant
Pigweed
Prostrate ngaio
Purple bladderwort
Ralph's kohuhu
Red-flowered vegetable
sheep
Sand-dune pincushion

Scree hebe
Snowball Spaniard
Southern salt horn
Spiny whipcord
Sprawling pohuehue
Sticky-stalked daisy
Tall pinatoro
Tangle herb
Toothed lancewood
Torlesse grass tree
Tufted haastia
Turepo — milk tree
Tutukiwi — hooded
orchid/elf's hood
Varnished koromiko
Wet rock hebe
Wi
Wild celery
Woollyhead
Wrinkled-leaved
pomaderris
Yellow buttons

Of Bog Pine and Pigmy

Native alpine plants

Bog pine
Coprosma
Eidelweiss
Everlasting daisy
Forget-me-not
Grass tree
Hebe

Mountain buttercup
Mountain daisy
Mountain heath
Mountain mikimiki
Mountain totara
New Zealand bluebell
Ourisia

Parahebe
Pigmy pine
Raoulia
Snowberry
Speargrass
Seneao

Of Dwarf Broom and Maori Onion

Native flowering herbs and small shrubs

Angelica Montana
Astelia
Chatham Islands forget-me-not
Blueberry
Dwarf broom
Geranium Traversii

Geum
Hibiscus Trionum
Kaka Beak
Kerikeri everlasting daisy
Koru
Kumarahou
Maori onion

New Zealand calceolaria
New Zealand iris
Olearia
Rock lily
Violets

From Creeping Lawyer to Porcupine Shrub

Native ground cover plants

Coprosma
Cotula
Creeping lawyer
Gunnera

Hebe
Mazus
Mercury Bay weed
New Zealand daphne

Parataniwha
Pentachondra pumila
Porcupine shrub
White rata

FAMOUS & INFAMOUS NEW ZEALANDERS

From JHC Sidebottom to Minnie Dean

William Larnach, creator of Otago's Larnach Castle, committed suicide in Parliament House.

Politician John A Lee served time in Borstal and Mt Eden Prison.

David Lange, at 41, became the second youngest New Zealand Prime Minister.

Maud Ruby Basham ('Aunt Daisy') was a dominant voice on radio for 25 years. She was only 1.5 metres tall.

Sir Brian Barrett-Boyes, a New Zealand pioneer in the field of heart surgery, himself underwent heart surgery.

William Jackson Barry was a nineteenth-century kiwi con man who, after selling offal meat to the gold miners at Tuapeka fields, toured New Zealand with a showbiz lecture group including 'Maori chiefs', an 'old whaler' and other people's lecture material.

Amy Bock (1859–1943) was New Zealand's most notorious female con artist. Among other escapades, she perfected up to seven different handwriting styles to enable her to send letters to herself from fictional relatives and backers, attesting to her strong financial state, thus allowing her to borrow money from others.

Richard Burgess was the leader of the evil Burgess gang that was responsible for 20-odd murders on the West Coast during the 1890s.

Minnie Dean, in 1895, was the only New Zealand woman to be executed.

Sir Edmund Hillary's middle name is Percival. Prior to becoming a mountain climber, he was a beekeeper.

Justice Peter Mahon made his famous criticism of Air New Zealand — 'An orchestrated litany of lies' — following his report into the Erebus air crash.

William Henry 'Bully' Hayes (1829–77) was notorious as a cheat and kidnapper of women.

Helen Clark was our first woman Deputy Prime Minis-ter. She was our second woman Prime Minister, after Jenny Shipley.

Archbishop Paul Reeves became New Zealand's first Maori Governor-General in 1985.

Gordon Coates was the first New Zealand-born Prime Minister.

William Ferguson Massey, who was Prime Minister from 1912 until his death, reacted to labour strife on the wharves by swearing in hundreds of farmers as special constables — Massey's Cossacks — to help break the strike.

The 'Flogging Parson' was the name given to Reverend Samuel Marsden when he was appointed as magistrate. The job required him to mete out physical punishment to the convicted.

Henare Kepa Te Ahururu, a constable in the Armed Constabulary, was the first of four Maori awarded the New Zealand Cross for helping settlers during the land wars.

Johannes Carl Anderson was the first librarian at the Alexander Turnbull Library.

Sylvia Ashton-Warner was one of New Zealand's leading novelists and educationalists.

Isabella Aylmer was an Englishwoman who wrote the second New Zealand novel, *Distant Homes*.

Sir Joseph Banks was an English botanist who travelled with Captain James Cook on his first exploration of the South Pacific.

Jean Batten, the world famous aviatrix, undertook solo flights from England to India, England to Australia, Australia to England, England to Brazil and from England to New Zealand.

James Keir Baxter is widely regarded as being New Zealand's most gifted poet.

Colonel Sir Charles Moihi Te Arawaka Bennett commanded the Maori Battalion.

Solomon Black was one of the first three men awarded the New Zealand Cross.

William Brame was the founder of the non-conformist Port Albert settlement.

Sir Ron Brierley founded Brierley Investments Ltd while still in his twenties.

Charles Brown, a close friend of the poet John Keats and an associate of Lord Byron, emigrated to New Zealand in 1841.

Thomas Brunner, one of New Zealand's most intrepid early explorers, was forced to eat his dog because of lack of food while searching for the source of the Buller River.

John Butler was the first ordained clergyman to settle in New Zealand as a missionary. In 1820, he supervised the first ploughing of New Zealand soil.

'Carbine' was New Zealand's first internationally successful racehorse.

'Cardigan Bay' was New Zealand's most famous pacer and the first in the world to earn a million dollars.

Welsh-born Stephen Carkeek was the first New Zealand inspector of customs.

Bob Charles, a left-hander, was New Zealand's most successful international golf professional.

Archibald Clark was the first mayor of Auckland. His son, James McCosh Clark was mayor of Auckland too.

William Colenso produced the first book printed in New Zealand: the *Epistles to the Ephesians and Philippians* in Maori.

Dame Whina Cooper is known as 'Mother of the Nation'.

James Crawford, a geologist, constructed a drainage tunnel 100 metres long from his Miramar property to Evans Bay. It is believed to be the first tunnel made in New Zealand.

William Davidson bred the first Corriedale sheep flock in New Zealand.

Ethel De Costa was New Zealand's first woman lawyer.

Bob Deans, the All Black who 'scored' the disputed try against Wales in 1905, died of complications following an appendectomy two months after playing a test match against the touring Anglo-Welsh rugby team in 1908.

Squash player Susan Devoy was the youngest player, at 20 years of age, to gain the 'first in the world' ranking.

Marmaduke Dixon was the first New Zealand farmer to ship wheat in bags to England.

Thomas Ellison, a lawyer, was actively involved in the rugby evolution of the wing forward.

Kate Evans was the first New Zealand woman, and possibly the first in the British Empire, to graduate with a BA.

Pianist Richard Farrell was one of New Zealand's few genuine child prodigies, learning to play the piano at four and writing his first composition at nine.

Sir James Fletcher was New Zealand's first industrialist.

Sir William Fox had four tenures as Prime Minister of New Zealand.

Bernard Freyberg was an outstanding field soldier in World War I; the commander of the New Zealand Division in World War II; and Governor-General of New Zealand between 1946 and 1952.

Samuel Frickleton single-handedly captured two German machine-gun posts in World War I, killing all enemy occupants as he did so.

Sir Harold Delf Gillies, who was born in Dunedin, was the most influential plastic surgeon of his era.

Sir George Gipps was, in essence, the first Governor of New Zealand, when he became Governor-in-Chief of New Zealand in 1839. His role terminated in 1841 when New Zealand became a Crown Colony.

Denis Glover, a leading poet and printer, was an excellent boxer.

Doris Gordon was largely responsible for the establishment of the Chair of Obstetrics and Gynaecology at the University of Otago Medical School.

David Gray was the perpetrator of the worst multiple murder in New Zealand's history in 1990, when he shot 13 men, women and children, before being shot by police.

Sir George Grey, the most influential political figure in New Zealand during the nineteenth century, was born in Lisbon, Portugal.

Sir Richard Hadlee, at the time of his retirement from international cricket in 1990, held the world record for the number of test-match wickets — 431.

William Hardham was the only New Zealander to win the Victoria Cross during the Boer War. A blacksmith in civilian life, he achieved the rank of farrier-major.

Thomas Heeney was the first New Zealand heavyweight boxer to challenge for a world professional boxing title.

Christine Hellyar is a controversial artist, whose work 'Country Clothesline' is one of the most notorious and polarising artworks to be seen in a New Zealand gallery.

Frederick Hilgendorf made a significant contribution to New Zealand agriculture by adapting wheat to local conditions.

Francis Hodgkins is the most internationally celebrated painter New Zealand has produced.

Sir Keith Holyoake, Prime Minister in 1957 and from 1960 to 1972, and later Governor-General of New Zealand, left school without any secondary qualifications. While still in his twenties he became president of the Golden Bay-Motueka Rugby Union.

Abraham Hort was the founder of the first Jewish congregation in New Zealand.

Alfred Hulme won the Victoria Cross after killing 33 German snipers on the island of Crete in 1941. Denis Hulme, his son, became a champion racing driver, and was the first New Zealander to win the world Formula One driving championship.

Keri Hulme, a poet, short-story writer and novelist, won the prestigious Booker prize for fiction in 1985, with *the bone people*.

Sir Thomas Hunter founded the New Zealand school dental service.

Robin Hyde, one of New Zealand's most acclaimed novelists and poets, took her own life a few days before the outbreak of World War II.

Rowena Jackson, New Zealand's most acclaimed ballerina, was noted for her brilliant turns — 'multiple fouettes performed sur place'. In this field she created a world record.

Billy T James, one of New Zealand's best-known comedians, became New Zealand's fourteenth heart transplant recipient in 1989. Sadly, he passed away in 1991.

Ron Jarden was both a brilliant All Black winger and a worthy New Zealand representative in the Admiral's Cup at Cowes, in his yacht, *Barnacle Bill*.

Reginald Judson won the three highest awards for gallantry — the Distinguished Conduct Medal, the Military Medal and the Victoria Cross — within a six-week period during World War I.

Newton King, founder of the large stock-and-station firm Newton King Ltd, was the brother of Truby King, deviser of the Plunket system for the welfare of mothers and babies.

Norman Kirk, New Zealand's Prime Minister from December 1972 until his death in office on 31 August 1974, had only a primary school education.

Dame Sister Mary Leo was New Zealand's best-known and most successful singing teacher, having among her pupils Malvina Major and Dame Kiri Te Kanawa.

Trevor Lloyd, an illustrator, was one of the first New Zealand artists to make etchings.

John ('Jack') Lovelock, the first of New Zealand's world-class middle- and long-distance runners, was a Rhodes Scholar, a doctor and the assistant director of a department of the Manhatten Hospital.

Sir David Low was the most famous cartoonist to come out of New Zealand.

Arthur Lydiard, the running coach, was the originator of the jogging craze that swept the world.

Colin McCahon is the leading name in contemporary New Zealand painting.

Donald McIntyre, the New Zealand bass-baritone of international standing, became the first 'English' singer to take on the roll of Wotan in Wagner's 'Ring Cycle'.

Jessie MacKay, a poet, also campaigned passionately for Prohibition and against vivisection and blood sports.

James McKenzie is a legendary, often mysterious figure in New Zealand history, for although the MacKenzie Country, MacKenzie Pass and MacKenzie River are all named after him, albeit with a different spelling, his date and place of birth and ultimate fate remain unknown. He was associated with the rustling of sheep in 1855 and served time, but escaped twice during a stipulated five-year sentence. However, after being recaptured and having served only nine months of his term, he was pardoned, whereupon it is believed he returned to Australia.

JHC Sidebottom was the overseer at Levels Station, Timaru, who set about tracking down and locating James McKenzie and the 1800 rustled sheep. Sidebottom and his two Maori sidekicks overpowered McKenzie, but the latter broke free and made for Lyttelton, where he was captured.

Mahuki Manukura founded a new religious cult, 'Te kau-ma-ra'. In 1890, he prophesied that the Maori Millennium would come on 2 November, and he and his followers moved to Te Kuiti during October to await the event. After stirring up trouble in the town he was jailed, not for the first time.

A few years earlier he had been jailed for a year when he tried to stymie the progress of the Main Trunk Railway survey.

George Mannering, an extremely durable New Zealand mountaineer, climbed the Matterhorn when he was 60. Ten years later he climbed Mount Torlesse in New Zealand's Southern Alps, then topped it all off by climbing Fog Peak near Lake Wanaka on his 79th birthday.

Eliza Melville, a lawyer, became the first woman city councillor in New Zealand, serving for 33 years on the Auckland City Council.

Ditlev Monrad was Prime Minister of Denmark in 1863, and after his country's defeat by the Germans over Schleswig-Holstein, he emigrated to New Zealand in 1865.

Edward Morgan, a boxer, won New Zealand's first gold medal at an Olympic Games. He remains the only New Zealand boxer to win an Olympic event. Initially Morgan was to fight in the lightweight division but because he had put on weight while travelling to the games site — Amsterdam — he had to fight as a welterweight.

John Morgan was a leading light in the development of a comprehensive and sophisticated Maori agricultural economy that flourished in the Southern Waikato during the late 1840s and 1850s. Two flour mills were constructed to process the large acreage of wheat and eventually produce was exported to Australia and California.

Sir Howard Morrison is the best-known Maori entertainer in New Zealand. As a member of the Howard Morrison Quartet he shared in the success of the group's first recording in 1958 — 'My Old Man's an All Black' and 'Battle of Waikato', which sold 78,000 copies.

Thomas Murphy was the only New Zealand-born boxer to win a world professional title, when he won the 1890 world featherweight title in San Francisco. Much earlier he had been expelled from school for hitting a teacher.

James Nairn, an influential New Zealand art teacher, attracted criticism for his nude life classes.

At the age of 45, George Nepia became the oldest New Zealander to play in a first-class rugby match, when he captained the Olympians against Poverty Bay in 1950.

Harold and Harry Nicholls, despite the apparent duplicity of Christian name, were two separate individuals who both played for the All Blacks.

Annaliese Coberger won the silver medal in the giant slalom at the Winter Olympics in 1992. It was the first medal won by an athlete from the southern hemisphere.

Samuel Parnell, a carpenter, refused to work more than eight hours a day, thereby helping to create the mood, in the 1840s, for the instigation of the eight-hour day. Because there was a shortage of carpenters Parnell was able to dictate his own terms.

Joseph Pawelka was one of New Zealand's most celebrated convicts. A butcher from Palmerston North, he married a woman six years his senior, although the marriage lasted only two months. Pawelka attempted suicide, was charged for the offence and that's when his problems really started.

Richard Pearse is believed to have been a world-beater at flying in a home-made aircraft. Reports suggest that he beat the Wright brothers by a long shot. Pearse's supporters claim that after a series of taxiing tests and short jumps, Pearse was able to get his craft airborne and it remained aloft until approximately one kilometre had been covered, at the end of which it nose-dived into the Opihi River.

William Pickering, some time after Richard Pearse, became director of the Jet Propulsion Laboratory in California, which produced the first successful US earth satellite, Explorer I. He was born in Wellington.

Whetoi Pomare was a Ngapuhi chief who led successful raids down through the North Island in the 1820s. However, this all came to an end when he was killed and eaten by Waikato Maori after they caught him off guard.

The Fifth Earl of Ranfurly was New Zealand's fifteenth Governor. His most telling contribution to New Zealand culture was the bestowing of the Ranfurly Shield for rugby competition between New Zealand provinces.

Alfred Hamish (AH) Reed was a noted New Zealand publisher who enjoyed walking long distances and climbing high mountains. He accounted for Mount Taranaki/Egmont when he was 80, Mount Ruapehu at 83 and Mount Ngauruhoe at 85. Someone suggested that he was almost as old as some of the mountains he conquered. He died at the age of 99.

Pauline Rhodes, a New Zealand artist, was concerned 'with space and the use of metal, especially the visual effect achieved by rusting'.

Williams Rhodes-Moorhouse, a London-born part-Maori, was the first airman to win the Victoria Cross.

John Rutherford was on board the *Agnes* when it was blown off course on the way to the Bay of Islands. It took shelter in Poverty Bay but all the crew were killed and eaten — all except Rutherford who was adopted by the Maori tribe, given a moko and several wives. He was finally rescued by an American ship and returned to England where he travelled for a time with a side-show — starring as a tattooed man.

Frank Sargeson, the best-known New Zealand short-story writer of his time, was born Norris Frank Davey in Hamilton.

Michael Joseph Savage, New Zealand's first Labour Prime Minister, was born in Victoria, Australia.

Mary Scott, a writer of light romantic novels, wrote her first book while living on a King Country farm. For some reason she used the pseudonym Marten Stuart.

Richard John Seddon, the longest-serving Prime Minister in New Zealand's history, was almost 20 stone when he died.

Maurice Shadbolt, the internationally published New Zealand writer, was educated at Te Kuiti and Auckland.

Alfred John Shout won the Military Cross and Victoria Cross.

George William Smith played for New Zealand at rugby and rugby League, won a series of New Zealand track-and-field titles, won the British 120 yards hurdles, set an unofficial world record in the 440 yards hurdles, and as an apprentice jockey won the New Zealand Cup on Impulse in 1894.

Peter Snell, New Zealand's greatest middle-distance runner, was born at Opunake.

Carl Sydow was a sculptor who, after a while, began using PVC tubing, roofing iron and other commercial materials in his works.

Eric Tindall played rugby and cricket for New Zealand. He later became an international rugby referee and an international cricket umpire.

Dame Catherine Tizard was the first woman to become Governor-General of New Zealand. Earlier she had been the first woman mayor of Auckland.

James Ward won the Victoria Cross in World War II. One of his acts of bravery involved clambering out along the wing of a Wellington bomber to insert a canvas engine cover into a hole near a burning engine. The act effectively blocked leaking fuel from fuelling the fire.

Marilyn Waring, who became an MP at the age of 23, worked as a post office technician, musician and barmaid after graduating from Waikato University.

Lawrence Carthage Weathers, New Zealand born, became a South Australian undertaker. He won the Victoria Cross posthumously in World War I.

Ernest Mervyn Taylor was New Zealand's finest wood engraver in the European tradition.

John Clarke (aka Fred Dagg) starred in a movie called *Dagg Day Afternoon*.

William Crush Daldy took the first cargo of New Zealand produce to Britain.

Learmonth White Dalrymple, a woman, was the prime motivator in setting up the first public high school for girls in the southern hemisphere — Otago Girls High — in 1871.

A Hamilton woman, Mrs GA Hurd-Wood, began a movement in 1926 that led to the setting up of the New Zealand League for the Hard of Hearing.

Dame Kiri Te Kanawa was born in Gisborne in 1944.

The Right Honourable The Marquess of Normanby was Governor-General of New Zealand between 1875 and 1879. He was replaced by Sir Hercules Robinson.

When Elizabeth Yates became Mayor of Onehunga in 1893 she became the first woman to be elected mayor of a municipality in the British Empire.

John Sheahan was the first New Zealand-born Pakeha MP and Cabinet Minister.

William Meagher was one of New Zealand's first cabinet makers.

Billy T James, the comedian, was born William James Taitoko.

James K Baxter, the poet, is buried at Jerusalem on the Whanganui River.

Charles Heaphy was awarded the VC for his 'total disregard for his own safety' during an attack by Maori near Paterangi Pa.

RELIGION

The Wrath of a Down Under God

In 1825, Rangi, a Waitangi chief, requested baptism as he lay dying, thereby becoming the first Maori convert to Christianity.

In 1865, the German-born Anglican vicar of Opotiki, CS Volkner, was hanged outside his church by Pai Marire. Volkner had been sending strategic information to the government about the movements of Maori forces.

On 4 July 1868, Te Kooti and his followers escaped from the Chatham Islands, with this day being recognised as the Ra-tapu (Sabbath) of the Ringatu Church.

Spiritualist seances caused great excitement in Dunedin in 1870. As a result, a Spiritual Investigations Society was established.

In 1882, there was a controversy in Auckland Protestant church circles over 'conditional immortality'.

In 1888, William Salmond, Professor of Moral and Mental Philosophy at Otago University, was found guilty of heresy because of his doubts about hell.

The first Lutheran church in New Zealand was set up near Nelson where German immigrants had settled.

In 1890, the Grand Lodge of Ancient, Free and Accepted Masons was established in Wellington to control the activities of freemasonry.

In 1893, a riot occurred outside Christchurch's Temple of Truth, after its preacher AB Worthington was found guilty of bigamy.

The Reverend Rota Waitoa was the first Maori deacon.

AR Fitchett, a Wesleyan minister, was refused membership of the Dunedin YMCA because he agreed with the theory of evolution.

In 1896, a census revealed that 29.8 per cent of New Zealanders — the highest ever recorded — attended church.

The 'Primitive Methodists', a fundamentalist offshoot of the Methodist church, evolved in England and became established in New Zealand. In 1899, the 'Primitive Methodists' declared that only citizens who abstained from alcohol could become members of the church in New Zealand.

Pai Marire, a Maori religious movement founded by the prophet Te Ua Haumene, was based on the belief that Maori were one of the lost tribes of Israel.

The first ritualistic controversy in the Anglican Church in New Zealand occurred when Kaiapoi parishioners complained about the behaviour of curate H Carlyon. The latter was 'adoring' the sacrament and encouraging the confession of sins.

The first bishop of the New Zealand Anglican diocese of Melanesia, J Patterson, was killed by islanders in the Solomon Islands.

An American, Mrs MC Leavitt, arrived in New Zealand to persuade women to back the temperance cause. The outcome was the Women's Christian Temperance Union.

The New Zealand Freethought Association was formed at a meeting in Dunedin. At the meeting the laws against blasphemy were denounced.

In 1917, a report exonerating the Post Office from charges of Catholic bias was released. MPs listened in horror to anti-Catholic letters alleging moral misconduct by priests and nuns, which had been read by the Post Office military censor.

In 1925, the Ratana church came into existence.

A Dallimore set up the Revival Fire Mission in Auckland. It generated notoriety for its dramatic emphasis on miracles.

The first Pentecostal healing mission began in the Wellington Town Hall. Its preacher was Smith Wigglesworth of England.

In 1930, John Dickie, the Principal of Knox Theological College, completed his 'Organism of Christian Truth', a major statement of theology.

In 1932, following the riot of the unemployed in Auckland, 'Uncle Scrim' (CG Scrimgeour) noted that the rioters' utilisation of battens from the Methodist Social Service Mission building was the 'best use the Methodist Church had been put to in the last 100 years'.

The Presbyterian General Assembly became concerned when a pacifist theological student was required for military training.

The first yoga group in New Zealand — the Balmoral Physical Culture and Yoga School, was established in 1936.

The first Jehovah's Witness church in New Zealand was set up at Waima, Northland.

Te Ake Rapana left the Ratana Church to found the Absolute Established Maori Church at Te Tii in the Bay of Islands.

Ormond Burton, a Methodist minister with pacifist beliefs, was imprisoned four times during World War II.

New Zealand's first congregational minister was the Reverend Barzillai Quaife.

In 1958, the Church of Jesus Christ of Latter-Day Saints (Mormons), opened their New Zealand temple at Templeview, Hamilton.

In 1959, the Methodists became the first religious group in New Zealand to admit women to the ordained ministry.

In 1959, Billy Graham, the American evangelist, drew crowds of 60,000 in Auckland, Wellington and Christchurch.

Lloyd Geering, a controversial theologian, was the principal of the Presbyterian Knox Theological College who suggested, in 1966, that the resurrection of Jesus Christ may not have been literally true.

The General Assembly of the Presbyterian Church disassociated itself from Geering's views and reaffirmed its belief in life after death. Geering subsequently resigned. He was charged with heresy in 1967.

An Apostolic Delegate to New Zealand was appointed by the Vatican in 1968.

In 1980, Dean Goffin, a respected New Zealand brass band composer, was made Territorial Commander of the Salvation Army in New Zealand.

In 1981, 25 per cent of New Zealanders did not acknowledge membership of any Christian church.

Orthodox and Unorthodox

Religious affiliations in New Zealand

The following summary presents the main religious affiliations returned at the 1971, 1976, and 1981 censuses.

Religious Profession	Number of Adherents			Percentage		
	1971	1976	1981	1971	1976	1981
Anglican (Church of England)	895,839	915,202	814,740	31.3	29.2	25.7
Presbyterian	583,701	566,569	523,221	20.4	18.1	16.5
Roman Catholic (incl. Catholic undefined)	449,974	478,530	456,858	15.7	15.3	14.4
Methodist	182,727	173,526	148,512	6.4	5.5	4.7
Christian n.o.d.	33,187	52,478	101,901	1.2	1.7	3.2
Baptist	47,350	49,442	50,143	1.7	1.6	1.6
Latter-Day Saints (Mormon)	29,785	36,130	37,686	1.0	1.2	1.2
Ratana	30,156	35,082	35,781	1.1	1.1	1.1
Brethren	25,768	24,414	24,324	0.9	0.8	0.8
Agnostic	9481	14,136	24,201	0.3	0.5	0.8
Atheist	9291	14,293	21,528	0.3	0.5	0.7
Salvation Army	19,371	22,019	20,490	0.7	0.7	0.6
Protestant n.o.d.	37,475	33,309	16,989	1.3	1.1	0.5

Jehovah's Witness	10,318	13,392	13,740	0.4	0.4	0.4
Assemblies of God	3599	5581	12,525	0.4	0.4	0.4
Seventh-Day Adventist	10,477	11,958	11,520	0.4	0.4	0.4
Pentecostal	1859	4846	6408	0.1	0.2	0.2
Church of Christ	8930	8087	6372	0.3	0.3	0.2
Ringatu	5635	6230	6117	0.2	0.2	0.2
Hindu	3845	5203	6078	0.1	0.2	0.2
Lutheran	5930	6297	5676	0.2	0.2	0.2
Indigenous Pentecostal	12	824	5295	—	—	0.2
Apostolic	2361	2693	4503	0.1	0.1	0.1
Congregational	7704	6600	3825	0.3	0.2	0.1
Eastern Orthodox Catholic	4319	4153	3813	0.2	0.1	0.1
Undenominational	3709	4222	3720	0.1	0.1	0.1
Buddhist	1370	2382	3693	—	0.1	0.1
Union Church	1154	3045	3399	—	0.1	0.1
Hebrew Congregational	3803	3921	3360	0.1	0.1	0.1
Spiritualist	1015	1731	2418	—	0.1	0.1
Samoan Congregational	8	566	2310	—	—	0.1
Uncertain	353	1029	2253	—	—	0.1
Islam	779	1415	2004	—	—	0.1
Reformed Church of New Zealand	1628	1358	1923	0.1	—	0.1
Christadelphian	1667	1686	1698	0.1	0.1	0.1
Bahai	350	981	1452	—	—	—
All other religious professions	19,664	36,961	36,414	0.7	1.2	1.1
No religion (so returned) and not specified	161,018	140,591	275,832	5.6	4.5	8.7
Object to state	247,019	438,511	473,115	8.6	14.0	14.9
TOTAL	**2,862,631**	**3,129,383**	**3,175,737**	**100.00**	**100.00**	**100.00**

	Census year		
Religious affiliation (total responses)	*1991*	*1996*	*2001*
Adventist	15,675	14,691	14,868
Anglican	732,048	631,764	584,793
Asian Christian	—	222	195
Baptist	70,155	53,613	51,426
Brethren	21,915	21,933	20,406
Buddhist	12,762	28,131	41,634

Catholic	498,612	473,112	486,012
Christian	79,317	186,891	192,165
Church of Christ and Associated Churches of Christ	4842	4233	3270
Evangelical, Born Again and Fundamentalist	5169	1584	11,019
Hindu	18,036	25,551	39,798
Islam/Muslim	6096	13,545	23,631
Jehovah's Witness	19,182	19,527	17,826
Judaism/Jewish	3126	4809	6636
Latter-Day Saints	48,009	41,166	39,912
Lutheran	4965	5007	4314
Maori Christian	56,055	45,450	63,597
Methodist	139,494	121,650	120,705
No religion	670,455	867,264	1,028,052
Object to answering	251,709	256,593	239,244
Orthodox	4263	6933	9588
Other Christian	3276	2766	3558
Other religions	19,863	10,176	18,783
Pentecostal	49,596	69,333	67,239
Presbyterian, Congregational and Reformed	553,386	470,442	431,547
Protestant	1785	2778	2784
Salvation Army	19,992	14,625	12,618
Spiritualism and New Age Religions	5196	9786	16,062
Uniting/Union Church and Ecumenical	1026	1728	1389
TOTAL PEOPLE	**3,316,005**	**3,405,306**	**3,468,813**

United We Stand

New Zealand religious sects

Agnostic
Apostolic
Assemblies of God
Atheist
Baptist
Brethren
Buddhist
Christadelphian
Church of Christ
Congregational
Destiny Church
Eastern Orthodox

Hare Krishna
Hebrew
Hindu
Humanist
Jehovah's Witness
Latter-Day Saints
  (Mormon)
Lutheran
Mohammedan
Orthodox
Pentecostal
Ratana

Reformed Church of New
  Zealand
Ringatu
Salvation Army
Seventh-Day Adventist
Spiritualist
Undenominational
Undenominational
  Christian
Union Church

AGRICULTURE & FARMING

From Chew Chong to Chewings Fescue

Siberian barley was grown at Kerikeri in 1815.

In 1849, a Scab Ordinance was proclaimed to control sheep scab.

Ragwort was first discovered in New Zealand near Dunedin in 1874.

W Anderson built the first portable, screw-press, self-bagging chaff cutter in 1876.

American barbed wire was imported for the first time in 1879.

In the 1880s, New Zealanders numbered 490,000 and sheep 13 million, an even higher sheep-per-person ratio than today.

The first farm cream separator was a 'Nakarov', introduced in 1884.

By 1884, gorse had spread to the Auckland province from the South Island.

Chew Chong, a Chinese immigrant trader, opened a butter factory in Taranaki in 1887.

New Zealand flax exports reached 21,000 tons by 1890.

SM Babcock's 'Babcock Tester', used to test milk for butterfat, was imported from the US in 1890.

In 1897, Stanko Jurakovich, a Dalmation, developed vineyards at Kumeu. In 1902, Assid Corban, a Lebanese, planted his first vineyard at Henderson, in West Auckland.

In 1906, James McGregor returned to Wanganui from China with Chinese gooseberry seeds and began propagating them.

Captain James Cook introduced goats into New Zealand as a source of food for visiting seamen.

Ostrich feathers sold for 12 shillings a pound in 1900.

Basic slag was used on pasture during fertiliser trials in 1904.

Anti-German feeling during World War I led to the word 'Holstein' being deleted from the official description of Friesian cattle.

A demonstration of an Australian shearing machine was given near Gisborne, where the power-providing steam engine was fuelled by wood and dags.

'Single Bangers' was the name given to the first International Harvester single-cylinder, friction-drive Mogul tractors. They had one reverse gear.

The New Zealand Pig Breeders Associa-tion listed 168 Berkshires, 25 Tamworths, 23 Yorkshires, six Devons and one Large Black in its 'Herd Book' of 1918.

By 1919, there were 130 tractors on New Zealand farms.

New Zealand's first sheepdog trials were held at Hakataramea.

By 1933, Young Farmers and Country Girls Clubs had been set up throughout New Zealand.

Fred Barnes was the New Zealand Broadcasting Corporation's first super-visor of rural broadcasts.

Chewings Fescue was a type of pasture that was very hardy and ideal for undeveloped land. It was developed by George Chewings, a Lumsden runholder.

A Hudson and H Hopewell undertook mole-draining research at Massey Agricultural College.

By 1937, 300,000 hectares of Maori land had been returned to Maori farmers.

In 1938, the first 'bobby calf' pool was started at Edendale, Southland.

Over one million New Zealand pigs were produced for market in 1937.

Gerald Loftus Peacocke was editor of the *Bee and Poultry Journal*.

The Ferguson tractor was developed by Harry Ferguson of Britain.

Aerial top-dressing was developed first in New Zealand. Tiger Moth aircraft were the first planes used in the new venture.

In 1940, the Women's Land Army was formed to provide back-up labour for male farm workers who had been called away to war.

The Te Kuiti Airtruck was a later development in the aerial top-dressing industry. It was actually built at Te Kuiti.

The kiwifruit started life as a Chinese gooseberry, and in recent years has been rebranded Zespri.

The first commercial planting of Chinese gooseberries (kiwifruit) took place at Te Kuiti, Otahuhu and Wanganui.

There have been three suspected New Zealand outbreaks of foot-and-mouth disease since World War II, but all were unfounded.

Reid and Gray won a gold medal for double-furrow ploughing at the Melbourne Exhibition.

Japan's entry into World War II led to the interruption of phosphate supplies from Nauru and Ocean Islands, thereby diminishing the amount of fertiliser application in New Zealand.

Te Puke is described as the 'Kiwifruit capital of the world'.

When herringbone milking sheds replaced walk-through sheds there was an increase in the speed of milking and a general reduction in stooping.

A mobile raspberry harvester was developed for work on horizontally grown canes.

Wool Away, a book by world-renowned New Zealand shearer Walter Bowen, was published in 1956.

In 1959, 70 aerial top-dressing operators, utilising 270 aircraft, strafed the New Zealand landscape with fertiliser.

The term 'kiwifruit' was used for the first time in 1959.

Boar-performance testing facilities were set up at Korakonui, near Te Awamutu.

Sileage making was improved with the development of precision chop machines and wilting procedures.

In the 1963–64 season, 25,000 cattle died from bloat.

The Bird Nuisance Act was passed to get rid of birds likely to destroy crops.

An inspection system designed to produce disease-free partridge pea seeds was introduced in 1966.

New breeds of bull imported into New Zealand in 1972 were Blond d'Aquitaine, Main Anjou, Limousin and Pie Rouge.

Microlight aircraft — 'the farm bikes of the air' — aid mustering and spraying on New Zealand farms.

The Potato Board was established in 1977.

In 1984, approximately 35 per cent of farmers' gross income derived from subsidies.

In 1997, the rabbit calicivirus was released in the South Island as a means of rabbit control.

Stroppy Shropshires and Raiding Rams

Sheep breeds in New Zealand

Border Leicester are sheep that first arrived in New Zealand in 1859. They have white faces and legs and Roman noses.

Borderdale are sheep developed in New Zealand in the 1930s by crossing Border Leicesters with Corriedales.

Cheviot are sheep first introduced in 1845 from the Scottish Highlands and the borderlands between England and Scotland.

Coopworth are sheep developed in the

1960s by crossing Border Leicester stock and Romneys.

Corriedale are the first sheep breed developed in New Zealand, using Lincoln and English Leicester rams and Merino ewes.

Dorset Down are sheep that were first introduced into New Zealand in 1921. They died out, but were reintroduced in 1947.

Dorset Horn and Poll Dorset are sheep that emanate from British stock. The Poll Dorset was developed from the Dorset Horn in Australia and was introduced into New Zealand in 1959.

Drysdale are sheep developed in New Zealand by geneticist Dr Francis Dry, with work beginning in the 1930s. The coarse wool produced now contributes much of the hard fibre used in New Zealand carpets.

English Leicester are sheep that were introduced into New Zealand in the early days of European settlement, and by the turn of the century were the third most common New Zealand breed.

Hampshire are sheep that were introduced into New Zealand in 1861 from Britain. Their fine downy wool is used for flannels, hand-knitting yarns and woollen hosiery.

Lincoln are sheep that were among the first to be introduced into New Zealand and soon became the North Island farmer's answer to the problems created by the picky-eating Merino. Despite this, the Lincoln was replaced by the Romney.

Merino are sheep that were first brought to New Zealand by Captain James Cook in 1773. They were reintroduced in 1834 by James Wright who farmed them on Mana Island. The Merino was used to establish sheep farming in this country and it was the major breed at the turn of the twentieth century.

New Zealand Half-breed are sheep that resulted from the crossing of Merino with Leicester, Lincoln or Romney.

Perendale are sheep that were developed in New Zealand by Sir Geoffrey Peren of Massey University, using Cheviot and Romney genes.

Polworth are sheep that were introduced into New Zealand in 1932, after evolving in Victoria, Australia in the 1880s.

Romney are sheep that constitute half the New Zealand flock and dominate the local meat and wool industries. They were first introduced in the 1850s and have become so much a part of the New Zealand scene that they are now referred to as New Zealand Romneys, a breed distinct from the originals that arrived from England.

Ryeland are sheep that were first introduced into New Zealand in 1903. They are one of Britain's most ancient breeds, but their numbers in New Zealand have dwindled.

Shropshire are sheep that were first introduced into New Zealand in 1864.

by crossing Southdown and Hampshire stock with the view of coming up with a sheep with a firm-handling carcass.

South Suffolk are sheep bred in New Zealand during the 1930s in response to international demands for a sheep with leaner meat.

Southdown are sheep that arrived in New Zealand in the 1840s, and they remain the fastest maturing and most compact of the sheep breeds used as terminal crossing sires (rams used to sire lambs for the meatworks).

Suffolk are sheep that were introduced into New Zealand in 1913, and have now become widespread throughout the country, being used as a terminal crossing sire for meat production.

Welsh Black and Red Poll

Cattle breeds in New Zealand

Angus are the most popular beef cattle in New Zealand. They are black, polled and stocky animals introduced from Eastern Scotland.

Ayrshire are the third most common dairy breed in New Zealand and were introduced from Scotland.

Brangus is a breed of cattle crossed between the Asian Brahman and the Scottish Angus, and arrived in New Zealand in the early 1970s.

Brown Swiss cattle became part of New Zealand dairy herds in 1975. Their large

They became popular with local farmers following the development of refrigerated shipping in 1882 because they were a dual-purpose animal. Since then their popularity has declined.

South Dorset Down are sheep that were registered in New Zealand in 1956 after crossbred progeny from Dorset Down rams and Southdown ewes became popular as fat-lamb sires.

South Hampshire are sheep that were developed in New Zealand in the 1950s, frames makes them suitable for dairy beef production.

Charolais have become established as a major beef breed since being introduced to New Zealand from Britain in the 1960s.

Chianina cattle were introduced into New Zealand in the mid 1970s from Tuscany. They are tall, white, beef-producing stock.

Friesian are cattle introduced to New Zealand from the Netherlands in 1884. They have become the most important dairy breed in New Zealand.

Galloways and Belted Galloways are beef cattle breeds imported from Scotland in 1947. Bred from a common ancestral stock, they are believed to be the oldest polled beef cattle in the world.

Herefords are the second most numerous of New Zealand's beef cattle breeds, being introduced to New Zealand in 1868. They are deep red, with white faces.

Hereford/Angus cross are black steers with white faces, a common sight in New Zealand.

Jersey are dairy cows, fawn, cream and white in colour, that were introduced in 1862. The Jersey was overtaken by the Friesian in the 1970s.

Limousin are cattle introduced in 1972 from Limoges, France. They are essentially a beef breed of even, light-red colour.

Luing are beef cattle introduced in 1973 from the island of Luing, Scotland.

Milking Shorthorns are cows that have been bred in New Zealand from English Shorthorns and Australian Illawarra milking Shorthorns, with an infusion of Lincolnshire Reds.

Murray Grey are cattle developed in Victoria, Australia and introduced to New Zealand in the early 1970s.

Red Poll are milk and meat cattle introduced into New Zealand in 1898.

Santa Gertrudis are cattle introduced into New Zealand in the early 1970s, the result of cross-breeding between Brahman and Shorthorn cattle.

Shorthorn are cattle originally known as Durham when they were introduced to New Zealand in 1814, when Samuel Marsden brought two cows and a bull from New South Wales. Shorthorns made up 90 per cent of all dairy and beef cattle in 1900.

Simmental are cattle first introduced into New Zealand in 1972 from England. They were originally a Swiss breed with good milk and high butterfat production.

South Devon are cattle introduced into New Zealand in 1970. They are one of the oldest beef breeds in Britain, with a copper to medium-red colour.

Taurindicus cattle have been specially bred in New Zealand for tropical climates, by mating Holstein Friesian cows with either purebred or cross-bred Sahiwal sires. The female offspring are exported and used in dairy development projects and also established dairy production systems.

Welsh Black are cattle first introduced into New Zealand in 1973. They are descendants of the cattle of the ancient Britons.

FISHING

Farms Without Grass

A commercial fishery for pilchard-smoking started in the Marlborough Sounds in the 1880s. However, it didn't thrive, and by 1900 the fish were used mainly as groper bait.

Rainbow trout were imported from California in 1883.

A fish hatchery was established at Purakanui in 1895.

American author Zane Grey became a fan of big-game fishing in the Bay of Islands and his accounts in *Tales of the Angler's Eldorado, New Zealand* no doubt popularised New Zealand and helped give it an international reputation for big-game fishing.

Attempts to develop a fishery for southern blue-fin tuna off Fiordland were unsuccessful.

In 1948, a lucrative export market in rock lobster tails to the US began.

In 1959, the first Japanese snapper long-liners appeared off the New Zealand coast, fishing beyond the three-nautical-mile territorial zone.

New Zealand's first dredge oyster beds were discovered at Port Adventure, Stewart Island.

The commercial production of rock oysters began when legislation was passed in 1964 enabling the leasing of tidal lands and harbour beds.

The Pacific oyster was discovered in northern North Island waters. It had been accidentally carried on spat sticks to oyster farms and soon outgrew the native rock oyster as the dominant species.

The Portobello Marine Fish Hatchery produced mature European turbot and lobsters and millions of native sole and flounder.

Sockeye salmon was introduced from Canada and became established in Lakes Ohau, Benmore, Aviemore and Waitaki.

Trout farming became a political issue in 1972 when the incumbent National

Government favoured the move. Following strident objections from keen anglers who feared the proposal could lead to the alienation of public fishing waters, the incoming Labour Government repealed much of the legislation.

Whirling disease was discovered in rainbow trout in the Waitaki hatchery in Otago.

With the opening up of European and Japanese markets, eel fishing became more popular.

TRADE

Thirty Jars of Pickled Oysters

The *Favourite*, a US sealing ship, carried 87,000 seal skins to China in 1804.

The purchase of dried Maori heads, which had formerly sold well in Sydney, was forbidden by law in 1831.

Maori sold kauri gum to ships visiting New Zealand, a trade practice that was to prosper for many years.

In 1853, New Zealand trade statistics were gathered for the first time. Timber and wool were the leading exports during that time.

In 1853, trade tariffs based on peculiar measurements were abolished and a flat ad valorem duty of 10 per cent was enforced on most items.

When the *Argo* touched land at Sydney its cargo contained 30 jars of pickled oysters. This represented the first recorded shipment from New Zealand.

In 1858, the importation of indecent books and paintings was prohibited.

The Beer Duty Act 1880 imposed a duty of threepence a gallon on beer brewed for sale.

The Beetroot Sugar Act 1884 enabled the payment of a halfpenny a pound for the first 1000 tonnes of beetroot or sorgum sugar.

The 'Long Depression', the first to hit New Zealand, lasted until 1895. Wool prices fell dramatically.

In 1908, New Zealand wool, mutton and tallow prices were affected by a financial crisis in England.

'Enemies' of New Zealand in World War I — Germany, Austria and Hungary — had restrictions placed on their imports into New Zealand.

The first attempt to ship frozen meat from New Zealand came to nothing when the refrigeration machinery failed.

New Zealand's terms of trade were badly affected by the Great Depression in 1932–33.

The opening of the Suez Canal helped New Zealand as a trading nation.

The Apple and Pear Marketing Board was established in 1948.

The waterfront dispute of 1951 adversely affected New Zealand's wool exports at the height of the wool boom, brought about by the Korean War.

In 1973 Britain joined the EEC, and existing and highly lucrative trading arrangements with New Zealand were terminated.

New Zealand imports crude oil from Saudi Arabia, Australia, the United Arab Emirates, Malaysia and Indonesia.

In 1981, the New Zealand Dairy Board announced that it had bought 100,000 tonnes of surplus US butter, to save New Zealand dairy export markets.

In 1985, the New Zealand dollar was floated on a 'free' basis. Exchange controls had been abolished the previous year.

BP, Caltex, Mobil and Shell have, in recent years, been the principal oil suppliers in New Zealand. In 1998, Challenge and Gull oil suppliers also entered the New Zealand market.

Nothing Great About the Great Depression

Booms and busts

With the depletion of the large goldfields, a period of depression and unemployment hit New Zealand.

In 1884, Julius Vogel was returned to power, in the hope that he would curb the fall in New Zealand's prosperity.

From 1879–95, New Zealand endured a slump known as the Long Depression. The Great Depression (c. 1928–39), by contrast, was greater.

There was an economic boom in New Zealand during World War I. However, following the war, wool exports fell 56 per cent, meat exports 25 per cent, butter exports 19 per cent and cheese 43 per cent.

At the height of the Great Depression 12 per cent of the labour force were unemployed.

Dramatic increases in oil prices — 70 per cent in October 1973 and 128 per cent in January 1974 — impacted on the New Zealand economy.

In January 1984, unemployment climbed to 83,597. As at December 2004, unemployment had fallen to a rate of 3.6%

Boom conditions became apparent in the first half of 1984, as a result of the tax cuts and government-funded development projects.

Sweating and the Sin of Cheapness

Workers' conditions

'Sweating' — long working weeks with low pay — became an issue during the 'Long Depression' from 1877 to the early 1890s.

Rutherford Waddell, a leading Dunedin clergyman, was a prime mover in improving the lot of workers when he sermonised against the 'sin of cheapness'.

In 1881, an Act of Parliament set the minimum age of female workers at 12.

In 1889, Dunedin tailoresses formed the first women's union in New Zealand.

The Truck Act 1891 prohibited the payment for labour in any form other than money.

The Employment of Young Boys and Girls Without Protection Act of 1899 made it illegal to employ children without pay.

William Pember Reeves, a Labour Minister, was the architect of the labour law system in New Zealand.

In 1931, during the Great Depression, unemployment numbers peaked at 79,435.

In the three years leading up to the 1938 General Election, unemployment fell from 57,000 to 14,000. The Labour Government was returned to power with an increased majority.

The Accident Compensation Act, leading to the establishment of the ACC, was introduced in 1972.

The Coal Miners Act, 1975, was the first New Zealand law to bring in industrial supervision in terms of inspections in the interests of safety.

In 1980, the Maternity Leave and Employment Protection Act allowed 26 weeks' unpaid leave.

Trouble at Mill

Unions and strikes

New Zealand's first industrial dispute occurred in 1840 when Samuel Parnell refused to build a storehouse for George Hunter at Petone, on the grounds that he was being asked to work more than an eight-hour day.

When Nelson labourers attacked a supervisor in 1841, it became New Zealand's first recorded instance of industrial violence.

A benevolent society of carpenters and joiners was formed in Wellington in 1842, thereby becoming the first New Zealand union of sorts.

Workers in Christchurch walked off the job in 1850, demanding more pay than Maori for the same work. They returned to work the next day after the powers that be threatened to replace them all with Maori.

The Trade Union Act of 1878 gave trade unions legal recognition and protection against prosecution for forming a trade union.

Christopher Leek was the prime mover when five railway workers formed the Amalgamated Society of Railway Servants in 1886. Later, this modest body became the National Union of Railwaymen.

In 1890, New Zealand had 200 unions and 63,000 union members. In this year the Public Service Association was formed.

The Federation of Labour took over the *Maoriland Worker* newspaper in 1910.

The government called up farmers as special constables against a background of industrial violence in 1912 and 1913.

The 1912 Miners' Strike at Waihi led to nasty confrontations. A policeman was shot. As strikers and non-strikers fought, Frederick Evans was badly beaten and he later died of his injuries.

'Big Jim' Roberts was secretary of the New Zealand Waterside Workers Federation in 1915.

The government passed the War Regulations Continuance Act in 1920, thereby extending World War I restrictions and censorship to counter threats of 'Bolshevism'.

In 1921, shearers' wages were cut by 20 per cent.

In 1925, there were 83 incidents of industrial action.

Fintan Patrick Walsh became the most influential figure in New Zealand union circles. In 1927, he took control of the Seaman's Union by leading a raiding party that physically threw out the union's secretary William Thomas Young.

Union membership decreased during the Great Depression.

The United Mineworkers of New Zealand was a communist-orientated organisation led by Angus McLagan.

'Massey's Cossacks', the special constables deputised from farming communities, were named after Prime Minister William Massey.

Prime Minister Michael Joseph Savage was a former brewery union official.

The militant Federation of Labour was dubbed the 'Red Fed' by the *Evening Post*, after a circular printed on red paper during a Wellington tramways dispute was distributed.

Prime Minister Fraser's government took over New Zealand's mines in 1942 during a miners' strike.

A large pay rise granted to Members of Parliament in 1944 led to a strike by railway and dairy factory workers.

There were 154 strikes in 1945 — a record at the time.

In 1951, Prime Minister Holland used the

waterfront dispute as an excuse to call a snap election.

The waterfront strike of 1951 was claimed by employers to be a strike, although the union insisted it was a lockout. The strike led to the loss of a record 1,157,390 working days.

Tom Skinner became president of the Federation of Labour in 1963.

Anne Berry applied to the Human Rights Commission in 1963, to enable her to join the New Zealand Fire Service.

Bill Anderson, secretary of the Northern Drivers Union, ended up in Mt Eden jail in 1974, after refusing to obey a Supreme Court injunction regarding picketing.

In 1978, Southland farmers slaughtered 1000 ewes in the main street of Invercargill as a protest against rising costs in meat works caused by industrial action.

Death threats were aimed at senior union officials during a Taranaki dairy industry strike in 1982.

Sonia Davies was elected as the first woman vice president of the Federation of Labour in 1983.

Jim Bolger was Minister of Labour in 1983.

Union membership had been made voluntary in 1984, but legislation enacted the following year made it 'obligatory' for workers to belong to a union if a union membership clause had been negotiated as part of a collective agreement or other award.

Making the Most of Things

Manufacturing

In 1918, the first dried milk was exported from New Zealand to Britain.

In 1921, the first motor vehicle assembly plant in New Zealand was built in Wellington by the Colonial Motor Company.

General Motors' car assembly plant was opened in Petone in 1926, with the first car produced being a Chevrolet sedan. Eventually Pontiacs, Buicks and Oldsmobiles rolled off the assembly line too. In 1957, General Motors produced New Zealand's first Holden car.

Todd Park, the largest vehicle assembly plant in New Zealand, was opened in 1975.

In 1984, General Motors closed its plant at Petone.

MINING & ENERGY

Let There be Light . . . and Ignimbrite

The mining of kauri gum began in Northland in the latter half of the nineteenth century. The gum was used in several industrial processes, including the manufacture of paint and polishes.

Pre-European Maori chewed the fresh gum, while dried gum was used as fuel. The ash from the burnt gum was used in dye making for tattooing.

The first discovery of coal in New Zealand was made in 1844 at Coal Point, Kaitangata. Several years later, Thomas Brunner found coal on the West Coast of the South Island.

Charles Ring was the first European to discover workable amounts of gold at Kupanga Stream, Coromandel.

In 1856, gold was discovered in the Collingwood-Takaka area.

When Gabriel Read collected seven ounces of gold from the Tuapeka River in Central Otago, the upshot was the New Zealand gold rushes.

The streets of Dunedin were the first in New Zealand to be lit by gas.

The first productive oil well in New Zealand — and the British Empire — was located at Moturoa, New Plymouth.

Moss Davies, a leading merchant and brewer, owned the first house to have electricity in Auckland.

The first hydroelectric power station of any significant size in New Zealand was built near Skippers Creek for the Phoenix Quartz Mine.

A hydroelectricity scheme on the Inangahua River supplied the power that enabled Reefton to have the first public electricity supply in New Zealand.

The first government-built dam on the Waikato River was the Arapuni Dam.

Maraetai was the largest dam built on the Waikato River.

The Wairakei geothermal power station was New Zealand's first, and the world's second, such power station.

In 1959, Kapuni No 1 well in Taranaki began producing New Zealand's first supplies of natural gas.

The Moawhango Tunnel feeding the Tongariro River power scheme is one of the longest hydro-tunnels in the world. It took 10 years to build.

Manapouri, one of New Zealand's largest hydroelectric power stations, feeds both the Bluff aluminium smelter and the national grid.

New Zealand's largest power station is the Huntly thermal station.

In 1969, oil condensate, natural gas and traces of heavy oil were discovered in significant quantities off the Taranaki coast.

In 1982, work on the controversial Clyde Dam in Central Otago commenced.

The Rangipo hydroelectric station is located completely underground.

On a Power Trip

New Zealand's principal power stations

Name	Location	Power Type	Capacity in MW
Huntly	On the banks of the Waikato	Gas or coal-fired (thermal)	960
Ohau	Ohau River	Hydroelectric	672
Manapouri	Lake Manapouri and Waiau River	Hydroelectric	600
New Plymouth	New Plymouth	Natural gas & oil-fired (thermal)	600
Benmore	Waitaki River	Hydroelectric	540
Clyde	Clutha River	Hydroelectric	432
Maraetai	Waikato River	Hydroelectric	360
Roxburgh	Clutha River	Hydroelectric	320
Tekapo	Tekapo River	Hydroelectric (thermal)	265.2
Whirinaki	Whirinaki, Napier	Diesel oil (thermal)	216–240
Aviemore	Waitaki River	Hydroelectric	220
Stratford	Stratford	Natural gas (thermal)	208
Arapuni	Waikato River	Hydroelectric	157.8

Wairakei	Wairakei	Geothermal	153
Tongariro	Tongariro River, Lake Rotoaira	Hydroelectric	120
Ohakuri	Waikato River	Hydroelectric	112
Waitaki	Waitaki River	Hydroelectric	105
Whakamaru	Waikato River	Hydroelectric	100
Aratiatia	Waikato River	Hydroelectric	90
Karapiro	Waikato River	Hydroelectric	90
Atiamuri	Waikato River	Hydroelectric	84
Matahina	Rangitaiki River	Hydroelectric	72
Tuai	Lake Waikaremoana	Hydroelectric	58
Waipapa	Waikato River	Hydroelectric	51
Piripaua	Lake Waikaremoana	Hydroelectric	40
Lake Coleridge	Rakaia River	Hydroelectric	35
Kaitawa	Lake Waikaremoana	Hydroelectric	34
Cobb River	Cobb River	Hydroelectric	32
Highbank	Rakaia River	Hydroelectric	25.2
Mangahao	Mangahao River	Hydroelectric	19.2
Arnold River	Arnold River	Hydroelectric	3.6

POLITICS

Of 'Sufferage' and Suffering

Initially New Zealand was a dependency of New South Wales.

The Second New Zealand Constitution Act of 1852 saw six provinces established: Auckland, New Plymouth, Wellington, Nelson, Canterbury and Otago. Hawke's Bay and Marlborough were created as provinces in 1859; Southland was absorbed into Otago province in 1870, and Westland was created in 1873.

In 1856, Henry Sewell formed New Zealand's first responsible ministry, thereby becoming regar-ded as New Zealand's first premier. Sewell's ministry lasted little more than a week.

Although he was con-sidered at least partly responsible for the out-break of the Maori-Pakeha wars in Taranaki in 1860, Edward Stafford established responsible government in New Zealand.

Wellington became the capital city of New Zealand in 1865.

Four Maori electorates were established in 1867, based on universal male franchise, because Maori land was communally owned.

In 1872, two Maori were appointed to the Legislative Council, although there had been objections by some members of the Council to the presence of 'honourable cannibals'.

The provinces were abolished in 1875.

A Manhood Suffrage Bill, which would have enabled every man 21 years of age and over, and who had resided in an electorate for at least six months, to vote, was defeated in 1876.

Elections in 1879 produced an urban-rural split in the vote and an indecisive result — after a very vigorous and occasionally violent campaign.

One time West Coast pub owner, Richard John Seddon, became so dominant in

POLITICS

New Zealand politics for at least a dozen years following his election in 1893, that he was nicknamed 'King Dick'.

A Farmers Union was formed in 1899 which became a strong influence in New Zealand politics, siding with, initially, the Reform Party and, later, the National Party.

The first working man to enter the New Zealand Parliament was Samuel Andrews, a Christchurch plasterer.

In 1901, the six colonies of Australia combined to form the Commonwealth of Australia. Although the Australian constitution contained a clause for New Zealand to join the federation, New Zealand decided to go it alone.

In 1902, the term 'Prime Minister' replaced 'Premier'.

In 1903, King Mahuta was appointed to the Legislative Council.

In 1907, fire destroyed Parliament Buildings, with only the General Assembly Library surviving.

In 1909, the Young Maori Party was established. It sought to work with European politicians to improve living conditions for Maori. Apirana Ngata, Maui Pomare and Peter Buck were pivotal members.

On 6 July 1912, the Liberal Government's 21 years in office ended. In a bizarre moment John Andrew Millar, favourite to become Liberal's new leader, but now ill and dressed in his pyjamas, crossed the floor with four other Liberal ministers to vote on a no-confidence motion.

During World War I, a Coalition National Government was formed by the Reform and Liberal parties.

In 1919, New Zealand became a founding member of the newly created League of Nations.

The Communist Party of New Zealand was formed in 1920.

The first Marxist organisation in New Zealand was the Petone Marxian Club.

The West Coast miners unions formed the New Zealand Federation of Miners, which by incorporating other unions became the New Zealand Federation of Labour. They rapidly became known as the 'Red Feds'.

When Elizabeth McCombs became New Zealand's first woman MP she was able to boost her late husband's tiny Lyttelton majority from 32 to 2699.

In 1931, the United Party and the Reform Party announced the formation of a coalition National Party to try to deal with the problems created by the Great Depression.

In 1933, Labour's leader Harry Holland died after climbing Taupiri Mountain while attending the tangi for Te Rata Mahuta, the Maori king. He was succeeded by his deputy, Michael Joseph Savage, who two years later became Prime Minister at the head of New Zealand's first Labour Government.

'Coats off with Coates' was one of the slogans peddled during the campaign to get Gordon Coates, a farmer, elected as new Reform Party leader and Prime Minister.

Parliamentary debates and discourses from the House of Representatives were first broadcast in 1936.

In 1939, John A Lee published in the journal *Tomorrow* an article suggesting that Prime Minister Savage was not only dying of cancer, but that he was also mentally ill.

John A Lee's Democratic Soldier Labour Party achieved over four per cent of the vote in the 1943 general election.

Mrs Mary Grigg, from mid-Canterbury, was National's first woman MP. She won a by-election necessitated by the death of her MP husband who was killed in active service in 1942.

In 1945, the first two women were appointed to the Legislative Council.

The Labour Government won the 1946 general election thanks to securing the four Maori seats.

The first state house, built by the Labour Government, was located at Miramar.

In 1947, Mabel Howard, Labour MP for Sydenham, became New Zealand's first woman cabinet minister when she became Minister of Health.

Hilda Ross of Hamilton was the National Party's first woman cabinet minister in 1949.

Mrs Iriaka Ratana of Western Maori became the first Maori woman MP in 1949.

W Lee Martin was the first farmer elected to Parliament as a Labour candidate.

In 1950, the New Zealand Parliament became a unicameral system, with the voting out of the Legislative Council — the Upper House. The intention was expressed to form a new Upper House in the future, but a second chamber has never eventuated.

The New Zealand Communist Party was the only communist party in the Western world to endorse Maoism in the Sino-Soviet dispute.

The ANZUS alliance between New Zealand, Australia and the USA was instituted in 1951. Its intention was to safeguard security in the Pacific.

In 1954, MP Mabel Howard waved a pair of women's bloomers in the debating chamber of Parliament, demanding to know why the quality was so poor, the price was so high and dimensions not given in inches.

The Social Credit Political League contested its first general election in 1954 and garnered 11 per cent of the vote.

The Waterfront Strike of 1957 lasted 151 days.

In 1957, New Zealander Leslie Munro became president of the United Nations General Assembly.

The Black Budget was foisted on the nation in 1958 and featured a doubling of taxes on beer, cigarettes, cars and petrol. It was not popular and the Labour Government, the 'foisters', lost the next election.

Sir Guy Powles became New Zealand's first ombudsman in 1962.

The Indecent Publications Act was passed in 1963.

RM Hutton-Potts was leader of the new Liberal Party (which was in fact very conservative), that polled one per cent of the vote in the 1963 election.

In 1966, the Socialist Unity Party was formed.

A national referendum in 1967 was overwhelming in its preference for three-yearly elections, as opposed to four-year Parliamentary terms of office.

In 1967, it became possible for a Maori to stand for election in a Pakeha seat, or a Pakeha to stand for a Maori seat in Parliament.

In 1969, the voting age in New Zealand was lowered from 21 to 20.

The Values Party was formed in 1972.

A price freeze on baby food, bread and underwear was imposed in 1973.

In 1974, an act was passed enabling all New Zealanders over the age of 18 to vote.

In 1975, Malcolm Douglas became the first MP since 1873 to be expelled from Parliament after being sworn in, thanks to an electoral petition and a recount of votes in the Electoral Court. Douglas, the Labour MP for Hunua, lost out to Winston Peters of National.

In early 1977, every New Zealander received a substantial pension at age 60, when the National Government honoured an election promise.

Gutter politics emerged in 1977 when Prime Minister Muldoon made accusations against Labour Agriculture Minister Colin Moyle, to the effect that the latter had been picked up by the police for suspected homosexual activities, and then misled his leader over the issue.

When Keith Holyoake became Governor-General in 1977 it was the first time in New Zealand's history that an active party politician had held the post.

Bruce Beetham, leader of the Social Credit Party, won a by-election in the Rangitikei electorate early in 1978, and in the general election later in the year held on to the seat to become Social Credit's only MP.

In 1980, Social Credit won East Coast Bays in a by-election.

The social upheaval caused by the 1981 Springbok rugby tour to New Zealand has been cited as a possible reason for National winning a narrow victory in the 1981 elections. A reaction against tour demonstrators was enough in some marginal electorates to tip the vote National's way.

The 1984 Labour Government voted to extend the Waitangi Tribunal's jurisdiction to claims extending back to 1840.

Following the sinking of the *Rainbow Warrior*, the French government denied any involvement for the best part of three months. The photographer who was killed in the sinking of the *Rainbow Warrior* was a Portuguese national.

Prime Minister Robert Muldoon, in a slightly inebriated state, announced a surprise early election in 1984.

In 1984, incoming Prime Minister David Lange devalued the New Zealand dollar by 20 per cent.

In 1984, Japan became New Zealand's biggest export market for the first time in local history.

Sue Wood of National was the first woman to lead a political party when she became National Party president.

In 1985, Labour, National and Social Credit MPs joined together in urging the New Zealand Rugby Union to decline an invitation to the All Blacks to tour South Africa. The urgings fell on deaf ears.

Robert Muldoon lost the leadership of the National Party to Jim McLay in 1985.

In 1985, David Lange achieved worldwide exposure for his government's nuclear-free policy by starring in the Oxford Union Debate.

Margaret Wilson was the first woman to be elected president of the Labour Party.

The USS *Buchanan* was refused entry to New Zealand ports as a result of David Lange's Labour Government abiding by its anti-nuclear policy.

In 1986, the Goods and Services Tax (GST) was introduced.

Homosexual Law Reform legislation was passed by Parliament in 1986.

The Government returned Bastion Point to Ngati Whatua in 1988, and paid $3 million as a resettlement grant.

CER, or closer economic relations with Australia, moved towards full free trade when a new agreement was signed in 1988.

The Labour Government began to disintegrate in the years 1988–90, with Rogernomics being reined back, Cabinet Minister Richard Prebble being sacked, Prime Minister David Lange resigning and being replaced by Geoffrey Palmer, and Palmer himself resigning two months before the 1990 general election, to be replaced by Mike Moore. Not surprisingly, Labour lost the election.

Jim Bolger, who had become leader of the National opposition in 1986, became New Zealand's new Prime Minister in 1990.

Ruth Richardson, who became Minister of Finance in Prime Minister Bolger's National Government, continued with a vengeance, the style of economic management championed by Roger Douglas under Labour. Despite dire social forecasts, she oversaw the reduction in welfare payments and became so unpopular (someone suggested Ruth was short for Ruthless), that Bolger eventually sacked her.

In 1996, Mixed Member Proportional representation (MMP), was introduced when incorporated in that year's general election. Winston Peters, of minor party

New Zealand First, held the balance of power; and in what critics described as an act of treachery, formed a coalition with National. In this way, National were able to retain power.

New Zealand's first MMP election in 1996 led to a 95 per cent voter turnout.

Jenny Shipley became New Zealand's first woman Prime Minister by deposing incumbent Bolger in 1997.

The Labour Party returned to power in 1999, thanks to a coalition formed with the Alliance Party. They were able to retain power in 2002 by forming a coalition with the Progressive Coalition and by gaining the support of the Green Party and United Future.

Helen Clark's Labour Government came to be known as the 'nanny state', because of its humourless 'I've got my eye on you' bossy style.

Thanks for Coming

Early royal visits to New Zealand

Queen Victoria's second son, Prince Alfred, the Duke of Edinburgh, was New Zealand's first royal visitor, in 1869. He arrived in New Zealand as captain of the Royal Navy's frigate HMS *Galatea*.

In 1870, the Duke of Edinburgh visited again on the *Galatea* as commander of a squadron of four ships.

The Duke and Duchess of Cornwall and York (later King George V and Queen Mary), visited New Zealand on the Royal yacht *Ophir* in 1901 while on a tour of the British Empire. The tour was a means to convey gratitude for support given in the Boer War.

In 1920, the Prince of Wales, who was to become King Edward VIII and the Duke of Windsor, arrived on HMS *Renown* to thank New Zealand for its World War I effort.

The Duke and Duchess of York, later King George VI and Queen Elizabeth, arrived on the HMS *Renown* in 1927.

In 1934, Prince Henry the Duke of Gloucester arrived on board the HMAS *Australia*.

Lord and Lady Mountbatten visited New Zealand in 1946 to thank the country for New Zealand's service during World War II.

Queen Elizabeth II and the Duke of Edinburgh toured New Zealand in 1953 in what was the first visit made to New Zealand by a reigning monarch.

In 1956, the Duke of Edinburgh visited New Zealand after opening the Melbourne Olympics. He was able to include the Chatham Islands in his itinerary, the only Royal visitor to do so.

In 1958, Queen Elizabeth the Queen Mother toured New Zealand.

In 1963, the Queen and Duke of Edinburgh toured New Zealand.

Queen Elizabeth, the Queen Mother, made an informal visit to New Zealand in 1966. In the same year, Prince Charles made a one-hour stopover in Auckland on his way to the Empire Games in Jamaica.

In 1968, the Duke of Edinburgh made a brief visit to New Zealand.

In 1970, the Queen, Duke of Edinburgh, Prince Charles and Princess Anne visited New Zealand on the occasion of the Cook Bicentenary.

In 1971, Princess Alexandra, the Queen's cousin, visited New Zealand with her husband, Mr Angus Ogilvy, to attend Auckland's centennial celebrations.

The Duke of Edinburgh visited in 1973 as president of the Royal Agricultural Society of the Commonwealth.

In 1974, the Queen, Duke of Edinburgh, Prince Charles and Princess Anne all visited New Zealand. The Duke opened the Commonwealth Games on 24 January and the Queen closed them on 2 February. Later in the year, Prince Charles made a 14-hour visit to represent the royal family at the funeral of Prime Minister Norman Kirk.

The Queen and Duke of Edinburgh visited in 1977 to celebrate the Queen's Silver Jubilee.

In 1979, Princess Anne visited in her capacity as president of the Save the Children Fund.

Princess Anne and her husband Captain Mark Phillips made a brief stopover in New Zealand in 1980, after attending Kiribati's independence celebrations. Later in the year, the Duke and Duchess of Kent made a brief visit.

In 1981, Prince Charles visited New Zealand, and later that year the Queen and Duke of Edinburgh toured following the Commonwealth Heads of Government Meeting in Melbourne.

In 1982, the Queen's third son, Prince Edward, arrived in New Zealand to attend Wanganui Collegiate.

Prince Charles, Prince of Wales, and Diana, Princess of Wales, visited New Zealand with their son, Prince William, in 1983.

In 1985, the Duke and Duchess of Gloucester visited New Zealand.

Reigning on Our Parade

Sovereigns of New Zealand

George III was King of England during the early years of New Zealand's history, ruling from 1760 to 1820. In the latter part of his reign, from 1810 to 1820, his son, the Prince of Wales, acted as Prince Regent because of his father's mental illness. He, in turn, later ruled as George IV.

William IV reigned from 1830–37; Victoria I from 1837 to 1901; Edward VII from 1901 to 1910; George V from 1910 to 1936; Edward VIII from 20 January to 11 December 1936; George VI from 1936 to 1952; and Elizabeth II from 1953 to the present day.

Monarch	Accession	Died	Age	Reigned (years)
HOUSE OF HANOVER				
Victoria	1837	1901	81	63
HOUSE OF SAXE-COBURG				
Edward VII	1901	1910	68	9
HOUSE OF WINDSOR				
George V	1910	1936	70	25
Edward VIII[1]	1936	1972	78	—
George VI	1936	1952	56	15
Elizabeth II	1952			

1. Abdicated; reigned 325 days.

Many Men and Two Women

Vice regal representatives

Vice regal representative[1]	Assumed office	Retired
DEPENDENCY		
Lieutenant-Governor		
Captain William Hobson, RN	30 Jan 1840	3 Jan 1841
CROWN COLONY		
Governor		
Captain William Hobson, RN	3 Jan 1841	10 Sep 1842
Captain Robert FitzRoy, RN	26 Dec 1843	17 Nov 1845
Captain George Grey	18 Nov 1845	31 Dec 1847
Governor-in-Chief Sir George Grey, KCB	1 Jan 1848	7 Mar 1853
SELF-GOVERNING COLONY		
Governors of New Zealand		
Sir George Grey, KCB	7 Mar 1853	31 Dec 1853
Colonel Thomas Gore Browne, CB	6 Sep 1855	2 Oct 1861
Sir George Grey, KCB	4 Dec 1861	5 Feb 1868
Sir George Ferguson Bowen, GCMG	5 Feb 1868	19 Mar 1873
Rt Hon Sir James Fergusson, BT	14 Jun 1873	3 Dec 1874
Marquess of Normanby, GCB, GCMG, PC	9 Jan 1875	21 Feb 1879
Sir Hercules George Robert Robinson, GCMG	17 Apr 1879	8 Sept 1880
Hon Sir Arthur Hamilton Gordon, GCMG	29 Nov 1880	23 Jun 1882
Lieutenant-General Sir William Francis Drummond Jervois, GCMG, GB	20 Jan 1883	22 Mar 1889
Earl of Onslow, GCMG	2 May 1889	24 Feb 1892
Earl of Glasgow, GCMG	7 Jun 1892	6 Feb 1897
Earl of Ranfurly, GCMG	10 Aug 1897	19 Jun 1904

Lord Plunket, GCMG, KCVO	20 Jun 1904	8 Jun 1910
DOMINION		
Lord Islington, KGMG, DSO, PC	22 Jun 1910	2 Dec 1912
Earl of Liverpool, GCMG, MVO, PC	19 Dec 1912	27 Jun 1917
Governors-General of New Zealand		
Earl of Liverpool, GCB, GCMG, GBE, MVO, PC	28 Jun 1917	7 Jul 1920
Admiral of the Fleet, Viscount Jellicoe, GCB, OM, GCVO	27 Sept 1920	26 Nov 1924
General Sir Charles Fergusson, BT, GCMG, KCB, DSO, MVO	13 Dec 1924	8 Feb 1930
Viscount Bledisloe, GCMG, KBE, PC	19 Mar 1930	15 Mar 1935
Viscount Galway, GCMG, DSO, OBE, PC	12 Apr 1935	3 Feb 1941
Marshall of the Royal Air Force, Sir Cyril Louis Norton Newall, GCB, OM, GCMG, CBE, AM	22 Feb 1941	19 Apr 1946
REALM		
Lieutenant-General the Lord Freyberg, VC, GCMG, KCB, KBE, DSO	17 Jun 1946	15 Aug 1952
Lieutenant-General the Lord Norrie, GCMG, GCVO, CB, DSO, MC	2 Dec 1952	25 Jul 1957
Viscount Cobham, GCMG, TD	5 Sept 1957	13 Sept 1962
Brigadier Sir Bernard Fergusson, GCMG, GCVO, DSO, OBE	9 Nov 1962	20 Oct 1967
Sir Arthur Espie Porritt, BT, GCMG, GCVO, CBE	1 Dec 1967	7 Sep 1972
Sir (Edward) Denis Blundell, GCMG, GCVO, KBE, QSO	27 Sep 1972	5 Oct 1977
Rt Hon Sir Keith Jacka Holyoake, KG, GCMG, CH, QSO	26 Oct 1977	27 Oct 1980
Hon Sir David Stuart Beattie, GCMG, GCVO, QSO, QC	6 Nov 1980	10 Nov 1985
Most Reverend Sir Paul Alfred Reeves, GCMG, GCVO, QSO	20 Nov 1985	29 Nov 1990
Dame Catherine Tizard, GCMG, GCVO, DBE, QSO	13 Dec 1990	3 Mar 1996
Rt Hon Sir Michael Hardie Boys, GNZM, GCMG, QSO	21 Mar 1996	21 Mar 2001
Dame Silvia Cartwright, PCNZM, DBE	4 April 2001	

1. Honours are specified only if held on retirement from office.

Many More Men and Two Women

Premiers and Prime Ministers

Premier/Prime Minister[1]	*Term(s) of office*
PREMIERS	
Henry Sewell	7 May 1856–20 May 1856
William Fox	20 May 1856–2 Jun 1856
	12 July 1861–6 Aug 1862
	28 Jun 1869–10 Sept 1872
	3 Mar 1873–8 Apr 1873
Edward William Stafford	2 Jun 1856–12 Jul 1861
	16 Oct 1865–28 Jun 1869
	10 Sep 1872–11 Oct 1872
Alfred Domet	6 Aug 1862–30 Oct 1863

Frederick Whitaker, MLC	30 Oct 1863–24 Nov 1864
	21 Apr 1882–25 Sep 1883
Francis Aloysius Weld	24 Nov 1864–16 Oct 1865
George Marsden Waterhouse, MLC	11 Oct 1872–3 Mar 1873
Sir Julius Vogel, KCMG	8 Apr 1873–6 Jul 1875
	15 Feb 1876–1 Sep 1876
Daniel Pollen, MLC	6 Jul 1875–15 Feb 1876
Sir Harry Albert Atkinson, KCMG	1 Sep 1876–13 Sep 1876
	13 Sep 1876–13 Oct 1877 (ministry reconstructed)
	25 Sep 1883–16 Aug 1884
	28 Aug 1884–3 Sep 1884
	8 Oct 1887–24 Jan 1891
Sir George Grey, KCB	13 Oct 1877–8 Oct 1879
John Hall	8 Oct 1879–21 Apr 1882
Sir Robert Stout, KCMG	16 Aug 1884–28 Aug 1884
	3 Sept 1884–8 Oct 1887
John Ballance	Liberal 24 Jan 1891–d 27 Apr 1893
Rt Hon Richard John Seddon	Liberal 1 May 1893–d 10 Jun 1906
PRIME MINISTERS	
William Hall-Jones	Liberal 21 Jun 1906–6 Aug 1906
Rt Hon Sir Joseph George Ward, BT, KCMG	Liberal 6 Aug 1906–28 Mar 1912
	United 10 Dec 1928–28 May 1930
Thomas Mackenzie	Liberal 28 Mar 1912–10 Jul 1912
Rt Hon William Ferguson Massey	Reform 10 Jul 1912–12 Aug 1915
	National 12 Aug 1919–d 10 May 1925
Sir Francis Henry Dillon Bell, CGMG, KC, MLC	Reform 14 May 1925–30 May 1925
Rt Hon Joseph Gordon Coates, MC	Reform 30 May 1925–10 Dec 1928
Rt Hon George William Forbes	United 28 May 1930–22 Sep 1931
	Coalition 22 Sep 1931–6 Dec 1935
Rt Hon Michael Joseph Savage	Labour 6 Dec 1935–d 27 Mar 1940
Rt Hon Peter Fraser, CH	Labour 1 Apr 1940–13 Dec 1949
Rt Hon Sidney George Holland, CH	National 13 Dec 1949–20 Sep 1957
Rt Hon Sir Keith Jacka Holyoake, GCMG, CH	National 20 Sep 1957–12 Dec 1957
	12 Dec 1960–7 Feb 1972
Rt Hon Walter Nash, CH	Labour 12 Dec 1957–12 Dec 1960
Rt Hon John Ross Marshall (later Sir)	National 7 Feb 1972–8 Dec 1972
Rt Hon Norman Eric Kirk	Labour 8 Dec 1973–d 31 Aug 1974
Rt Hon Wallace Edward Rowling (later Sir)	Labour 6 Sept 1974–12 Dec 1975
Rt Hon Sir Robert David Muldoon, GCMG, CH	National 12 Dec 1975–26 Jul 1984
Rt Hon David Russell Lange	Labour 26 Jul 1984–8 Aug 1989
Rt Hon Geoffrey Winston Russell Palmer (later Sir)	Labour 8 Aug 1989–4 Sep 1990
Rt Hon Michael Kenneth Moore	Labour 4 Sep 1990–2 Nov 1990
Rt Hon James Brendan Bolger	National 2 Nov 1990–12 Oct 1996
	Coalition 12 Oct 1996–8 Dec 1997

Rt Hon Jennifer Mary Shipley   Coalition 8 Dec 1997–10 Dec 1999
Rt Hon Helen Clark   Labour 10 Dec 1999 –

1. Honours are specified only if held on retirement from office.

From Te Tai Tokerau to Te Tai Tonga

Maori electoral districts

Te Tai Tokerau. Includes Ngamotu Karaka
   (Three Kings Islands)
Tamaki Makaurau
Waiariki
Tainui

Te Tai Hauauru
Ikaroa-Rawhiti
Te Tai Tonga (includes Wellington, whole
   of South Island, Chatham Islands and
   Stewart Island)

Sharing the Spoils

General electoral districts

Aoraki
Auckland Central
Banks Peninsula
Bay of Plenty
Christchurch Central
Christchurch East
Clevedon
Clutha-Southland
Coromandel
Dunedin North
Dunedin South
East Coast
East Coast Bays
Epsom
Hamilton East
Hamilton West
Helensville
Hutt South
Ilam
Invercargill
Kaikoura

Mana
Mangakiekie
Mangere
Manukau East
Manurewa
Mount Albert
Mount Roskill
Napier
Nelson
New Lynn
New Plymouth
North Shore
Northcote
Northland
Ohariu-Belmont
Otago
Otaki
Pakuranga
Palmerston North
Piako
Port Waikato

Rakaia
Rangitikei
Rimutaka
Rodney
Rongotai (includes
   Chatham Islands)
Rotorua
Tamaki
Taranaki-King Country
Taupo
Tauranga
Te Atatu
Tukituki
Waimakariri
Wairarapa
Waitakere
Wellington Central
West Coast Tasman
Whanganui
Whangarei
Wigram

A Two-horse Race

General election results — 1984–99

Political Party	1984	1987	1990	1993	1996	1999
ACT	–	–	–	–	8	9
Alliance	–	–	–	2	13	10
Democrats	2	–	–	–	–	–
Green Party	–	–	–	–	–	–
Labour	56	57	29	45	37	49
National	37	40	67	50	44	39
New Labour	–	–	1	–	–	–
New Zealand First	–	–	–	2	17	5
United New Zealand	–	–	–	–	1	1

You Can Trust the Public Trust

Government departments

Agriculture and Forestry, Ministry of: Te Manatu Ahuwhenua Ngaherehere

Archives New Zealand

Audit New Zealand: Te Mana Arotake

Child, Youth and Family Services, Department of: Te Tari Awhina I te Tamaiti, tae atu ki te Whanau

Civil Defence and Emergency Management, Ministry of: Te Rakau Whakamarumaru

Commerce, Ministry of: Te Manatu Tauhokohoko

Conservation, Department of: Te Papa Atawhai

Consumer Affairs, Ministry of: Manatu Kaihokohoko

Corrections, Department of

Courts, Department for: Te Tari Kooti

Crown Law Office

Culture and Heritage, Ministry for: Te Tanatu Taonga

Customs Service, New Zealand: Te Mana Arai O Aotearoa

Defence, Ministry of: Manatu Kaupapa Waonga

Defence Force, New Zealand: Te Ope Kaatua O Aotearoa

Economic Development, Ministry of

Education, Ministry of: Te Tahuhu o te Matauranga

Education Review Office: Te Tari Arotake Matauranga

Environment, Ministry for the : Te Manatu mote Taiao

Fisheries, Ministry of: Te Tautiaki I nga tini a Tangaroa

Foreign Affairs and Trade, Ministry of: Manatu Aorere

Housing, Ministry of: Te Whare Ahuru

Inland Revenue, Department of: Te Tari Taake

Internal Affairs, Department of: Te Tari Taiwhenua

Justice, Ministry of: Te Manatu Ture

Labour, Department of: Te Tari Mahi

Land Information New Zealand: Toitu te Whenua

Maori Development, Ministry of: Te Puni Kokiri

National Library of New Zealand: Te Puna Matauranga o Aotearoa

National Provident Fund

The Office of Treaty Settlements: Te Tari Whakatau Take e pa ana ki te Tiriti o Waitangi

Pacific Island Affairs, Ministry of

Police, New Zealand: Nga Pirihimana o Aotearoa

Prime Minister and Cabinet, The Department of the

Public Trust Office

Research, Science and Technology, Ministry of: Te Manatu Putaiao

Serious Fraud Office, The: Te Tari Hara Taware

Social Development, Ministry of: Te Manatu Whakahiato ora

State Services Commission: Te Komihana O nga Tari Kawanatanga

Statistics New Zealand: Te Tari Tatau

Transport, Ministry of: Te Manatu Waka

Treasury, the: Kaitohutohu Kaupapa Rawa

Women's Affairs, Ministry of: Te Minitatanga mo nga Wahine

Youth Affairs, Ministry of: Te Tari Taiohi

Nuclear-free in Te Puke

Organisations and bodies, local and otherwise

Some Borough Councils in 1981 declared themselves 'nuclear-free', which was a huge relief to citizens of towns like Te Kuiti, Te Awamutu and Te Puke.

Brownies, of Girl Guide fame, used to be called Fairy Scouts. To qualify for membership, girls were expected to be able to lace their boots, tell the time and skip on both the left and right foot.

Local authorities are answerable to their electorates through triennial local body elections.

Every parliamentary elector is automatically qualified as a residential elector of a local authority.

Ratepayers who are not residents are entitled to enrol and vote in any region, district or community in which they pay rates.

Most boards and councils pay their chairperson or mayor an annual salary, while other members are paid a combination of a daily meeting allowance and an annual salary.

Of Bodies and Boundaries

Local government

Territorial Authorities
NORTH ISLAND

Cities	Council members[1]
North Shore	16
Waitakere	15
Auckland	20
Manukau	21
Hamilton	14
Napier	13
Palmerston North	16
Porirua	14
Upper Hutt	11
Hutt	13
Wellington	19

Districts	
Far North	11
Whangarei	14
Kaipara	11
Rodney	13
Papakura	13
Franklin	15
Waikato	15
Waipa	13
Otorohanga	8
Waitomo	11
Thames-Coromandel	10
Hauraki	13
Matamata-Piako	12
South Waikato	11
Taupo	13
Tauranga	14
Western Bay of Plenty	13
Rotorua	13
Whakatane	16
Kawerau	9
Opotiki	11
Gisborne[2]	15
Wairoa	10
Hastings	15
Central Hawke's Bay	11
New Plymouth	17
Stratford	11
South Taranaki	13
Ruapehu	14
Wanganui	13
Rangitikei	12
Manawatu	14
Horowhenua	11
Tararua	9
Kapiti Coast	14
Masterton	11
Carterton	9
South Wairarapa	10

SOUTH ISLAND

Cities	
Nelson[2]	12
Christchurch	25
Dunedin	15
Invercargill	13

Districts	
Tasman[2]	14
Marlborough[2]	13
Kaikoura	8
Buller	12
Grey	9
Westland	13
Hurunui	10
Waimakariri	15
Selwyn	14
Banks Peninsula	10
Ashburton	13
Timaru	13
Mackenzie	11
Waimate	12
Waitaki	16
Queenstown-Lakes	12
Central Otago	14
Clutha	15
Southland	13
Gore	12
Chatham Islands Council	9

1. Based on October 1998 elections. Figures include mayors.
2. Unitary authority.

Regional Councils
NORTH ISLAND

	Council members[1]
Northland	8
Auckland	13
Waikato	14
Bay of Plenty	11
Hawke's Bay	9
Taranaki	10
Manawatu-Wanganui	11
Wellington	14

SOUTH ISLAND

	Council members[1]
West Coast	6
Canterbury	14
Otago	12
Southland	11

1. Based on October 1998 elections. Figures
   include mayors.

LAW & ORDER

Keeping Kiwis in Line

An anti-shouting law existed during World War I to stop 'shouting' in public bars and to reduce drunkenness.

The Constitution Act of 1846 enabled the division of New Zealand into separate provinces, each with a Governor and a House of Representatives. However, the act was never acted upon. The main provinces were to have been New Ulster and New Munster, as the North and South Islands were then known, and Stewart Island was to have been New Leinster.

In the early days, Maori were excluded from all jury service, apart from those criminal cases where both the perpetrator and the victim were Maori.

In 1893, voting rights were extended to all New Zealand women. Voting rights were also granted in the same year to all people aged 21 years or over who had been living in New Zealand for a year.

The New Zealand Colony became known as a Dominion in 1907.

The Tohunga Suppression Act of 1907 made it a crime to mislead any Maori by professing to possess supernatural powers in terms of curing disease or predicting the future.

The office of Governor of New Zealand was changed in 1917 to that of Governor-General.

Sir Charles Perrin Skerrett was New Zealand's fifth Chief Justice.

The Crimes Act of 1908 stipulated six major punishments: death, imprisonment with or without hard labour, flogging, whipping and fine.

In 1941, imprisonment with hard labour for life replaced the death penalty for murder. Just under 10 years later the death penalty was reintroduced.

In 1942, women were first permitted to undertake jury service — if they so desired.

Between 1900 and 1957, 27 men were executed by hanging in New Zealand.

The New Zealand Official Secrets Act made it an offence to communicate government information. The Official Information Act of 1982 made it an offence not to communicate information.

The Indecent Publications Tribunal was established in 1963.

Accident Compensation came into force in 1972–73. Only suicide and intentional self-injuries were excluded from its parameters.

The New Zealand Security Intelligence Service gained official recognition in 1969.

The Wanganui Computer Centre was established in 1976 to record information on law-breakers.

Murder and Mayhem

Crime and punishment

The first criminal sitting of the New Zealand Supreme Court — in 1842 — ordered the hanging of Bay of Islands chief Maketu for the murder of a European woman, her two children and a half-caste servant.

In 1848, the first European to be executed in New Zealand for murder, since the founding of Auckland, was former Royal navy worker Joseph Burns, who was found guilty of murdering three people.

In 1856, Charles Marsden was hanged outside Mt Eden jail for the murder of a Maori woman.

Public hangings were abolished in New Zealand in 1858.

The Burgess Gang (Richard Burgess, Thomas Kelly and William Levy) were hanged at Nelson jail in 1866 for murdering four people at Maungatapu Mountain.

Hostility between Irish religious factions flared in Timaru, when Irish Catholics opposed a march organised by Protestant Orangemen.

The Convicts Prevention Act was passed in 1867 in an attempt to prevent Australia's convicts entering New Zealand.

In 1868, the Duke of Edinburgh survived an assassination attempt in Sydney. New Zealand Royalist Irish gold miners went to Westport to celebrate the survival, and on the way back were set upon by Irishmen not kindly disposed towards British rule. The Irishmen, being fearful of a government backlash, gathered at Addisons Flat, but an armed clash was averted. Nonetheless, the incident became known as the 'Battle of Addisons Flat'.

A national civil police system was established with the passing of the Police Force Act in the 1880s.

Edward Terry, who was obsessed with the perceived problem of alien immigration, confessed to murdering Joe Kum Yung, a Chinese immigrant. Terry spent most of his incarceration in mental hospitals.

When an Auckland prostitute, Frances Marshall, was stabbed to death, claims of New Zealand's own 'Jack the Ripper' were mounted. However, no further related crimes were committed and no one was ever charged with the murder.

Flogging was abolished in 1883.

A Constable Nash is believed to have been the first New Zealand policeman.

Thomas Hall received life for attempting to poison his wife with antimony in 1886.

In 1887, John Cuffrey and William Penn were hanged for shooting Robert Taylor on Great Barrier Island.

Louis Chemis, in 1889, was charged with murder. His death sentence was later commuted to life imprisonment, and in 1897 he was released under a Queen Victoria Jubilee amnesty. In 1898, Chemis blew his head off with dynamite on Mount Victoria.

Arthur Bently Worthington, a religious imposter, attempted to hold a public meeting in Christchurch in 1897. Such was the disregard in which Worthington was held that the entire police force was required to take station to control the hostile crowd of 6000. Even then, a magistrate was obliged to read the Riot Act to allow Worthington to depart unscathed.

In 1897, a prisoner was put in irons for the last time in New Zealand.

The Habitual Criminals and Offenders Act, passed in 1906, was intended to help curb the activities of persistent criminals.

John Pawelka was a particularly elusive prisoner, escaping from custody on several occasions. His final escape — from Wellington's Terrace Jail in 1911 — saw the back of him. He was never heard of again.

Arrows on prison clothing were abolished in 1913.

During World War I, all European males between the ages of 20 and 46 were deemed liable for military service. Those who failed to register were fined or imprisoned.

Fourteen conscientious objectors to the war were forced to the battle front, even after serving prison sentences.

Labour politicians were often opposed to the Conscription Act during World War I. Indeed, leading Labourites, Peter Fraser and Robert Semple, were jailed for their beliefs.

Elspeth Kerr, a Devonport nursing home proprietor, was charged with attempting to poison her foster daughter with a substance called veronal, or barbitone.

Matching horseshoe prints were the critical evidence used in gaining a conviction in a murder case at Pukekawa. At this time, 1920, attempts were still being made to discredit the value of fingerprints as evidence.

The Ponsonby postmaster was murdered in 1920.

A man from Newlands was hanged in 1923 for murdering three newborn children found buried on his property.

In 1924, Borstal Institutions, based on the British model, were established in New Zealand. They catered exclusively for young offenders.

A bank robber was shot and killed by a bank teller after robbing the Remuera BNZ in 1931. The teller was charged with manslaughter but the case was dismissed.

Seven people died in a house fire at Mimatangi in 1931. One of the dead,

Thomas Wright, was found with a gun-shot wound to the head. The case was never solved.

Six people died in 1932 when a young farm worker in the King Country shot his farm boss and family for refusing to permit him to marry. The number of victims increased to six when the worker shot the arresting policeman and, finally, himself.

West Coast farmer, Eric Stanley Graham, who killed seven men before being mortally wounded by a policeman's bullet, became overwhelmed by feelings of persecution.

In 1939, a charge of interfering with a dead human body was believed to be the first of its kind in the European history of New Zealand.

Capital punishment was abolished in New Zealand in 1941, although the newly elected National Government reinstated the death sentence when they came to power in 1950.

Two prisoners escaped from Mt Eden prison by blasting a hole in the prison wall, using explosives they had smuggled into their cell, under their fingernails, after working in the prison quarry.

'The Battle of Manners Street', sparked off when US servicemen refused to let Maori servicemen drink in the Wellington Allied Services Club in 1943, was considered to be New Zealand's bloodiest riot.

In 1946, after a known homosexual was found murdered at the entrance to the Adams Bruce chocolate factory in Wellington, no conviction was ever made.

Auckland tailor George Horry was the first person in New Zealand to be found guilty of murder despite the absence of a body.

Traffic officer John Kehoe was shot and killed while chasing a speeding driver.

Arthur Rottman, the Ruahine axe murderer, accounted for three victims.

In 1954, Pauline Parker and Juliet Hulme murdered Parker's mother in a landmark case in Christchurch.

William Giovanni Silveo Fiori was the first person to be hanged in New Zealand since the reintroduction of capital punishment in 1950.

1 June 1951 became known as 'Bloody Friday' after exchanges between the police and waterside workers that involved fence palings, bricks and bottles.

Frederick Foster, who shot his girlfriend in an Auckland milkbar, was sentenced to death. He developed appendicitis shortly before his scheduled execution date, but following an emergency operation he was hanged before the wound had healed.

In 1954, corrective training and preventative detention were introduced.

Walter Bolton, who had been convicted of poisoning his wife with arsenic, became the last person to be hanged in New Zealand.

In 1957, the second Labour Government had promised to abolish the death penalty, and when they became the government it meant that Angelo La Mattina, convicted of murdering the manager of the Garibaldi Club in Wellington, had his death penalty commuted to life imprisonment. A change of government saved his life.

George Wilder, a convicted burglar and thief, became a folk hero for his ability to effect jail escapes and to remain at large for long periods of time.

The Armed Offenders Squad was established in 1964.

Hilda Jefferson was the first woman to be chosen as foreman of a jury in a murder trial.

Mt Eden Prison was severely damaged by fire in 1965 after prisoners rioted following an attempted break-out.

One of the bank robbers who held up the Avondale BNZ in 1965 was declared to be suffering from paranoid schizophrenia. Despite this, he was sentenced to seven years' jail, where very soon he was declared insane.

In 1968, a New Plymouth schoolboy shot and killed the headmaster of his school.

In 1968, Paremoremo Prison began operating as a maximum security prison.

During protest action relating to New Zealand's involvement in the Vietnam War, a spate of bombings — the worst in fact in the country's history — affected 13 military bases and other 'conservative establishments'.

Women picketed men-only bars and the Miss Auckland Beauty Contest during the emergence of the Women's Movement.

In 1972, a 21-year-old refused to undergo compulsory military training because of his opposition to the Vietnam War. He was sentenced to 10 days' jail after he failed to attend a medical examination: he served three of those days.

Ernie Abbott, caretaker of the Wellington Trades Hall, died when a suitcase bomb exploded in the building. Neither a motive nor a guilty party has ever been found.

In 1973, 500 policemen clashed with 400 anti-Vietman War demonstrators attempting to storm the US Naval Support Force's base near Christchurch Airport.

Dr WB Sutch, at one time Secretary of Industries and Commerce, was acquitted of charges under the Official Secrets Act in 1974.

Dean Wickcliffe was the first person to escape from Paremoremo Prison, in 1976.

In 1978, Arthur Allan Thomas was pardoned after serving nine years in jail for the Crewe murders.

New Zealander Terence John Clark, alias Alexander James Sinclair, was convicted in England in 1981 of the murder of New Zealand drugs boss Christopher Martin Johnstone.

In 1984, two South Auckland taxi drivers were murdered in separate incidents.

Two French agents were arrested and imprisoned in New Zealand in 1985 after the sinking of the *Rainbow Warrior*.

David Gray, the Aramoana mass murderer, used a 223 Norinco semi-automatic assault rifle to kill his victims in 1990.

Brian Schlaepfer shot six members of his family, and then himself, at Paerata in 1992.

Raymond Ratima of Masterton killed seven people in 1992.

There were 43 murders in New Zealand in 1992.

David Bain was convicted of killing five members of his family at Dunedin in 1994.

The South Auckland serial rapist confessed to his crimes in 1995.

Stephen Anderson shot six people at Raurimu in 1997.

In 2000, the average cost of keeping a person in prison in New Zealand was $52,525 per year.

In 2000, there were 14,639 convictions for violent offences in New Zealand.

In 2000, 83 per cent of all New Zealand criminal cases that resulted in convictions were associated with males.

In terms of ethnicity, 47 per cent of all convicted cases in 2000 involved Europeans. Maori accounted for 42 per cent, Pacific people nine per cent and offenders of some other ethnicity accounted for the remaining two per cent.

The Police National Headquarters' fingerprint section holds more than 500,000 sets of fingerprints.

In New Zealand in 1880, there were 17,837 recorded criminal offences, of which 93.8 per cent were resolved. In New Zealand in 2001, there were 424,286 recorded criminal offences, of which 42.9 per cent were resolved.

In 2002, New Zealand Police were deployed overseas in East Timor, Bougainville and the Solomon Islands.

When Punishment was Capital

Those executed in New Zealand

Maketu, Wiremu Kingi	Auckland	7 March 1842
Burns, Joseph	Auckland	17 June 1848
Maroro	Wellington	19 April 1849
Good, William	Wellington	17 June 1850
Bowden, William	Auckland	27 April 1852
Marsden, Charles	Auckland	12 February 1856
White, John	Auckland	11 July 1856
Killey, John	Auckland	18 March 1858
Collins, James	Wellington	30 January 1862
Taherei	Picton	10 July 1863
Harper, Richard	Auckland	22 September 1863
Ruarangi	Auckland	18 April 1864
Okoroa, Nikotema	Auckland	18 April 1864
McLean, Alexander	Auckland	21 October 1864
Jarvey, William Andrew	Dunedin	24 October 1865
Jones, John	Dunedin	6 April 1866

Stack, James	Auckland	7 April 1866
Mokomoko	Auckland	17 May 1866
Kahupaea, Heremita	Auckland	17 May 1866
Te Rahui, Hakaraia	Auckland	17 May 1866
Propiti, Horomoana	Auckland	17 May 1866
Kirimangu, Mikaere	Auckland	17 May 1866
Burgess, Richard	Nelson	5 October 1866
Kelly, Thomas	Nelson	5 October 1866
Levy, Philip (William)	Nelson	5 October 1866
Wilson, Robert	Nelson	20 December 1867
Swales, John Densley	Lyttelton	16 April 1868
Whakamau	Wellington	23 March 1869
Peri, Hamiora	Wellington	16 November 1869
Noble, Anthony	Hokitika	16 February 1871
Cedeno, Simon	Lyttelton	5 April 1871
Kereopa	Napier	5 January 1872
Eppwright, Joseph	Auckland	29 July 1873
Dyer, Charles	Auckland	30 October 1874
Nutana	Auckland	19 February 1875
Mercer, John Robinson	Lyttelton	7 May 1875
Woodgate, William Henry	Picton	25 January 1877
Curtin, Martin	Auckland	6 February 1877
Te Mohi, aka Patiti Mohi	Auckland	23 May 1877
Walsh, James aka Welsh	Invercargill	19 February 1879
Ah Lee	Dunedin	5 November 1880
Tuhiata	Wellington	29 December 1880
Hiroki, Wiremu	New Plymouth	8 June 1882
Winiata, Taurangaka	Auckland	4 August 1882
Donohue, John	Hokitika	11 June 1884
Edwards, Rowland Herbert	Napier	15 July 1884
Caffrey, John	Auckland	21 February 1887
Penn, Henry Albert	Auckland	21 February 1887
Te Piri, Haira	Napier	13 May 1889
Wata, Makoare	Napier	28 September 1889
Scott, Alexander James	Auckland	22 May 1893
Dean, Williamina	Invercargill	12 August 1895
Bosher, Stephen	Wellington	21 April 1897
Sheehan, William	Lyttelton	21 July 1897
Philpott, Frank	Wellington	23 March 1898
Clements, Charles	Dunedin	12 April 1898
Enoka	New Plymouth	2 May 1898
McLean, Alexander	Lyttelton	31 August 1901
Ellis, James	Wellington	28 February 1905
Kaka, Tahi	Auckland	21 June 1911
Biddle, Alfred Mortram	Lyttelton	13 December 1913
Rottman, Arthur	Wellington	18 March 1915

Bennier, Frank Edward	Wellington	19 January 1918
Eggers, Frederick William	Lyttelton	5 March 1918
Gunn, Dennis	Auckland	22 June 1920
Thorne, Samuel John	Auckland	20 December 1920
Te Kahu, Hakaraia	Auckland	10 October 1921
Tuhi, John	Wellington	19 April 1923
Cooper, Daniel Richard	Wellington	16 June 1923
Scott, Robert Herbert	Auckland	17 April 1924
Munn, Arthur Thomas	Auckland	29 July 1930
Coats, George Errol	Wellington	17 December 1931
Tarrant, Edward	Wellington	6 March 1933
Edwards, John Hubert	Auckland	11 December 1933
James, George Edward	Wellington	15 December 1933
Bayly, William Alfred	Auckland	20 July 1934
Price, Charles William	Wellington	27 June 1935
Fiori, William Giovanni Silveo	Auckland	13 March 1952
Te Rongapatahi, Eruera	Auckland	14 September 1953
Whiteland, Harry	Auckland	21 December 1953
Foster, Frederick	Auckland	7 July 1955
Te Whiu, Edward Thomas	Auckland	18 August 1955
Allwood, Harvey Eric	Auckland	13 October 1955
Black, Albert Laurence	Auckland	5 December 1955
Bolton, Walter James	Auckland	18 February 1957

Doin' Time

Penal institutions — 2001

Institution	Capacity	Institution	Capacity
MALE PRISONS		Rimutaka	491
Auckland Central Remand Prison		Rolleston	320
(privately operated)	272	Tongariro/Rangipo	442
Auckland (Paremoremo)	645	Waikeria	905
Christchurch	778	Wanganui	382
Dunedin	59	Wellington	120
Hawke's Bay Regional	568		
Invercargill	172	FEMALE PRISONS	
Manawatu	278	Arohata	152
Mt Eden	381	Christchurch Women's	98
New Plymouth	108	Mt Eden (women's division)	94
Ohura	100		

EDUCATION

Tomorrow's Schools and the University of Hard Knocks

The 'school of hard knocks' relates to the business of becoming 'educated' by being 'knocked about' by often painful life experiences.

The first mission school was opened in the Bay of Islands in 1816.

In 1841, a Father Petitjean opened the first Roman Catholic English school in Auckland.

Otago University, New Zealand's oldest, initially refused affiliation with the University of New Zealand, thereby losing its right to confer degrees under its own name. Before Otago University finally reneged and came under the auspices of the University of New Zealand in 1874, it granted just one degree under its own name. The lucky and unique recipient was one AW Williamson who came away with a BA.

Compulsory education for children was introduced in New Zealand in 1877.

Auckland University had an initial roll of 100 students when it opened in 1883.

In 1908, a special school for mentally handicapped boys opened at Otekaike in Otago.

The Native Schools Act sanctioned the education of Maori and half-caste children or adults in Maori schools.

Massey University began life as Massey Agricultural College in 1928, before becoming the Massey University of Manawatu in 1964 and finally, in 1966, Massey University. It derives its name from former Prime Minister, William Ferguson Massey.

The Summer Institution for the Deaf and Dumb was the world's first government-funded school for the deaf.

In August 1988, the devolution of power from the education bureaucracy to local communities — 'Tomorrow's Schools' — was introduced. It was a revolutionary move in education.

U3A, the University of the Third Age, commenced in New Zealand in 1990. Its aim is to increase educational opportunities for retired New Zealanders.

Lincoln University, which originally came under the auspices of Canterbury University, became a university in its own right in 1990.

Suspensions and expulsions, as well as an apparent rise in the frequency of bullying of both staff and pupils, became increasingly common in New Zealand secondary schools in the 1990s.

'Tomorrow's Schools' led to some strange aberrations, like the situation at Cambridge High School in 2003 where it was found that the school's library had been closed, in favour of an Internet café.

SCIENCE & TECHNOLOGY

Of Atoms and Bigger Things

Seismographic readings began in New Zealand in 1900.

Prothallus of *Phyllogossum drummondii* was discovered by APW Thomas of Auckland University.

In 1908, the Nobel Prize in Chemistry was awarded to Ernest Rutherford.

Leonard Cockayne established the Cockayne Plots to study the ecology of pasture types on depleted tussock grassland in Central Otago.

Plastic Surgery of the Face was written by HD Gilles, a New Zealand-born plastic surgeon.

In 1911, while working at McGill University, Ernest Rutherford performed an experiment which demonstrated that an atom contained a positively-charged nucleus.

In 1925, C Hercus, W Benson and C Carter established the relationship between endemic goitre and soil iodine.

The Department of Scientific and Industrial Research was set up by an Act of Parliament in 1926.

FW Dry was appointed lecturer in Agricultural Zoology at the newly instituted Massey Agricultural College. Dry became known as the father of wool biology. He was largely responsible for the mutation of the New Zealand Romney into the Drysdale sheep.

When Ernest Rutherford won the Nobel prize, Sweden printed a postage stamp to honour the occasion.

By 1932, researchers under Rutherford's supervision had developed the proton accelerator which eventually split the atom.

In 1940, FH Smirk was appointed professor of medicine at Otago Medical School.

The use of DDT insecticide for the control of grass grub and porina was officially sanctioned in 1948. It was later deemed to be unacceptable.

The first functional electron microscope was set up in New Zealand in 1949 when a Metropolitan-Vickers EM 2 was established at the DSIR's Dominion Physical Laboratory.

HC Smith discovered barley yellow dwarf virus, a serious disease in cereals in New Zealand. He later discovered the perithecial stage in the life cycle of dry rot in brassicas.

In the 1950s, the notion of growing exotic fruit in New Zealand, including the Chinese gooseberry (which later became the Kiwifruit and then Zespri), gained headway.

Geothermal tests were carried out in 1950 with the view to developing the Wairakei geothermal area near Taupo into a possible source of electricity.

KM Harrow discovered the process whereby boric acid could be used for the preservation of Pinus radiata timber.

In 1959, an analytical ultra centrifuge was constructed by the DSIR using, amongst other things, 'odd bits of naval weaponry'.

The Earthworm Fauna of New Zealand was published by KE Lee.

The first New Zealand university Department of Earth Science was founded at Waikato University.

The DSIR's Climate Laboratory was opened by the Queen in 1970.

In 1972, the eighth international radio-carbon dating conference was held at Lower Hutt.

Maurice Wilkin, who was born in Pongaroa in the Wairarapa, and moved to England at the age of six, won the Nobel Prize for Medicine in 1972.

In 1981, the association of a Lolium endophyte with the sheep disease, ryegrass staggers, was made.

Although the electric fence was developed in both the USA and New Zealand, scientists at Ruakura Research Centre and Hamilton-based Gallagher Group were able to lay claim to a distinctively New Zealand development — mains energisers which send out a safe but high-current pulse.

Unleaded regular grade petrol was introduced to New Zealand in 1987. The sale of leaded petrol was banned in 1996.

The distribution of natural gas occurs only in the North Island.

About 70 per cent of New Zealand's coal production occurs in the South Island.

Landfill gas is used to produce energy at plants in Auckland and Wellington.

In 1993, a wind energy unit was set up in the Wellington suburb of Brooklyn.

In 1996, the Hau Nui wind farm, generating 3.5 megawatts, was set up in the Wairarapa.

Marsden Point, Whangarei, is New Zealand's only oil refinery, producing petrol, diesel, aviation kerosene, fuel oils and bitumen.

A serious power failure in Auckland in 1998 lasted several months and caused considerable disruption.

Professor Alan Macdiarmid of New Zealand won the Nobel Prize in chemistry in 2000, for helping discover that certain 'hi-tech' plastics can conduct electricity. A wide range of electronic and communication devices, like cellphones, have benefited from such discoveries.

At the beginning of 2001, New Zealand's remaining crude oil and condensate reserves were dominated by the Maui field with more than 60 per cent of available supply. The Kapuni, Kupe and McKee fields were the remaining significant fields.

The Mangahewa gas field is the least significant supplier of oil and condensate reserves.

At the year ended March 2001, New Zealand's self-sufficiency in oil production was 34 per cent.

Roughly one-third of Marsden Point's refined production is piped to Wiri in South Auckland for use in the Auckland area.

In early 2001, 45 per cent of all New Zealanders over the age of 10 had access to the Internet from home.

Giving the World the Crimped Hairclip

New Zealand inventions

An Invercargill blacksmith invented a self-sealing lid for treacle tins at the turn of the twentieth century. The same lid is now used for tins of paint the world over, but unfortunately the inventor failed to patent his invention.

Aviator, Richard Pearse, invented ailerons — the horizontal rudders on wings — and a tricycle undercarriage, which he utilised on his aircraft.

The Taranaki gate, built from barbed wire, conventional wire and fence battens, is believed to be a distinctly New Zealand invention.

The crimped hairclip is thought to have been invented by a New Zealander.

William Bacon, a Wellington businessman, invented a patent lock which, once it had been sold to an American company, became widely known as the Yale lock.

The spare wheel and tyre for cars was an idea realised by an Oamaru engineer, FR Dennison, in 1907.

In 1958, Sir Brian Barrett-Boyes and his cardiac team at Greenlane Hospital successfully replaced damaged heart valves with artificial valves. It was a world first.

John Britten invented a racing bike with largely his own components, which set all sorts of world records.

For option 73 please press 2, followed by the hash key

The new technology

Over 67 per cent of New Zealanders have mobile phones.

By 1998, 83 per cent of New Zealand primary schools and 94 per cent of secondary schools had Internet access.

Fifty-five per cent of Chatham Islanders have access to a fax machine, the highest figure in New Zealand.

Cellphone distraction has led to several serious car accidents.

In 1992, New Zealand computer programmers developed the world's first real-time 3D graphics for inclusion in a live sports telecast.

Laser technology developed in New Zealand in the 1960s.

The world's first postal franking machine was the work of Christchurch mechanic Ernest Moss in 1911.

In 1928, John A Hart invented the Thermette, a water boiler that burnt twigs and newspaper.

A Timaru pharmacist, CA Murdoch, invented the tranquilliser rifle in the 1950s.

In the early 1950s, CWF 'Bill' Hamilton invented the jet boat. He was also involved with the development of earth-moving machinery, hydraulic pumps, valves and cylinders, mobile cranes and garden sprinklers.

In 1971, Claudio Petronelli, a hairdresser, and Gavin Park, a pharmacist, invented a childproof pill box.

In 1973, John A Hough invented the Tullen snips, cutters that can account for anything from thin steel to human hair.

RUOK, M8

Text messaging terms

A?	eh?
AFAIK	As far as I know
AKA	Also known as
ASAP	As soon as possible
AYT	Are you there?
B	Be
B10	Beaten
B4	Before
B4N	Bye for now
BB	Bye Bye
BB10	Be back in 10 mins
BCNU	Be seeing you
BK	Big kiss
Bwd	Backward
BYKT	But you knew that
CALQL8	Calculate
CELEBR8	Celebrate
CHLYa!	Chill ya!
CIO	Cut it out
CU	See you
CUL	See you later
CW2CU	Can't wait to see you
D8	Date
DBD	Don't be dumb
DBV	Don't be vulgar
DGT	Don't go there
DITY	Did I tell you?
DKDC	Don't know don't care
DL	Download
DOB	Date of birth
DUK	Did you know?
EZ	Easy
EZ2CY	Easy to see why
F2F	Face to face
F2T	Free to talk
F8	Fate
FAQ	Frequently asked questions
FAT	File allocation table
FOAF	Friend of a friend
FR8	Freight
FUBR	Fouled up beyond recognition
G2G	Got to go
GFI	Go for it
GL	Get lost
GOWI	Get on with it
GR8	Great
GYST	Get your stuff together
H&K	Hugs and kisses
H2	How to
H8	Hate
HABO	Have a better one
HAGO	Have a good one
HAND	Have a nice day
Hot4U	Hot for you
HUH	Have you heard
ICYR	I see you are
IH8U	I hate you
IOHiis4U	I only have eyes for you
IOOH	I'm out of here
IOU1	I owe you one
JAM	Just a minute
JAS	Just a second
JM5c	Just my five cents' worth
KISS	Keep it simple stupid
KIT	Keep in touch
KOTL	Kiss on the lips
KWIM	Know what I mean
L8	Late
L8r	Later
LFW	Lost for words
LOL	Lots of laughs
LYMY	Love you miss you
M8	Mate
MAY	Mad about you
MHOTY	My hat's off to you
MO	Modus operandi
MOB	Mobile
MYOB	Mind your own business
N1!	Nice one!
NAG	Not a good idea
NE	Any
NIMBY	Not in my backyard
NOTY	No thank you
NOYB	None of your business

NTL	Nevertheless		TAG	Take a guess
OH	Off hand		TAH	Take a hint
OIC	Oh I see		TGIF	Thank God it's Friday
On4It	On for it		TIA	Thanks in advance
ONNA	Oh no, not again		TIC	Tongue-in-cheek
OO	Over and out		TINWIS	This is not what I said
OOC	Out of character		TOY	Thinking of you
OOP	Out of print		TT4N	Ta ta for now
OTOH	On the other hand		TU	Totally understand
PAW	Parents are watching		TYT	Take your time
POV	Point of view		U	You
QT	Quality of service		UP4IT	Up for it
R	Are		UPD8	Update
R8	Rate		URT1	You are the one
RAE	Raise an eyebrow			
RU	Are you			
RUOK	Are you OK?			
SAL	Such a laugh			
SIABH	Sorry I'm busy helping			
SIT	Stay in touch			
SNAFU	Situation normal all fouled up			
SOD?	Single or dating?			
SOHF	Sense of humour failure			
SOL	Simply out of luck			
SOME1	Someone			
SOS	Someone special			
SOT	Short of time			
SPOC	Single point of contact			
SUL	See you later			
SUM1	Someone			
SUS	See you soon			
SWAK	Sealed with a kiss			
SWALK	Sealed with a loving kiss			
SWIM	See what I mean			
SYL	See you later			
SYS	See you soon			
TA	Thanks again			
TA4N	That's all for now			

Try These at Home

Households with computers

Percentage of households with a personal computer, 1988–2001

Year ended 30 June	Percentage
1988	9
1989	11
1990	11
1991	13
1992	15
1993	16
1994	18
1995	21
1996	24
1997	27
1998	32
2001	47

TRANSPORT

Getting Around Down Under

The first recorded visit of a whaling ship to New Zealand was that of the *William and Ann*, which visited Doubtless Bay in 1792.

In 1822, the sloop *Snapper* was the first deep-sea vessel to enter Bluff Harbour.

The *June* was the first merchant steamer to visit New Zealand, when it arrived at the port of Auckland in 1847.

The paddle steamer *Governor Wynyard* was the first power-driven ship to be built in New Zealand. It was launched at Auckland and was subsequently used for trading purposes on the Tamaki River.

In 1857, a ferry service across the Clutha River was established.

The first Act of Parliament empowering rail construction in New Zealand occurred in 1860. The Act enabled work to commence on the Christchurch to Lyttelton tunnel.

New Zealand's first steam railway was a 7.2-kilometre line from Christchurch to Ferrymead.

The Dun Mountain Railway in the Nelson district is reputed to be the first railway in New Zealand. On 3 February 1862, 14 months before steam trains began running on the Christchurch to Ferrymead line, a horse-drawn tramway began operation from the Dun Mountain chrome ore mines to the port of Nelson. When the mountain line was closed, an urban section was retained, operating a passenger tram service that continued until the rails succumbed to fatigue in 1901.

In earlier times, before bridges were built over rivers and estuaries, ferries were a common part of the New Zealand transport systems. A major river crossing on the Clutha River at Port Molyneux still depends on a ferry, but, in general, ferries are a thing of the past.

The first Cobb and Co. coach ran from Dunedin to Gabriels Gully (1862). In the same year, a night coach began operating on the Dunedin to Tuapeka road.

With the opening of the first alpine road through Arthurs Pass, coaches were able to service the goldfields on the West Coast.

Tom and Harry Newman began a mail coach service in Nelson from Foxhill to Murchison.

The first coach between the Hermitage and Fairlie was a six-in-hand affair run by the Mount Cook Hermitage Company.

In 1864, a wooden railway between Invercargill and Makarewa was opened, but, because of operating difficulties, was abandoned in 1866.

Construction on the Auckland to Drury railway began in 1865. It was erected to carry troops and materials to the Waikato Wars.

In 1867, the first passenger train travelled through the Christchurch to Lyttelton tunnel.

The Tararu Tramway in Thames is considered to be New Zealand's second street tramway.

The first public railway in Auckland was a 13.8-kilometre section to Onehunga. It was later extended to Onehunga wharf.

The first scow in New Zealand was built in 1873 by Septimus Meiklejohn at Omaha in Northland. In the following 50 years, scows contributed more to the development of the country than any other form of transport.

The slowest passage made by an immigrant ship occurred when the *Bebington* arrived in Auckland 154 days after leaving London.

Between 1877 and 1893, a horse-drawn bush tramway linked Greymouth and Kumara on the West Coast of the South Island. The three-hour trip was highlighted by a link across the Taramakau River on a river cage suspended from a cable.

The Rimutaka Incline, where locomotives utilised a gripping device on a central third rail, was built in 1879.

Glen Eden station was originally established in 1879 to serve Waikumete Cemetery, located directly behind the station.

Between 1880 and 1886, private railways proliferated, although they were worked by New Zealand Railways or taken over on completion. The lines concerned were Waimea Plains, Gore to Lumsden, Duntroon and Hakataramea, Rakaia and Ashburton Forks, Waimate and Waihao Downs, and Thames Valley and Rotorua.

A line was built from the Wairoa River in Northland in the 1880s, to serve the kauri forests near Kaihu.

The Seaman's Union was formed in 1880.

A short-lived horse tramway linking the harbour ferries with Cheltenham Beach on Auckland's North Shore was opened in 1886.

By the end of the nineteenth century, the Wanganui River was regarded as the Rhine of New Zealand because of its physical attractions and large numbers of river craft. A regular service was instigated in 1891, when the *Wairere* travelled upriver from Wanganui to Pipiriki. In 1903, this service was extended as far as Taumarunui, which was then the southern terminus of the Main Trunk line. To break the journey downstream to Pipiriki, a houseboat was moored some 50 kilometres south of Taumarunui to serve as an overnight stopover.

In 1895, the *Penguin* became the first ship allocated to the Steamer Express Service between Wellington and Lyttelton.

Wellington businessman and politician William McLean imported the first motor car into New Zealand in 1898.

Early bicycles with hard tyres were called 'Bone Shakers'.

Prior to the arrival of heavy trucks and tractors, teams of bullocks (bulls without bollocks), were yoked in pairs to provide motive force.

Before the Main Trunk line was in operation, Auckland to Wellington train travellers caught the 'Boat Train' from Auckland to Onehunga Wharf, whereupon they caught a boat bound for New Plymouth. The New Plymouth-Wellington line was up and running by then, and by transferring to the New Plymouth-Wellington Express they were able to reach the capital.

The first New Zealand trunk line to be completed was that between Christchurch and Invercargill.

In 1900, the first electric tram service was established in Dunedin.

A year later, Timaru engineer Cecil Wood developed a combustion engine and built New Zealand's first motorcycle. In 1901, Wood built a motor car and drove it around the streets of Timaru.

George Hemming procured a steam-driven 'Locomobile' and was the first to drive a car from Auckland to Rotorua, and later from Auckland to Napier.

The first motor-car journey from Wellington to Napier was credited to a Mr Oates, who drove a Benz vehicle.

The Auckland Automobile Association was formed in 1902.

The Wanganui Fire Brigade was the first to be motorised in Australasia.

A referendum in Auckland in 1903 approved the running of Sunday trams.

Car registration became compulsory in New Zealand in 1905.

In 1908, a few months before the completion of the North Island Main Trunk line, a special train — 'The Parliamentary Special' — used a temporary linking track to make the journey from Wellington to Auckland. The intentions of the Parliamentarians were twofold: to visit the US Great White Fleet in Auckland, and to attend a performance of 'Mother Goose'. However, the train was late and they missed the performance.

The last spike completing the North Island Main Trunk was driven at Manganui-o-te-Ao, on 6 November 1908.

The first regular passenger trains between Wellington and Auckland took nearly 20 hours to complete the journey.

New Plymouth was the last New Zealand city to introduce an electric tram service.

In 1908, 12 Ford Model Ts were shipped to New Zealand, each of them selling for £425.

When the first through passenger service from Auckland to Wellington ran in 1909, second-class passengers were charged 21 shillings and twopence, and first-class 30 shillings and one penny.

New Zealander Bertram Ogilvie is credited with inventing contra-acting ailerons for aircraft, over which he took worldwide patents.

The Dunedin and Roslyn Tramway Co. instigated New Zealand's first electric tram service from Ross Street near the Town Belt to Maori Hill.

The historic Dunedin railway station was designed by NZR engineer George Troup.

In the early part of the twentieth century, members of the Otorohanga Rugby Club once convened a full (everyone had had a few) committee meeting in the carriage of the mixed goods train trundling between Te Kuiti and Otorohanga.

In 1910, the Grafton Bridge in Auckland was opened. It was the southern hemisphere's largest reinforced-concrete single-span bridge.

Vivian Walsh made the first controlled powered flight in New Zealand, at Papakura in 1911.

In 1912, the first driver's licence was issued.

When the Mount Cook Motor Company purchased a Leyland truck for use as a goods carrier it was considered to be the first heavy motor truck on New Zealand roads. It was affectionately known as the 'Red Lorry'.

The steamer *Earnslaw* began service on Lake Wakatipu in 1912.

In 1914, the idea of building a light railway line between Te Kuiti and Piopio was approved in principle — and one assumes, in Wellington. However the idea was shelved and then cancelled altogether.

The first plane to fly over Auckland City was the *Britannia* in 1914.

Count Von Luckner, a prisoner during World War I on Motuihe Island, made his escape by launch. He was later recaptured in the Kermadec Islands.

The Wellington and Manawatu Railway was the first to introduce electric lights and dining cars on trains. Initially the dining car was not connected to the rest of the train, and passengers were forced to board the dining car at one stop and return to their seats at another.

The *Providence* was the first ship to be built in New Zealand.

In 1920, the Department of Railways set up an operation in Frankton, Hamilton to build prefabricated houses for railway workers and their families. Eventually the works were expanded to include houses for other state servants. The scheme was scrapped in 1929, following complaints by the forces of private enterprise, to the effect that unfair competition was being displayed.

Various claims have been made that Richard Pearse, a South Canterbury farmer, was the first person in the world to achieve powered flight.

Experiments in aerial sowing of farmlands

were conducted from a hot-air balloon at Marshlands near Blenheim.

The first woman to ride as an aeroplane passenger in New Zealand was a Miss Lester.

The AB steam engine was capable of 3590 lbs of draw-bar power.

In the old days, race trains were not competing trains hurtling down parallel tracks, but trains that took punters to horse-race meetings.

New Zealand Rail had designated non-smoking carriages long before ASH and other PC bodies reared their smokeless heads. Ironically passengers in non-smoking carriages got a lungful of smoke anyway when steam engines pulled trains through tunnels and windows were left open.

Over 33,000 New Zealanders have died on New Zealand roads since records began in 1921.

Petrol brands in earlier times: Texaco, BP, Shell, Europa, Atlantic, Caltex, Big Tree, Voco, Plume, Peak.

The first parachute descent from an aircraft in New Zealand was made by Albert Eastwood on 22 February 1922.

Wigram Airport was originally named Sockburn.

The tramway line to the Auckland Zoo was opened in 1923.

In 1924, the largest and fastest motor liner in the world, the *Aorangi*, was launched.

The first radio beacon in Australasia was constructed at Cape Maria Van Diemen.

In 1925, balloon tyres replaced solid and high-pressure pneumatic tyres.

In 1929, the *Rangitane*, *Rangitata* and *Rangatiki* were delivered to the New Zealand Shipping Company.

The first flight between Wellington and Auckland involved a Supermarine Channel flying boat. Including stops at Kawhia and Wanganui, the flight took eight hours.

The Post and Telegraph Department used a Cadillac car to collect mail in Wellington, the first time a motor vehicle had been used in such a way.

The Te Kuiti oxidation ponds provided water, albeit sullied, to help the local fire brigade extinguish a fire on a passing diesel engine.

An AB locomotive somehow slipped its moorings on the Waitara branch line and steamed off under its own steam. The driver, having visited the toilet, was forced to break into a sprint in order to catch up with his errant motive force.

The railway line between Napier and Gisborne is forced to traverse the runway of Gisborne Airport, creating certain problems. Basically, trains give way to planes.

Trains used to have guards' vans attached to them.

The General Manager of New Zealand Railways used to travel around the country in a six-cylinder, petrol-driven inspection car on rails.

In the old days of steam trains, babies' bottles and baby food used to be reheated in the driver's cabin, and nappies dried on the whistle cord, before being handed back to grateful mothers.

In 1931, Guy Menzies, in a single-engine Sports Avion, became the first solo pilot to cross the Tasman from Australia to Harihari, New Zealand.

The first woman to fly the Tasman was Jean Batten.

The Napier earthquake put paid to the city's trams. Buses took over as the city was rebuilt.

In 1935, Pan American Airways began regular flying-boat services between San Francisco and Auckland.

For 20 years the famous dolphin 'Pelorus Jack' used to escort ships across Admiralty Bay towards French Pass in the Marlborough Sounds.

The Motor Vehicles Amendment Act of 1936 brought in a speed limit of 30 mph in built-up areas.

Union Airways of New Zealand Ltd commenced its operations with an air service between Palmerston North and Dunedin in 1936.

The building of the Mangere Bridge was delayed for two years because of the longest industrial dispute in New Zealand's history.

The Road Code was first published in 1937.

The first zebra pedestrian crossing was installed in New Zealand in Petone.

In 1938, Auckland's first trolley-buses emerged when the Farmers Trading Company set up a free shoppers' service from Wyndham Street to Hobson Street.

Riverboats plied the Waikato and Waipa Rivers until World War II.

In 1939, the last steamer on the Clutha River ceased operations.

After the completion of the railway to Gisborne, the Hawke's Bay seaports of Wairoa and Waikokopu were closed.

In 1940, the *Orion*, a German raider, laid mines near Auckland. This vessel destroyed the *Niagara* and *Turakina* and together with another raider, the *Komet*, sank the *Rangitane*.

The construction of the North Island Main Trunk, between Frankton and Te Awamutu, was delayed when work gangs were whisked away to help fortify New Zealand's shores against a perceived Russian invasion. Also, before the line could continue, solid ground had to be found at the bottom of a 'hungry hole' near Ohaupo — a seemingly bottomless pit that swallowed more than 100 tons of ballast.

Once, high winds in South Canterbury buckled a towering pine tree over so that it landed on a goods wagon carrying a new tractor. Amazingly, as the wind blast eased, the old pine, still rooted, righted itself, taking the tractor with it. Rescue gangs were confronted by the sight of a tractor sitting halfway up a pine tree.

The *Northerner* express travelled both north and south, and the *Southerner* express, which doesn't travel at all any more, used to go south and north.

During the 1950 Auckland Empire Games, 1500 Aucklanders and others travelled by several trains along the laid-back Cambridge branch, in order to see the rowing events at Lake Karapiro.

Give Way signs at intersections and crossings were first introduced in 1956.

The rail tunnel linking Lyttelton with Christchurch was reputedly the first tunnel to be excavated through the rim of a volcanic crater.

Auckland's last trams ran in 1956.

The 'notional railway' was set up in 1957 between Nelson and Blenheim, after the closure of the Nelson line in 1955. The government paid the freight and passenger operators on the road a subsidy equal to the difference between their normal rates and those of New Zealand Railways. It was a railway with no lines.

The first Holden car to be assembled in New Zealand hit the road in 1957.

Two goats attacked a diesel engine on the Opunake branch line in the 1960s.

When the Alliance Freezing Works at Invercargill ran out of steam because of the late delivery of a new boiler, the Ferrymead Railway Musuem in Christchurch donated their KB968 steam engine to provide steam.

Motor vehicle accidents have claimed nearly twice as many New Zealand lives as World War I.

Breath and blood tests for suspected drunk drivers were introduced in 1967.

Columbus New Zealand, New Zealand's first container ship, entered service in 1971.

When the refreshment rooms at Taumarunui Station were closed in 1975, all passengers off the Auckland to Wellington express, plus 100 locals, stormed the rock cake citadel for the 'last cuppa'.

Some tourists believe that Main Trunk station names like Oio and Kiokio equate to numbers 0-1-0 and K10-K10.

In 1996, 42.7 per cent of New Zealand households owned one car. That figure had decreased to 40.8 per cent in 2001, although the figure for two cars per household had increased from 33.5 per cent to 35.9.

The use of hidden speed cameras was introduced in 1997.

In 2000, Air New Zealand had in its fleet, eight 747-400s, nine 767-300 ERs, four 767-200 ERs, nine 737-300s and nine 737-200s serving international and domestic routes.

New Zealanders are regarded as the most prolific pleasure-boat owners in the world.

In 2001, 13.1 per cent of New Zealand households owned three or more cars. In the same year, 10.1 per cent didn't own a car at all.

In New Zealand it costs, on average, 51.1 cents per kilometre to own and operate a car under 1300 cc. That makes a total annual cost of $6132, or $118 per week, if the car is driven 12,000 kilometres a year, the New Zealand average.

Oldsmobiles for Young and Old

Cars seen on New Zealand roads

Alfa Romeo
Alldays and Onions
Argyll
Ariel
Audi
Austin
Bean
Benz
BMW
Buick
Cadillac
Chevrolet
Chrysler
Citroën
Clyno
Daewoo
Daihatsu
Daimler
Darracq
Datsun
De Dion
De Soto
Essex
Fiat
Ford

Graham-Paige
Hillman
Holden
Honda
Hudson
Humber
Hupmobile
Hyundai
Isuzu
Jaguar
Jowett
Kia
Land Rover
Locomobile
Marmon
Mazda
Mercedes Benz
Mitsubishi
Moon
Morgan
Morris
Nash
Nissan
Oakland
Oldsmobile

Peugeot
Plymouth
Pontiac
Porsche
Rambler
Renault
Riley
Rudge
Rugby
Saab
Singer
Studebaker
Subaru
Sunbeam
Suzuki
Toyota
Triumph
Vanguard
Vauxhall
Volkswagen
Volvo
Wolseley
Kiwi-built cars —
    Carlton, Marlborough,
    Trekka, Anziel Nova

Yank Tanks and Dungers

Unofficial names for vehicles

Hoonmobile — car likely to be driven by a hoon

Rustbucket — a rust-ravaged car

Guard's van — a variation on Vanguard, a popular family car of the 1950s

Jalopy — run-down car

Mark II — Ford Zephyr

Poor man's Mark II — Ford Consul

Beetle — traditional Volkswagen

Maigret's machine — front-wheel-drive Citroën

Bubble — Baby Austin

Yank Tank — large American sedan

Dunger — an old, clapped-out car, aka a 'bomb'

The Ugly Duckling — Citroën 2 CV

Scareships and Flying Saucers

UFOs over New Zealand

The earliest twentieth-century sighting of a UFO was the balls of light and cigar-shaped craft seen in many parts of New Zealand. Kiwis referred to the latter as 'Scareships'. The Kelso Aerial Mystery, as the event was called, occurred in 1909.

Two Gore dredge hands who worked the nightshift not only saw what looked like an airship, but they clearly saw two figures on board.

The Kelso Aerial Mystery of 1909 led to reports of 'strange lights' from Kelso (obviously), Balclutha, Invercargill, Kaitangata, Owaka, Kaka Point, Gore, Dunedin, Winslow, Timaru, Winchester and Christchurch.

The suggestion was made that the flying object associated with the Kelso Aerial Mystery could have contained a German spy from the yacht *Seestern*.

Halley's Comet was expected to arrive in 1910, and this produced a heightened awareness of 'things in the sky'. This was one rational account for the events of 1909: that people's imaginations were becoming heightened too.

In 1919, a Mr Church had been hunting rabbits when he noticed a grey-coloured disc-shaped object in a creek bed. It was about 4.5 metres across and had a ramp on one side.

In either 1944 or 1945, a Mrs Church of Christchurch saw a dome-shaped object on the ground. Three beings were sighted, including one outside the craft.

In 1945, a Mr Bray of Taumarunui saw a cigar-shaped object with red, yellow and orange lights fly past at midnight.

On the night of 6 December 1952, there were several sightings of UFOs over New Zealand — to wit, a pair of green and blue discs. Many mentioned a slight hissing sound as the discs passed overhead.

Many years later the 1952 'sightings' were revealed as being an elaborate student hoax, with students given specific instructions as to what to report to the media regarding the 'phenomenon'. There never were lights in the sky, just co-ordinated and convincing reports of false sightings that were fed to newspapers.

'Believers' in UFOs duly recorded the 1952 'sightings' in their logbooks and for 30 years the events of 1952 held surprising credibility.

In March 1978, Ken Nichol, one of the participants in the 1952 Grand Interplanetary Hoax, revealed that the exercise was a sophisticated student prank.

John Scott, now Sir John Scott, Professor of Medicine at Middlemore Hospital, was the mastermind behind the 1952 hoax.

In 1978, New Zealanders subscribed $23,000 to buy shares in a project that would promise flights on a flying saucer and an eventual share of the profit. The New Zealand promoter of the scheme claimed that the craft, which were apparently already in existence, could travel from Britain to New Zealand in 30 minutes.

The 'flying saucers' involved in the 1978 UFO scam were referred to as 'levity discs', in an attempt to negate the negative press associated with 'flying saucers'.

Close Encounters of the Third Kind, Steven Speilberg's blockbuster movie, arrived in New Zealand in 1978, igniting renewed interest here in UFO phenomena.

In December 1978, it was reported that a Christchurch-bound Argosy freight aircraft had been followed by a large white light with a red tinge to it, off the Kaikoura coast near Clarence. The Wellington Control tower confirmed that a strange object had tracked the plane for nearly 20 kilometres. Several pilots, at different times, confirmed the sightings. One of the objects was photographed by a TV crew.

New Zealand made world history in respect of the Kaikoura incident, for it was the first time a UFO had been logged by radar and camera, by reliable observers.

The RNZAF discounted the Kaikoura sightings, attributing them to 'natural but unusual atmospheric phenomena'.

A Dr Neil Cherry believed the sightings were mirages caused by dysfunctional weather conditions.

Also in December 1978, Captain Bill Startup of Blenheim flew a Safe Air Argosy over Kaikoura and an Australian TV crew filmed an object similar to the previous sightings.

BUSINESS & FINANCE

Business as Usual and Unusual

From the 1960s to the 1980s, New Zealand's Gross National Product (GNP) saw us plummet from fifth in the world to twentieth of OECD countries.

When Equiticorp failed in 1989, it had 2000 employees and owed an estimated $5.6 billion. It was the classic 'fat cat' financial organisation. The company didn't make anything as such — it didn't make tangible widgets, but rather specialised in mergers and takeovers in the style of the mid-1980s. It was caught out by the 1987 share-market crash, having bought New Zealand Steel from the government just before the crash.

The BNZ nearly collapsed in the 1980s.

In 1987, when the share-market collapsed, prices dropped by 59 per cent in four months. Despite the scare, 1987 also saw the drawing of the first Lotto prize.

In October 1986, GST was introduced at 10 per cent and sales tax was abolished.

In the 1990s, Brierley Investments Ltd (BIL), recorded New Zealand's largest-ever financial loss of close to $1 billion.

The Amusement Tax — No Laughing Matter

Taxation

Death duties were introduced in New Zealand in 1866, because of the high cost of the land wars with Maori.

A gift tax was introduced in 1881.

In 1917, beer duties were reviewed, with the rate increasing dependent on alcohol content.

The amusements tax, first introduced in 1917, was abolished in 1965.

In 1984, road user charges were increased by 46 per cent.

Life Savings and Death Duties

Banking and finance

The Union Bank of Australia, New Zealand's first bank, commenced operation in Wellington in 1840. In the same year, New Zealand's local bank, the New Zealand Banking Company, opened at Kororareka (Russell).

Alexander Kennedy was the first manager of the New Zealand Banking Company, Kororareka.

Government rags, Shin plasters, Flash notes and Assignats were some of the unflattering names given to debentures planned for release in 1844. There was little confidence in their value.

In 1846, New Zealand's first savings bank, the Wellington Savings Bank, was set up.

The Auckland Savings Bank began operations in 1847.

The Colonial Bank of Issue, a state-run bank with the sole right to issue notes, opened in 1850 — and closed in 1856.

The first deposit into the New Plymouth Savings Bank was lodged by Waitera Te Karei.

James MacAndrew was a prominent figure in the failed attempt to get the Bank of Otago up and running.

The Bank of New Zealand was founded in 1861. In the same year, the Bank of New South Wales commenced in New Zealand, after purchasing the Oriental Bank.

The National Bank began operations in 1862.

The Hokitika Savings Bank started in 1866.

The Commercial Bank of Australia began operations in 1912.

Counterfeiting was rife during the Great Depression.

The first New Zealand coin issued in 1933 was the half crown.

The Reserve Bank of New Zealand became the country's central bank in 1934.

New Zealand's first pennies and halfpennies, bearing the date 1940, began circulating in 1939.

In 1951, the Bank of Australasia merged with the Union Bank to form the ANZ Bank.

Decimal currency was introduced in New Zealand in 1967.

In 1976, Securitibank collapsed.

In 1982, the Bank of New South Wales and Commercial Bank of Australia merged to become Westpac Banking Corp.

New Zealand became the first country in the world to link all trading banks by a national computer network.

MEDICAL MATTERS

Of GPs, DDT and HIV

William Williams was the first doctor to arrive in New Zealand — in 1826.

Dr Samuel Ford was the first European doctor to study the Maori phenomenon of makutu, where seemingly healthy Maori die due to supernatural forces.

In 1840, John Johnson was appointed New Zealand's first Colonial Surgeon.

Four thousand Maori died in the great measles epidemic of 1854.

The Contagious Diseases Act of 1869 was unable to control the spread of venereal disease in early New Zealand.

Training for nurses in New Zealand was set up by Truby King in 1888. By 1893, New Zealand could claim the world's first state-registered nurse.

The New Zealand Foundation for the Blind was set up in 1890.

Before 1893, the age of sexual consent for girls was 12 years of age.

The Lunatics Ordinance put forward the notion of a universal system of asylums for all classes of society.

The first case of plague was diagnosed in Auckland in 1900.

The Tohunga Supression Act was passed with a view to stamping out the practice of Maori medicine.

In 1901, registration of New Zealand nurses became compulsory.

Children were prohibited from smoking in New Zealand, by legislation passed in 1903.

The registration of midwives was made compulsory in New Zealand in 1904.

In 1905, the first state maternity hospital was established.

The Quackery Prevention Act was introduced in 1908 to prevent the sale of patent medicines.

The Mental Defectives Act changed classifications of the mentally handicapped, and terms like 'lunatic' and 'insane' were scrapped.

In 1915, a pension for coal miners' phthisis was introduced. This was the first case of compensation being allocated for an occupational disease.

The worldwide influenza epidemic of 1918 claimed the lives of approximately 8600 New Zealanders. The New Zealand Department of Public Health constructed inhalation chambers to disinfect throats and lungs.

The 1918 influenza epidemic claimed more New Zealand men than women and country towns suffered more casualties than the cities.

Mining towns were the worst hit communities during the 1918 flu epidemic.

A school dental service was set up in 1919.

Peter Buck was the first director of the Division of Maori Hygiene, within the Health Department.

The Homeopathic Echo was New Zealand's first medical journal.

Emily Siedeberg was the first woman in New Zealand to gain a medical degree.

New Zealand's first health camp for undernourished children was established at Turakina, Wanganui.

Until 1920, abortion was a taboo subject in New Zealand.

Pensions for the blind were introduced in 1924.

The first sanatorium for the treatment of tuberculosis patients was established in Cambridge.

The Crippled Children's Society was formed in 1935.

The Plunket Society, originally set up as the Royal New Zealand Society for the Health of Women and Children, was the brainchild of Truby King, under the patronage of Lady Plunket, the wife of the Governor-General.

A report lodged in 1936 found that about one in every five pregnancies was aborted, of which 4000 were induced by criminal abortionists or women themselves.

In 1936, the maternal death rate from abortion in New Zealand was around the 25 per cent mark — among the highest in the world.

In 1937, free milk was made available in schools.

In 1937, there was another influenza scare in New Zealand, with 19 fatalities.

In 1947, North Island schools were closed because of a polio epidemic. They remained closed until April 1948.

Meals on Wheels were first associated with a service provided by the St John's Ambulance Association in Auckland. Eventually Hospital Boards took over this role.

The first experiments relating to the use of fluoride in public water supplies were conducted in Hastings.

The Salk vaccine was successful in halting the incidence of polio.

In the late 1960s, the New Zealand Asthma Society, the Arthritis and Rheumatism Foundation, and the National Heart Foundation of New Zealand were formed.

The Lawson quintuplets were born in 1965.

The use of DDT on farm land was prohibited in 1968.

New Zealander William Liley performed the world's first successful intra-uterine blood transfusion.

Heart disease and cancer were the main causes of death in New Zealand in the 1970s.

The concept of 'granny flats' was introduced in 1980, under the auspices of the Housing Corporation.

New Zealanders regarded as sufficiently mentally ill to require incarceration were detained in prisons pending the establishment of the colony's first mental hospitals in Auckland (1853), and Wellington (1854). Following the 'normalisation' and 'de-institutionalisation' movements of the 1980s when psychiatric hospitals were closed, many ill people requiring incarceration were again detained in prisons.

In New Zealand, Children's Health Camps provide services for 3000 children annually.

Aids became a notifiable disease in New Zealand in 1983 and the first case was notified in 1984.

The New Zealand AIDS Foundation was registered as a charitable trust in New Zealand in 1985.

By 1987, there were 21 cases of Aids in New Zealand, and 283 people were HIV-positive.

On a typical day in New Zealand, 42,700 New Zealanders will see a general practitioner.

New Zealand has been a world leader in combating Sudden Infant Death Syndrome (SIDS or cot death). In this country, the SIDS mortality rate fell from 4.4 per 1000 live births in 1988 to 1.2 per 1000 in 1998.

Obesity in New Zealand increased by 11 per cent in a 1989 survey to 17 per cent in a later survey in 1997.

In 1998, cancer was the cause of 28.7 per cent of all deaths in New Zealand. The lungs, large bowel and prostate were the most common cancer sites for New Zealand males, while the breasts and large bowel were the most prevalent sites for women.

In 1998, an estimated 117 New Zealanders died from alcohol-related diseases and conditions.

By the end of 2000, 729 New Zealanders had been diagnosed with Aids.

The majority of people diagnosed with

Aids in New Zealand have been male (94 per cent). Eighty-eight per cent of these cases were exposed to AIDS through homosexual contact.

It is estimated that every year 4700 smokers and 400 non-smokers (passive smokers) die in New Zealand.

In 2001, a medical abortion pill was approved for use in New Zealand.

Unintended hospital injuries in New Zealand are comparable with Australia and the United Kingdom.

Water is reported as being the most popular drink for New Zealanders, with 80 per cent drinking water at least three times a day.

Low-fat dairy products are more popular with New Zealand women than men.

Those New Zealanders who get the least sleep are those with children under the age of one.

Maori spend more time than non-Maori playing organised sport.

Currently, 82 per cent of New Zealand abortions are undertaken in Christchurch, Wellington and Auckland.

SARS (Severe acute respiratory syndrome) was declared a notifiable disease in New Zealand in 2003.

Great Expectations 1880–1997

Life expectancy

Period	Male	Female
	Years	
1880–91	54.4	57.3
1892–95	55.3	58.1
1896–1900	57.4	60.0
1901–05	58.1	60.6
1906–10	59.2	61.8
1911–15	61.0	63.5
1921–22	62.8	65.4
1925–27	64.0	66.6
1931	65.0	67.9
1934–38	65.5	68.4
1950–52	67.2	71.3
1955–57	68.2	73.0
1960–62	68.4	73.8
1965–67	68.2	74.3
1970–72	68.6	74.6
1975–77	69.0	75.4
1980–82	70.4	76.4
1985–87	71.1	77.1
1990–92	72.9	78.7
1995–97	74.3	79.6

MILITARY MATTERS

Gunboats up the Waikato

At the time of sighting the North Island near Poverty Bay, James Cook was a Lieutenant commanding the converted Whitby collier *Earl of Pembroke*. The boat had been renamed HMS *Endeavour Bark*. The Royal navy already had a sloop named *Endeavour*.

The first British soldiers set foot on New Zealand soil at Kororareka in the Bay of Islands in 1827 but it was not a propitious landing. The soldiers' brig, the *Wellington*, had been taken over by its convict manifest on their way to Norfolk Island. Puzzled Maori looked on as the convicts delighted in drilling the soldiers — members of the 57th Regiment. Before too long the situation had been salvaged as local whalers charged and rescued the soldiers and the status quo on board the *Wellington* returned.

Maori referred to the first British soldiers as the 'Red Tribe', because of the colour of their uniform.

In 1834, the crew of the HMS *Alligator* attacked the pa at Waimate, in an attempt at a show of force to Maori.

Gunboats up the Waikato River were used to defeat Maori at the Battle of Rangariri.

The gunboat *Sandfly* helped defend the garrison at Maketu.

The first European New Zealanders to see active service were the 75 Auckland volunteers who took part in the attack on Ohaewai pa in 1845.

One of the few times during the New Zealand Wars when militia or volunteers actually fought, occurred in Taranaki during the Battle of Waireka.

On 10 January 1846, the pa at Ruapekapeka was attacked, and the following day, a Sunday,

the breach was made while most of the Maori defenders were otherwise detained attending a church service.

The flagstaff at Kororareka (Russell) was cut down four times. Hone Heke was involved in all lopping episodes. The flagstaff then stayed down until after Hone Heke's death in 1850.

More than 100 Europeans died in the battle for Ohaewai pa. There were very few Maori casualties.

The last British regiment left New Zealand in 1870.

The final skirmish of the New Zealand Wars occurred at Mangaone, south of Waikaremoana, in 1872.

In 1880, Lieutenant-Colonel Peter Scratchley recommended the building of fortifications at Auckland, Wellington, Lyttelton and Dunedin in response to the fear of Russian expansion in the South Pacific.

In 1881, the Parihaka Crisis led to the deployment of 950 volunteers to join the Armed Constabulary force.

In 1885, the New Zealand Cabinet offered the British Government 1000 troops, a quarter of whom would have been Maori, to fight in Afghanistan. The offer was declined.

British regiments who served in the New Zealand Wars of 1843–47 and 1860–72 were: 80th South Staffordshire, 96th Manchester — 'The Bendovers', 99th Wiltshire — 'The Moonrakers', 58th Rutlandshire, 65th Second Yorkshire North Riding — 'The Royal Tigers', 12th Suffolk — 'The Old Dozen', 40th Second Somersetshire — 'The Excellers', 57th West Middlesex — 'The Diehards', 14th Buckinghamshire — 'Lord Wellington's Bodyguard', 43rd Monmouthshire Light Infantry — 'The Light Bobs', 70th Surrey — 'The 70th Glasgow Greys', 18th Royal Irish, 68th Durham Light Infantry — 'The Faithful Durhams'.

The South African, or Boer War, first impacted on New Zealand when 214 men and their horses sailed from Wellington.

New Zealand was the first colony to offer assistance to Britain in the Boer War.

In 1901, during the Boer War, Trooper IE Baigent rescued a fellow New Zealander at Bastard's Drift. Baigent was later awarded the Distinguished Conduct Medal.

Sixteen New Zealand troops were killed in a railway accident at Machavie, during the Boer War.

New Zealander Lieutenant R McKeich became the last casualty of the Boer War when he was shot in Orange Free State, during a skirmish with the Boers who later claimed they were unaware that a state of surrender had been announced.

At the outset of World War I, Britain accepted New Zealand's offer of an Expeditionary Force. This group was the largest body of men ever to leave New Zealand. They became known as the 'Main Body'.

The New Zealand Army Nursing Service was formed in 1913, and during World War I, 519 nurses served overseas.

In 1914, the HMS *Philomel*, *Psyche* and *Pyramus* provided an escort for the ships carrying troops to occupy German (now Western) Samoa.

The first New Zealand soldier to die in World War I was Private William Ham of Wanganui.

Almost 10 per cent of the New Zealand population and 42 per cent of males aged between 19 and 45 years of age saw active service in World War I.

New Zealand paid a heavy price in World War I, with 16,697 Kiwis losing their lives in the various campaigns.

During World War I, New Zealand pilots trained at their own expense at private flying schools, before joining the Royal Flying Corps, the Royal Air Force or the Royal Naval Air Service.

When the hospital ship *Marquette* was torpedoed in the Mediterranean in 1915, 11 New Zealand nurses drowned.

Second Lieutenant Rhodes-Moorhouse, a part-Maori serving as a pilot in the Royal Flying Corps, was killed during a bombing raid in France in 1915. He was awarded New Zealand's first air Victoria Cross.

In 1918, four members of the Barnes family were killed in World War I. The youngest son was exempted from war service.

Of the 8556 New Zealanders who served in Gallipoli, 2721 died and 4752 were wounded.

In 1926, the total numbers of the New Zealand Army Permanent Force were 102 officers and 391 other ranks. The Territorial Force, with its compulsory component, numbered 821 officers and 21,218 other ranks.

In 1929, the New Zealand Air Force airlifted supplies to the Murchison area which had been ravaged by earthquakes, thereby becoming the Air Force's first emergency relief operation. Its first active operation occurred in 1930 when an Air Force Moth seaplane was part of the arsenal sent aboard the HMS *Dunedin* to Samoa, to quell an uprising.

In 1931, following the Napier earthquake, sailors from the HMS *Veronica*, *Dunedin* and *Diomede* worked willingly in earthquake relief efforts.

During the Korean War, 33 New Zealand soldiers died, from a total of 3794.

New Zealand contributed one million pounds towards the establishment of the Singapore Naval Base.

The New Zealand Division of the Royal Navy, at the outbreak of World War II, comprised the cruisers HMS *Achilles* and *Leander* and the minesweeper HMS *Wakakura*.

The New Zealand Navy vessel the *Achilles* played a pivotal part in the demise of the German pocket battleship *Graf Spee* in 1939. Along with Royal Navy cruisers *Ajax* and *Exeter*, the *Achilles* caused severe damage to the *Graf Spee* at the mouth of the River Plate, between Uruguay and Brazil. Eventually the Germans scuttled the crippled *Graf Spee* and blew her up. Four New Zealanders from the *Achilles* died in the skirmish.

When the HMNZ *Leander* was struck by torpedoes in the Battle of Kolombangara, 28 of the crew lost their lives.

At 9.30 p.m., September 3 1939, New Zealand joined Britain, Australia, France and India in declaring war on Germany.

When the voluntary enlistment commenced for New Zealanders in World War II, 5419 enlisted on the first day.

Enlistment for Maori was voluntary during World War II.

The coastal vessel *Holmwood* was sunk by the German raider *Komet* in 1940, while sailing from the Chatham Islands to Lyttelton.

On 11 June 1940, New Zealand declared war on Italy.

Private GR Osborne was the first New Zealander killed in World War II — the victim of a thermos bomb in North Africa.

As a result of their bravery during the campaign in Crete, Second Lieutenant CH Upham and Sergeant AC Hulme were awarded the Victoria Cross.

The distinctive army 'lemon squeezer' hat was developed by Lieutenant Colonel WG Malone.

When the HMS *Neptune* was sunk in 1941, by mines in the Mediterranean, 150 New Zealanders lost their lives. It was the New Zealand Navy's worst loss in World War II.

The Women's Auxiliary Air Force (the WAAFs), was established in 1941.

Sergeant Pilot JA Ward of Wanganui was awarded the first air Victoria Cross won by a New Zealander in World War II.

The Short Singapores were the RNZAF's first flying boats.

New Zealand pilots were involved in the 'Dam Buster' raids on the Ruhr and Weser Valleys in Germany.

The Women's Royal New Zealand Naval Service was established in 1942.

In 1942, the merchant navy vessel *Awatea*, while serving as a troopship, sank after being bombed off the coast of Algeria.

On the same day the Japanese attacked Pearl Harbor, they also shelled Ocean Island in the Pacific where New Zealand citizens operated a radio station.

In 1942, reconnaissance flights by Japanese aircraft were made over Wellington and Auckland.

A total of 11,625 New Zealanders died in World War II. Most of the fatalities occurred in the Middle East and Mediterranean theatres of war.

After displaying further gallantry in the capture of Ruweisat Ridge in North Africa, Charles Upham, now a captain, was awarded a bar to his Victoria Cross.

When the Italian ship *Nino Bixio* was torpedoed in the Mediterranean while transporting prisoners of war from North Africa to Europe, included in the numbers of those who lost their lives were 120 New Zealand soldiers.

Under the terms of conscription during

World War II, 306,000 men were called up.

Five hundred women enlisted in the Womens' Royal New Zealand Naval Service during World War II.

During World War II, 640 nurses served overseas.

Of the 5000 New Zealand women who served in the Women's Auxilliary Army Corps (The WAACs), in World War II, over 900 served overseas.

The first Maori to be awarded the Victoria Cross was Second Lieutenant Ngarimu.

In 1943, New Zealand troops were the first to enter Tunisia in North Africa.

Thirty Wellington Bombers were the basis of the Number 75 New Zealand Squadron which became the first Commonwealth squadron to be formed within the Royal Air Force. Six aircraft from the squadron took part in the first major bombing raid on Germany in World War II.

'Cobber' Kain of Wellington was the first Allied air ace of World War II. He was credited with shooting down 17 enemy aircraft in the first months of hostilities. Sadly, he lost his life in June 1940 in a flying accident in France.

One pilot in every 12 who flew in the Battle of Britain was a New Zealander.

The Germans' surrender became effective from 12.01 a.m. on 9 May 1945.

Charles Upham was the only soldier to win the Victoria Cross twice during World War II.

Approximately 10,000 New Zealand women joined the services during World War II.

During the Korean War, New Zealand sent two frigates to patrol Korean waters.

The RNZAF was involved in top-dressing trials in 1946.

In 1948, six frigates, the HMS *Loch Shin*, *Loch Achray*, *Loch Morlech*, *Lock Eck*, *Loch Achanalt* and *Loch Katrine* were bought from Britain by the New Zealand Navy and renamed HMNZS *Taupo*, *Kaniere*, *Tutira*, *Hawea*, *Pukaki* and *Rotoiti*.

The Chief of Air Staff, Air Vice Marshall LM Isitt, represented New Zealand at the signing of the Japanese surrender on the USS *Missouri* in Tokyo Bay.

In 1948, after the Russians had sealed off the land routes to Berlin, the Berlin Airlift began. Three New Zealand crews flew Dakotas between Lubeck and Berlin for 13 months.

The Australian Government gifted four minesweepers to New Zealand: HMNZS *Kiama*, *Stawell*, *Inverell* and *Echuca*.

Invitations for recruits for a special New Zealand force to assist with the Suez Canal crisis received 907 applications. In the end, the force was not sent.

During the waterside workers' industrial dispute in 1951, all three New Zealand armed services provided personnel to work on New Zealand's wharves.

In 1951, the RNZAF received its first operational jet, a de Havilland Vampire.

The first flight by an RNZAF plane occurred when a Hercules flew from Christchurch to McMurdo Sound.

During the Christmas Island nuclear tests of 1957, HMNZS *Pukaki* and *Rotoiti* kept a watching brief.

Compulsory military training in New Zealand was discontinued in 1958.

In 1960, two New Zealand Army officers served with the United Nations force in the Congo.

Thirty-five New Zealanders lost their lives during the Vietnam War. Close to 4000 New Zealand soldiers — all volunteers — served in the campaign.

The first RNZAF helicopter pilots were deployed during the Vietnam War. One-third of the 30 pilots who served in Vietnam received awards for gallantry.

The HMNZS *Irirangi*, not a seagoing vessel, but the Navy's wireless-telegraphy station, was set up on the landlocked plateau of Waiouru.

In 1968, the New Zealand Government ordered 14 Skyhawk ground attack aircraft.

An RNZAF Orion created a world record endurance flying record of 20 hours, 15 minutes.

The RNZAF's first jet was a Gloucester Meteor.

New Zealand troops were withdrawn from Vietnam in 1971.

The Vampire aircraft was withdrawn from service in 1972.

The HMNZS *Otago* sailed from Auckland in 1973, as a protest against nuclear testing by the French at Mururoa Atoll.

Industrial disputes disrupted commercial airline operations in New Zealand and Australia in 1981. RNZAF and RAAF aircraft stepped into the breach and carried more than 4000 passengers across the Tasman.

HMNZS *Canterbury* was awarded the Wilkinson Sword of Peace in recognition of its role in assisting the Royal Navy during the Falklands War of 1982–83.

Lest We Forget

New Zealand war casualties

War	Killed	Wounded
South Africa (Boer War) 1899–1902	228	166
World War I — 1914–1918	16,697	41,362
World War II — 1939–1945	11,625	17,000
Korea — 1950–1953	41	81
Malaysia — 1948–1966	26	30
Vietnam — 1964–1972	35	187

DISASTERS

Off the Beaten Track

In 1809, the sailing ship *Boyd* was plundered and burned by Maori in Whangaroa Harbour. All but four of the ship's complement of 70 were killed and eaten.

In 1828, the *Enterprise* bound from Sydney to Hokianga was wrecked north of Hokianga Heads. The crew survived only to be killed by Maori.

The *Alma*, in 1856, was the first steamer to be wrecked on the New Zealand coast.

In 1863, the HMS *Orpheus* ran onto the Manukau Harbour bar. Of the 259 officers and men on board, 189 lost their lives. It was New Zealand's worst maritime disaster.

The *Pride of Yarra* was in collision with the paddle steamer *Favourite* in Otago Harbour in 1863 and 12 passengers drowned.

The *City of Dunedin* was lost while bound for Nelson in 1865 and 40 lives were lost.

In 1865, a clipper named *Fiery Star* caught fire and was forced to change its course from Australia to London and head for the Hauraki Gulf. Seventy-eight people on board, including the captain, several crew and all the passengers were lost at sea after taking to the lifeboats.

On 21 February 1879, 35 men died in a coal-mining accident at Kaitangata.

High winds blew a passenger train off the Rimutaka rail incline in 1880, killing three children and seriously injuring another 21 passengers.

In 1881, the passenger steamer *Tararua* struck a reef and 131 people died.

Mt Tarawera erupted in 1886, destroying the world-famous Pink and White Terraces and killing 153 people.

In 1894, the steamer *Wairarapa* struck a cliff on Great Barrier Island in heavy fog and 121 died.

The Brunner coal mine was the scene of the worst mine disaster in New Zealand

history, when 67 men were killed in March 1896.

In 1902, while bound for Hong Kong with the remains of 499 Chinese who had died in New Zealand, the *Ventnor* struck a rock and sank.

In 1903, the Waimangu geyser in Rotorua erupted, killing four people.

In 1907, the *Dundonald* ran aground on Disappointment Island.

Seventy-five lives were lost when the *Penguin* was wrecked in 1909.

A mudslide on White Island killed 11 workers in 1914.

In 1918, a combination of cyclonic winds and bushfires devastated the Raetihi district. Nine timber mills and hectares of forest were wiped out and 120 homes and much of the town of Raetihi fell victim to the fire. Townsfolk were forced to leap into the Whanganui River to save themselves.

Seventeen passengers on the Auckland–Wellington Express were killed when the train ran into a sudden landslide in 1924.

In 1929, Murchison was close to the epicentre of a major earthquake that killed 17 people and virtually destroyed the town. Surrounding land, to the extent of 80 square kilometres, was raised nearly half a metre.

A mountain guide and four women were killed in a storm at Tasman Glacier in 1930.

The Napier earthquake of 1931 was one of New Zealand's worst disasters, claiming 256 lives. In Napier itself, 161 people died, while Hastings (93) and Wairoa (2) also suffered casualties.

In 1936, the inter-island ferry *Rangatira* ran aground and began taking on water. She was negotiated stern first into Wellington Harbour and was able to berth safely.

The first aviation fatality in New Zealand occurred when a pilot was killed in a Canterbury Aviation Co. biplane.

In 1938, an excursion train was derailed at Ratana, near Wanganui, killing six passengers and the fireman.

In 1938, a cloudburst hit Wairoa and 21 people drowned.

In a mining accident at Glen Afton, Huntly in 1939, 11 miners lost their lives.

In 1942, an American Flying Fortress crashed after taking off from Whenuapai, Auckland, killing 11 airmen. Official disclosure of the disaster was not made until a year after the accident. In 1943, 14 airmen were killed near Whenuapai when a Liberator Bomber crashed. In 1944, two Lockheed Hudson Bombers of the Royal New Zealand Air Force disappeared off the New Zealand coast. Both disasters were kept secret.

In 1942, a Union Airways Electra 10A crashed on Mt Richmond near Nelson after receiving an incorrect radio bearing. Five people died, representing the first fatalities on a New Zealand passenger airliner flight.

In the same year, an Air Travel (NZ) Ltd DH Dragonfly crashed into the sea off the West Coast of the South Island, killing four passengers.

In 1942, a fire swept through Seacliff Mental Hospital, killing 39.

Twenty-one passengers were killed in 1943 when the Cromwell to Dunedin Express was derailed due to excessive speed applied by a drunken engine driver. The latter was sentenced to three years' jail on a charge of manslaughter.

The Ballantyne department store fire in Christchurch in 1947 killed 41 people and incurred damage of $1 million. All 41 victims were staff members.

The 1947 floods in the Wairarapa were regarded as the worst in 50 years.

In 1948, six passengers were killed and 61 injured when the Picton–Christchurch express derailed at Blind River near Seddon.

A tornado struck Hamilton in 1948, killing three and injuring 18.

In 1949, 15 people died when an NAC Lodestar crashed near Waikanae on a flight from Auckland to Dunedin.

On Christmas Eve 1953, 151 people died when the Wellington–Auckland express plunged into the swollen Whangaehu River at Tangiwai.

In 1957, a Safe Air Bristol Freighter crashed on the Russley golf course near Christchurch airport, killing two people.

A Bay of Plenty Airways Aero-Commander crashed on the summit of Mt Ruapehu in 1961, killing all six people on board.

In 1962, a DH Dragonfly aircraft disappeared on a scenic flight over Fiordland. The five on board were presumed dead.

All 23 people on board an NAC DC-3 died in 1963 when the plane crashed in the Kaimai Ranges en route from Auckland to Tauranga. The cause of the crash was attributed to a severe downdraught.

Fifteen people died in a bus crash on the Brynderwyn Hills in 1963.

In 1966, the collier *Kaitawa* sank near Cape Reinga with the loss of all 29 people on board.

The inter-island ferry *Wahine* sank in a freak storm in Wellington Harbour, with the loss of 51 lives.

Cyclone Giselle struck the North Island in 1968.

In 1970, the Kaimai rail tunnel excavation site experienced a cave-in and four workmen were killed.

In 1978, heavy flooding led to the evacuation of 2000 residents on the Taieri Plains in Otago.

The Erebus disaster of 1979 was New Zealand's worst air accident. Of the 257 casualties, 213 were positively identified.

The Greenpeace ship *Rainbow Warrior* was bombed at its Auckland berth in 1985.

The Soviet cruise ship *Mikhail Lermontov* sank in New Zealand waters in 1986.

The 1987 Bay of Plenty earthquake

measured 6.5 on the Richter scale.

Cyclone Bola created great devastation in the North Island in 1988.

A viewing platform collapsed at Cave Creek on the West Coast in 1995, killing 14 young New Zealanders.

Be Careful Out There

Accidents in New Zealand

Road crash casualties and rates

	Persons killed	Persons injured
1991	650	16,767
1992	646	16,121
1993	600	15,108
1994	580	16,600
1995	582	16,870
1996	514	14,796
1997	539	13,375
1998	501	12,412
1999	508	11,999
2000	462	10,962

International comparisons — motor crash death rates, 1999

	Persons killed per 100,000 population	Persons injured	Persons killed per 10,000 vehicles
New Zealand	508	13.3	2.0
Australia	1759	9.3	1.4
United Kingdom	3564	6.0	1.3
United States of America	41,611	15.3	2.0
Japan	10,372	8.2	1.3
Canada	2972	9.7	1.7
Germany	7772	9.5	1.5
Sweden	580	6.6	1.3
France	8487	14.4	2.5

DISASTERS

Drownings

Activity	Year ended 31 December									
	1991	1992	1993	1994	1995	1996	1997	1998	1999	2000
RECREATIONAL										
Boating	15	22	35	14	23	22	18	16	13	24
Surf sports	1	–	1	1	1	–	–	4	3	4
White-water sports	1	4	–	5	2	1	–	–	2	–
Recreational fishing	11	8	12	11	8	1	13	5	9	6
Underwater sports	9	7	7	11	12	7	10	8	4	11
Swimming	18	7	12	17	22	19	18	26	19	11
Other recreational	2	4	4	8	9	7	6	4	4	3
NON-RECREATIONAL										
Immersion accidents	30	30	25	32	23	35	33	39	31	30
Road accidents	22	15	18	16	25	15	12	13	11	10
Other transport	1	–	1	2	–	–	–	4	2	–
Commercial fishing	6	7	10	1	4	18	–	12	3	4
Other commercial	2	–	2	–	5	1	1	1	1	6
Rescuing others	4	5	2	–	1	1	2	3	2	4
Suicides and homicides	24	20	24	13	20	13	25	14	17	19
Miscellaneous	1	1	1	1	4	–	–	1	–	2
TOTAL	**147**	**130**	**154**	**132**	**159**	**140**	**138**	**150**	**121**	**134**

Deaths from external causes 1996–1998

	1996 Number	1997 Number	1998 Number
Motor vehicle crashes	537	550	529
Other transport accidents	68	67	60
Accidental poisoning	26	27	11
Accidental falls	267	242	199
Accidents caused by machinery	14	17	13
Accidents caused by fire and flames	35	33	20
Accidents caused by firearms	6	0	6
Accidental drowning and suffocation	91	118	102
Suicide and self-inflicted injury	540	561	577
Homicide	69	69	57
All other external causes	82	99	98
TOTAL	**1735**	**1783**	**1672**

Incidents attended by fire brigades

Year ended 30 June	2000/01
Fires	
Fires relating to structures	5499
Mobile property fires	2622
Vegetation fires	4325
Chemicals, flammable liquids and gases fires	79
Miscellaneous fires	6698
Total	**19,223**
Fatalities (all fires)	44
Hazardous emergencies	
Flammable liquid, gas incidents	591
Chemical, biohazard, radioactive incidents	93
Mobile properties hazardous incidents	4195
Other	944
Total	**5823**
Special service calls	
Animal rescue	329
Repair roof	224
Other, including assisting ambulance or police	5193
Total	**5746**
Natural disasters	
Earthquake	0
Volcanic eruption	2
Tsunami, tidal waves	5
Flood	621
Wind storm, tornado, cyclone etc	502
Natural disasters — not classified above	6
Total	**1136**
False alarms	
Good intent	6874
Malicious	1796
Defective apparatus/installation	6679
Accidental operation	5968
Other	3391
Total	**24,708**
Other emergencies	
Over-pressure, rupture, explosives, over-heating	349
Rescue, emergency, medical call	1478
Mutual aid, cover moves	21
Total	**1848**
ALL INCIDENT TYPES	**58,484**

Slipping, Stumbling, Skidding, Tripping

Causes of accidents — 1981

Accident	Cases
Aggression (intentional) of:	
Another person	2015
Sheep	164
Cow	149
Dog	146
Horse	142
Other	201
Total	**2817**
Loss of balance by:	
Self	5216
Horse	113
Another person	56
Other	47
Total	**5432**
Collapse, cave-in, or slip of:	
Other persons (including scrum)	110
Stack of objects or goods	94
Other	402
Total	**606**
Dropped (by victim or another):	
Heavy object	352
Log or plank	84
Other	570
Total	**1006**
Explosion, eruption or ignition of:	
Petrol or petrol product	105
Oil, grease	68
Other	381
Total	**554**
Failure or malfunction of:	
Ladder	256
Brakes	179
Tyre	147
Motorcycle or scooter	137
Door, gate, lid, bonnet etc	102
Jack	85
Pedal cycle or tricycle	67
Car	53
Chainsaw	72
Chain	50
Other	1591
Total	**2739**
Failure of material etc:	678
Moving into hazardous position (incl against, over edge of, into path of etc):	
Another person	886
Car	576
Door, gate, lid etc	532
Subsidence	410
Ball	318
Sharp object	308
Log, plank	209
Hole, well	180
Tree, branch	238
Stone, rock	253
Sporting implement (not ball)	126
Fence, railing, wall, etc	202
Heavy object	145
Glass (already broken)	151
Hot liquid	96
Glass door	126
Truck, tanker	86
Motor mower	84
Dog	51
Motorcycle, scooter	70
Cliff, bank, mountain, etc	102
Bed of sea, river, pool, etc	110
Awkward object	207
Trench, ditch	92
Horse	55
Bone	71
Cow	61
Thorn (included in wool)	67
Nail etc (including protruding)	85
Jungle gym, playground equipment	57
Lamp post, pole, road sign etc	81

Table	65
Knife	60
Window, porthole (including pane)	68
Parked vehicle	55
Chair, stool etc	53
Carcass (including frozen)	57
Other	2982
Total	**9375**

Inherent part of activity:
Practical joke, horseplay or startled, by:

Another person	299
Horse	84
Self	51
Other	214
Total	**648**

Loss of control or misoperation
(not by victim) of:

Car	3239
Motorcycle, scooter	278
Truck, tanker	212
Van, utility	105
Sporting implement (not ball)	71
Door, gate, lid, etc	82
Pedal cycle, tricycle	66
Bus, trolleybus	82
Knife	51
Other	875
Total	**5061**

Loss of control or misoperation
by victim of:

Knife	3893
Motorcycle, scooter	2128
Car	801
Pedal cycle, tricycle	663
Heavy object	421
Axe, slasher, cleaver etc	373
Horse	344
Chainsaw	389
Log, plank	271
Hammer, sledgehammer	295
Door, gate, lid etc	238
Spanner, wrench	250
Circular saw (hand-held)	248
Awkward object	171
Sharp object	84
Hose	93
Skis	165
Ladder	131
Handpowered vehicle	70
Motor mower	86
Roller skates	105
Hand saw	72
Tractor	77
Carcass (including frozen)	148
Sheep	51
Skateboard	53
Drill (powered)	63
Sporting implement (not ball)	65
Tree branch	67
Trailer (not caravan)	63
Drum	53
Crowbar, lever	58
Ball	56
Food cutter, slicer, slitter	88
Welding, etc torch	51
Box	52
Pipe (length of)	55
Other	3248
Total	**15,539**

Slipping, stumbling, skidding
or treading on:

Water	1336
Loose metal, gravel	812
Ice, snow	252
Stone, rock	158
Oil	326
Mud	178
Litter (excluding broken glass)	78
Glass (already broken)	63
Log, plank	78
Other	716
Total	**3997**

Natural disaster:	*14*

Overmeasure (acute) of:

Movement	13,405
Other	603
Total	**14,008**

DISASTERS

Overmeasure (prolonged or repetitive) of:

Movement	1777
Other	63
Total	**1840**

Quarrel, fight or struggle: 643

Medical misadventure: 98

Slipping on:

Stairs, steps	1482
Floor	1247
Ground	1046
Path, footpath (paved)	327
Grass, field (not lawn)	285
Rocks, cliff, bank, etc	326
Ladder	192
Undefined surface	175
Log or plank	104
Shower floor	118
Truck, tanker	98
Roof	99
Lawn	70
Verandah, balcony, deck etc	116
Road	74
Bath	72
Deck of ship	83

Kerb	56
Fence, railing, wall etc	58
Mat, rug	57
Playground equipment	54
Other	1670
Total	**7809**

Tripping or stumbling over:

Stairs, steps	1009
Ground	565
Floor	366
Path, footpath (paved)	415
Kerb	209
Mat, rug	187
Subsidence	175
Stone, rock	106
Undefined surface	159
Road	96
Log, plank	80
Grass, field (not lawn)	63
Other	1713
Total	**5143**

Unconsciousness, collapse, or incapacity of:

Self	579
Other	53
Total	**632**

Environmental hazards:

Wind	312
Noise	337
Microbe, virus etc	72
Undertow, wave etc	158
Other	271
Total	**1150**

Involvement of apparel, etc:

Clothing	136
Other	100
Total	**236**

Unwitting aggression of:

Another person	1079
Self	300
Cow	53
Other	156
Total	**1588**

Ill-defined: 9512

Other: 4831

TOTAL ACCIDENTS **103,860**

Did the Earth Move for You?

Earthquake fatalities

Date	Location	Magnitude (Richter scale)	Deaths
1843 (8 July)	Wanganui	7.5	2
1848 (16 Oct)	NE Marlborough	7.1	3
1855 (23 Jan)	SW Wairarapa	8.1	5
1901 (16 Mar)	Cheviot	7.0	1
1914 (7 Oct)	East Cape	7.0–7.5	1
1929 (16 June)	Murchison	7.8	17
1931 (3 Feb)	Hawke's Bay	7.9	256
1934 (5 Mar)	Pahiatua	7.6	1
1968 (24 May)	Inangahua	7.0	3
TOTAL			**289**

PERFORMING ARTS

End of the Golden Wether

Theatre and drama

In 1853, George Buckingham's family — Rosetta, George, Walter and Conrad — debuted with a series of popular musical entertainments at Auckland's Oddfellow's Hall.

In 1890, the great English comedian JL Toole and his company visited New Zealand.

In 1893, the London Gaiety Burlesque Company visited New Zealand and a Dunedin newspaper made suggestive comments about the young ladies of the company. The ladies in turn attacked the editor of the newspaper with horse-whips.

Vaudeville was established in New Zealand by 1899 with touring companies formed by John Fuller and Percy Dix. Top acts that toured New Zealand were comedian Harry Lauder, Paul Cinquevalli — 'the greatest juggler on the face of the earth', strong-man Eugene Sandow, and magician Carter the Great.

In 1904, Mel B Spurr, an English entertainer, toured New Zealand.

In 1920, a touring theatrical company starring Allan Wilkie and Frediswyde Hunter-Watts included a small part played by Ngaio Marsh, who would later gain international fame as a writer of detective stories.

Sybil Thorndike starred in *Captain Brassbound's Conversion*, during a New Zealand tour.

The newly formed New Zealand Players performed *Dandy Dick* in 1953.

In 1959, Bruce Mason gave the first performance of his solo work *The End of the Golden Weather*. This famous New Zealand theatrical work received a send-up of sorts in later years when *The End of the Golden Wether*, based on the demise of a precious and rare sheep, performed in deserted wool sheds in the central North Island.

Downstage Theatre produced *Well Hung* by New Zealand playwright Robert Lord.

Foreskin's Lament, Greg McGee's landmark play, emerged in 1980. No one voiced much opposition to its title, although in recent years *The Vagina Monologues* and *Puppetry of the Penis* have caused deeper rumblings.

In 1983, *Footrot Flats* toured the country before touring Australia in 1985.

In 1984, a planned production of *Songs to Uncle Scrim* by Mervyn Thompson at Wellington's New Depot theatre was cancelled after opposition by feminists.

Glide Time by Roger Hall was the first broadly popular New Zealand play.

Pavlova Comes to New Zealand

Ballet

Anna Pavlova, the Russian ballerina, toured New Zealand in 1926.

The New Zealand Ballet became known as The Royal New Zealand Ballet.

Paul Gnatt, a former dancer with the Royal Danish Ballet, founded the New Zealand Ballet Company in 1953.

In 1967, the wardrobe and equipment store of the New Zealand Ballet and New Zealand Opera was destroyed by fire.

The Limbs Dance Company was formed in 1977.

LITERATURE

A Good Keen Man Alone

John Mulgan, author of the iconic novel *Man Alone*, committed suicide in Cairo in 1945.

Barry Crump wrote *A Good Keen Man* in 1960 and *A Good Keen Girl* in 1970.

Michael O'Donnell, an Irishman living in the New Zealand bush, once wrote an unauthorised autobiography about his life.

Sir George Grey wrote *Polynesian Mythology*, 'an ancient Traditional History of the New Zealand race, as furnished by their Priests and Chiefs'.

Samuel Butler's *First Year in Canterbury Settlement* was compiled and published in London by his father from letters sent home to him. An unflattering review of the book in the *Christchurch Press* was believed to have been the work of Butler himself, who was not in favour of the book's publication.

What is regarded as New Zealand's first novel — *Taranaki* — was a love story written against the background of the New Zealand wars. Its author was Major W Storey and it was published in 1861 by WC Wilson, part owner of the *New Zealander*.

WC Wilson later founded the *New Zealand Herald*.

Poenamo, the memoir of John Logan Campbell, one of Auckland's founding fathers, became a New Zealand classic.

Musings in Maoriland revealed Thomas Bracken as a national poet. His hymn, 'God Defend New Zealand', produced the lyrics for the national anthem.

In 1890, Jessie Weston wrote *Ko Meri*, a novel about upper-class Auckland society and the social difficulties of an educated half-caste girl.

Philosopher Dick, the adventures and contemplations of a New Zealand shepherd, was written by George Chamier.

William Pember Reeves wrote *The Long White Cloud*, a history of New Zealand, which was published in London in 1898.

The first edition of *Who's Who in New Zealand* was founded and edited by GH Scholefield.

Feminism entered New Zealand fiction in the 1890s when Edith Grossman wrote the novel, *The Heart of the Bush*.

Brown Bread From a Colonial Oven was written by BE Baughan.

Eileen Duggan was the first New Zealand-born poet to achieve international recognition.

In 1920, Jane Mander's first novel, *The Story of a New Zealand River*, was published in New York and London.

Katherine Mansfield was born Katherine Mansfield Beauchamp. She was New Zealand's first native-born writer to gain an international reputation, and was briefly married to a singing teacher.

The Garden Party, a collection of short stories, was Katherine Mansfield's best-loved work. In 1923, suffering from failing health, she checked into the Gurdjieff Institute for Harmonious Development of Man, where she died three months later.

In 1926, *The Butcher Shop* by Jean Devanny was banned by the government for 'indecency'. It spoke of passion and murder on a sheep station near Taihape.

Elsdon Best's *The Maori*, published in 1924, was widely accepted as being the most authoritative account of pre-European culture in New Zealand.

Walter D'Arcy Cresswell was in the habit of going from door to door in an effort to sell his poetry.

In 1932, AH and AW Reed became the first New Zealand firm to concentrate on book publishing.

The New Zealand Women Writers Society was founded in 1932 by Nellie E Donovan-Hair and Miss NE Coad.

Frank Sargeson was the first writer to use New Zealand colloquial language.

M Escot wrote only one novel — *Show Down* — which showed touches of maturity.

Denis Glover, co-founder of Caxton Press, wrote *Arawhata Bill*, a work that afforded Glover folk-hero status.

Brown Man's Burden, was written by Roderick Finlayson in 1938.

In 1939, the *New Zealand Listener* began publishing.

David Blackburn Paul, a Hamilton bookseller, set up a publishing house specialising in New Zealand books. Later the firm became Longman Paul Ltd.

Dwarf with a Billiard Cue was written by Kendrick Smithyman in 1978.

Ruth France, primarily a novelist, also wrote poetry under the pseudonym Paul Henderson.

In 1959, the biennial Katherine Mansfield Memorial Award was established by the Women Writers Society and sponsored by the Bank of New Zealand.

Playwright Bruce Mason's best-known play about Maori was *The Pohutakawa Tree*.

Noel Hilliard's *Maori Girl*, published

in 1960, was the first novel highlighting the social impact on Maori when they moved from the country to the cities.

In 1961, Vladimir Nabokov's *Lolita* was deemed to be indecent by the Supreme Court and Appeal Court. In 1964, the newly established Indecent Publications Tribunal overturned these decisions.

Maurice Shadbolt's novel *Among the Cinders* is believed to be the largest seller of all New Zealand novels, with 150,000 copies having been printed.

Ngaio Marsh of Christchurch wrote detective novels that won her a worldwide reputation.

Smith's Dream, a novel by CK Stead, was made into the movie *Sleeping Dogs*.

Janet Frame's first published work was *The Lagoon* (1951). One of her later novels was *Scented Gardens for the Blind*.

JC Beaglehole's *Life of Captain Cook* was published three years after his death. The final segments of the book were assembled by his son, TH Beaglehole. Beaglehole senior had, in 1970, been awarded the Order of Merit, the highest award made to a New Zealand writer.

AH Reed, the founder of the Reed publishing house, received a knighthood for his efforts, at the age of 99. He died soon after.

In 1976, the first New Zealand Book awards were announced.

Gordon McLauchlan published *The Passionless People* in 1976, a landmark sociological study of New Zealanders.

Sam Hunt's poetry became widely known when it was published by Penguin in 1980.

In 1985, Keri Hulme won Britain's prestigious literary award, the Booker Prize, for *the bone people*.

Ronald Hugh Morrieson wrote *Cross My Heart and Cut My Throat*.

Barry Crump was born at Papatoetoe.

Noel Virtue, the New Zealand novelist, worked for several years as a zookeeper.

In the early days, the *Edmonds Cookery Book* was sent free and unsolicited to every engaged New Zealand couple.

It's All Part of My Day

Newspapers and magazines

The *New Zealand Listener*, at its peak, was selling 340,000 copies a week.

In 1861, the *Otago Daily Times* was established as New Zealand's first daily newspaper.

The *Waikato Times* was first published as a tri-weekly in Ngaruawahia, in 1872. It moved to Hamilton in 1875 and became a daily newspaper in 1900.

The *Whangarei Comet* was an early Northland paper, but it didn't survive.

The *New Zealand Referee* was started in Christchurch by Phineas Selig and AE Bird.

New Zealand Truth was first published in 1905.

Point Blank was the initial name of *Straight Furrow*, the official publication of the New Zealand Farmers Union, and later the New Zealand Federated Farmers.

The *New Zealand Woman's Weekly* is New Zealand's most successful periodical for women.

The emergence of the *New Zealand Listener* led to the failure of the privately owned *Radio Record*, which had had exclusive access to radio programmes since the early 1930s.

Cue magazine, designed to compete with the *New Zealand Listener*, ceased operations after 17 issues.

The *New Zealand Journal of Agriculture* was initially a free publication.

The *New Zealand Free Lance* began as an offshoot of Auckland's *Observer* and *Free Lance*.

The *Auckland Weekly News* was modernised in the mid 1960s, but as the *Weekly News* it was unable to survive.

A national magazine called *The New Zealand Girl* began publishing in 1936.

New Zealand has 25 daily newspapers, a high number in relation to its population.

The *New Zealand Herald*, with an average daily circulation of approximately 500,000 in 2003, is far and away the leading daily newspaper. The biggest provincial paper is the *Waikato Times*, with a daily circulation of over 40,000 copies.

More than 1.6 million New Zealanders over the age of 15 read a newspaper on a daily basis.

New Zealand has approximately 120 community newspapers.

The *Evening News*, the Dannevirke daily newspaper, had a circulation of 2273 as at December 2001, the second smallest figure of New Zealand's daily papers. The smallest circulation was that of the *Westport News* (2167).

New Zealand *Woman's Day*, the magazine, had a weekly circulation figure of close to 150,000 copies in 2001.

In 1993, the *New Korea Herald* became the first Korean language paper to be published in New Zealand.

The *Chinese Express*, a family newspaper, was first published in New Zealand in 1992. Other Chinese newspapers published in New Zealand are the *Mandarin Times*, *Chinese Herald*, *Asian Times*, *New Times*, *Epoch Times*, *Capital Chinese News* and *Homeland Voice*.

Landfall, the New Zealand literary magazine, was launched in 1947.

COMEDY

Do Your Gumboots Lose Their Flavour (in the Woolshed Overnight)?

By the turn of the twentieth century at least four musical comedies written by New Zealanders had been produced. They were *Tapu*, *The Belle of Cuba*, *The Gay Hussar* and *Prime Bulbo*.

Fred Mills was one of New Zealand's earliest humorists.

Following World War I, the Diggars, led by Pat Hanna and Stan Lawson, toured extensively.

Playwright Roger Hall was born in Britain six months before Hitler invaded Poland.

New Zealand's first sketch-comedy TV show was 'In view of the circumstances'.

Roger Hall used to do a very good Keith Holyoake impersonation.

John Clarke, aka Fred Dagg, came from Manawatu. A documentary on the Dagg family, written by John Clarke and John Banas, appeared on TV's 'Country Calendar'.

Knickers, Knackers and Knockers, a New Zealand satirical show, ran for 18 months at the Downstage Theatre.

New Zealand's first TV sitcom was 'Buck House'.

Commercial radio performances by Fred Dagg began on Lindsay Yeo's 2ZB show.

The LP *Fred Dagg's Greatest Hits* was released in 1975. It sold 80,000 copies in three weeks.

In the same year, John Clarke produced his first book, *Fred Dagg's Year*. It cost $1.95 and had advance orders for 30,000 copies.

'The Gumboot Song', a single recording by Fred Dagg, made it to number six on the New Zealand charts and remained on the list for almost four months.

Fred Dagg undertook a national tour in 1976.

Arthur Baysting invented the comic persona Neville Purvis.

'A Week of It' first appeared in 1977.

David McPhail was born in Christchurch in 1945, the day before Germany surrendered.

AK Grant was born in Wanganui.

Annie Whittle was a very good fencer, winning the Sydney Rose Bowl for most promising newcomer at the national championship. She also lived in Germany for four years where she sang with 'Gran's Chicago Foot Warmers'.

David McPhail and Jon Gadsby were approached by Channel 7 in Australia regarding a possible series across the ditch. However, spending cuts kiboshed the scheme.

The TV sitcom 'Letter to Blanchy' was written by David McPhail, Jon Gadsby and AK Grant.

Diamond Lil was the alter-ego of Marcus Craig.

Guy Cater is a New Zealand magician-comedian-hypnotist.

Colin Parris was the voice of Rob Muldoon on Radio Hauraki's 'Robman and Brian' series. He was all set for time on TV when he, apparently, said the word 'shit' live, although he claims he said 'ship'.

Earlier Arthur Baysting, as Neville Purvis, was credited with being the first person to say 'fuck' on TV.

Colin Parris released a record in 1979 called *The Rise And Fall Of A Young Christmas Turkey*, a parody of Prime Minister Muldoon singing Christmas carols. Later, in 1987, he developed a character called Buddy Oath for the inaugural Rugby World Cup and another recording was made.

Mika is a cabaret artist who used to be known as Neil Gudsell. One of his most popular embodiments was a character called 'Ricky the skateboarder' whose catch-cry was 'Oosh-ba-doosh'.

Debbie Dorday was an accomplished New Zealand dancer and comedian.

'Lynn of Tawa' (Ginette McDonald), was first presented in 1968, pre-dating Fred Dagg.

Michael McDonald, brother of Ginette McDonald, wrote the 'Lynn of Tawa' scripts. He also wrote and directed 1991's 'Visual Symphonies', a 10-part tour by Lynn of Tawa through parts of New Zealand and Australia.

Lynn of Tawa was named Miss Tawa Aluminium Extrusions for 10 successive years.

Billy T James, who spent his early life in Cambridge, was often very shy offstage. He played Dexter Fitzgibbons in the TV show 'Radio Times'.

Laurie Dee, the singer-entertainer, was also known as Michael Laurence Herdman.

Billy T James claimed that the keys to speaking Japanese were feeling cold, and having constipation and amnesia.

In the film *Came a Hot Friday*, Billy T James played the role of the Tainuia Kid.

On the 'Billy T James Show', Billy T James once produced a microwave oven made out of an old TV set. One viewer wrote in inquiring how to make such a device.

Billy T James received an MBE. He died in 1991 at the age of 45, despite heart by-pass surgery and a heart transplant.

The Topp Twins are well known for their Camp Leader and Camp Mother skits.

The Topp Twins' theatre show *Topp Secret* ran for six weeks in London.

In 1996, the Topp Twins appeared in their own TV series, 'The Topp Twins — Do Not Adjust your Twinset'.

Ken and Ken were characters developed by the Topp Twins.

When the Topp Twins toured New Zealand in 1989 they moved from town to town by tractor, which towed a caravan.

The Front Lawn was a comedy duo made up of Don McGlashan and Harry Sinclair. *Reason for Breakfast* was one of their better-known reviews.

The Lounge Bar was a short film made by The Front Lawn that revolved around a bar, a man wearing a headbrace, a woman, a singer and a bartender.

Jennifer Ward-Lealand joined The Front Lawn in 1988.

Songs from the Front Lawn and *More Songs from the Front Lawn* were albums recorded by The Front Lawn.

Harry Sinclair wrote and directed TV's four-minute comedy-dramas, *Topless Women Talk About Their Lives*.

Funny Business, a retinue of Auckland comedians, performed at the Windsor Castle pub in Parnell for two years, after setting up in November 1984.

'Funny Business' became a TV series in 1986.

Comedian Peter Rowley had tuna bombs thrown at him in Motueka while operating as support act for rock group the Narcs.

Two Auckland pubs — Abby's and Kitty O'Brien's were popular venues for comedy in Auckland.

Mr Fungus was a Wellington comedian.

The Shenanigan Brothers were Christchurch comedians.

Leonard Deogood was a Charlie Chaplin impersonator who starred in several short New Zealand comedy films in the 1920s.

Roger Hall's *Middle Age Spread* was made into a movie in 1979.

The film *Goodbye Pork Pie* (1981), a New Zealand comedy, was still being shown on a television channel in India up until a few years ago.

Billy T James' persona as the Tainuia Kid in *Came a Hot Friday* has been described as being a cross between a 'mischievous Taniwha-worshipping Maori and a Mexican patriot'.

In the movie *Footroot Flats — A Dog's Tale* the vocal cast was Peter Rowley as Dog, John Clarke as Wal, Peter Hayden as Cooch, Irish Murphy as Cheeky Hobson, Fiona Samuel as Pongo, Rawiri Paratene as Rangi, Brian Sergent as Spit Murphy, Marshall Napier as Hunk Murphy, Dorothy McKegg as Aunt Dolly and Billy T James as Pawai.

Old Scores, a light-hearted movie involving a rugby rematch between the All Blacks and Wales, starred Tony Barry, John Bach, Martyn Sanderson, Windsor Davies and former All Blacks Grizz Wyllie, Waka Nathan, Grahame Thorne, Steve McDowell and Ian Kirkpatrick.

John Gadsby wrote the script for the TV series 'Rabbiters Rest'.

Glide Time, Roger Hall's play, was staged as *Flexi-time* in Australia.

Theatresports, which arrived in New Zealand in 1987, has become more popular than the stand-up comic movement.

'Skitz' the TV comedy series ran for three years.

Ted Kavanagh, a New Zealander living in England, wrote every episode of Tommy Handley's famous 1940s show, *It's That Man Again*.

The 'Robman and Brian' satirical radio series was written by Matt Elliott and Ian Watkin.

Gary McCormick formed his own political party called The Pull Yourself Together Party.

FILMS

Goodbye Pork Piecart

One of New Zealand's earliest feature films was *The Test*, based on William Satchell's *The Ballad of Stuttering Jim*. It was not rugby-related.

In 1896, during a performance of *Godfrey's Vaudeville Co* at the Auckland Opera House, 'Professors' Hausmann and Gow presented a programme of films projected by Edison's Kinematograph. This represented the first public screening of movies in New Zealand.

Film-making in New Zealand began when the official opening of the Auckland Exhibition in 1898 was filmed by AH Whitehouse.

By 1900, AH Whitehouse had made 10 films, each with a running time of less than a minute.

In 1901, the New Zealand Government commissioned the Salvation Army to film the visit of the Duke and Duchess of Cornwall and York.

In 1908, the Royal Pictures Syndicate established New Zealand's first permanent movie show at His Majesty's Theatre, Wellington.

Rudall Hayward made his first feature film, *My Lady of the Cave*, when he was 21 years of age.

Gaston Méliés, a Frenchman, visited New Zealand in 1912 to film shorts of Rotorua and other scenic attractions.

The first issue of *New Zealand Animated News*, a weekly newsreel, occurred in 1913.

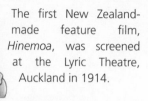

The first New Zealand-made feature film, *Hinemoa*, was screened at the Lyric Theatre, Auckland in 1914.

William Joliffe was New Zealand's first Censor of Cinematograph Films.

Rawdon Blandford took a leading role in *The Test*, filmed in 1916.

In the late 1920s, Rudall Hayward travelled around New Zealand making 'community comedies', like *A Daughter of Dunedin* and *A Daughter of Te Kuiti*.

Rudall Hayward made a two-reel comedy in 1921: *The Bloke from Freeman's Bay*. His uncle considered the film to be so bad he offered Rudall £150 to burn it.

The Romance of Sleepy Hollow had its first screening in Auckland. Amateur actors from Auckland made up the cast.

The Birth of New Zealand, directed by Harrington Reynolds, had its first screening in Palmerston North in 1922.

Rudall Hayward's *Rewi's Last Stand* was first made as a silent movie in 1925. It was later remade with a soundtrack.

In 1925, the Government Publicity Office's first feature-length film, *Glorious New Zealand*, was released.

The Te Kooti Trail was produced by Rudall Hayward for Whakatane Flims Ltd.

Rudall Hayward's first 'community comedy', *Military Defaulters and Others*, was screened at Hamilton. Its original title, 'Hamilton's Hectic Husbands', was rejected by the film censor.

Producer Lee Hill also indulged in 'community comedies', coming up with *Susie of Stratford*, which was screened, fittingly, at Stratford.

Hill and Hayward experienced a clash of venues when they arrived in Nelson at the same time to produce 'community comedies'. *Nellie of Nelson* and *Natalie of Nelson* were the respective results.

The first New Zealander to produce a 'talkie' was Edwin Coubray, with a horse-racing drama called *Carbine's Heritage* in 1927.

The Bush Cinderella, by Rudall Hayward, was first screened in 1928.

In 1929, the Paramount Theatre in Wellington became the first New Zealand theatre to change to 'talkies'.

Alexander Markey's Maori movie *Hei Tiki* was screened in New York.

One Hundred Crowded Years, was the name given to the New Zealand Centennial film, produced by the Government Film Studios in 1940.

The National Film Unit was established in 1941. Its first release was *Country Lads*.

The National Film Unit eventually became part of the Information Section within the Prime Minister's Department.

The movie *The Seekers*, filmed partly in New Zealand, had its international premiere in Wellington. It starred British actor Jack Hawkins and Laya Raki.

The film *Broken Barrier* caused controversy when it was released in 1952 because of its depiction of a romance between a Pakeha journalist and a Maori woman.

John O'Shea produced *Runaway* and *Don't Let It Get You* in the 1960s.

Goodbye Pork Pie grossed over $1.2 million during local screenings.

Hinge Film Productions were responsible for *Test Pictures*, first screened at the 1975 Wellington Film Festival.

The year 1975 saw the release of Geoff Murphy's *Wild Man* and Roger Donaldson's *Sleeping Dogs*.

In 1980, the New Zealand movie *Nutcase* was released.

Strange Behaviour, filmed on location in New Zealand, was released in the USA in 1981. It was later released in New Zealand with the title *Dead Kids*.

Bruno Lawrence won the Best Actor Award at the Manila International Film Festival for his role in *Smash Palace*.

In 1983, La Cinémathèque Française presented 'Panorama du cinema de Nouvelle-Zelande', a retrospective season of New Zealand films.

Vincent Ward, the Kiwi director, received international acclaim for *Vigil* in 1984.

Death Warmed Up was released in 1984.

Jane Campion was best known for *The Piano*, although she had earlier, in 1990, become internationally known for *An Angel at My Table,* which was based on Janet Frame's autobiography.

The highly successful *Once Were Warriors* was based on the novel by Alan Duff.

Peter Jackson won a major prize at the 1994 Venice Film Festival for *Heavenly Creatures*.

The Lord of the Rings trilogy of films is made up of 'The Fellowship of the Ring', (2001), 'The Two Towers' (2002) and 'The Return of the King' (2003).

Special effects for *The Lord of the Rings* films comprised 10,000 prosthetic faces and 1800 pairs of hobbit feet.

A total of 23,000 New Zealanders worked on the production of the *Lord of the Rings* film trilogy.

The Lord of the Rings: 'The Return of the King' was only the second film to break the US one-billion-dollar box-office mark. At the 2004 Academy Awards it won all 11 awards for which it was nominated.

Wild Man and The Lunatic's Ball

Distinctive New Zealand film titles

My Lady of the Cave (1922). Rudall Hayward.
Venus of the South Seas (1924). James Sullivan.
The Bush Cinderella (1928). Rudall Hayward.
Rangi's Catch (1973). Michael Forlong (UK).
God Boy (1976). Murray Reece (Telemovie).
Wild Man (1977). Geoff Murphy.
Squeeze (1980). Richard Turner.

Smash Palace (1982). Roger Donaldson.
The Scarecrow (1982). Sam Pillsbury.
Battletruck (1982). Harley Cokliss.
Death Warmed Up (1984). David Blyth.
Pallet on the floor (1984). Lynton Butler.
Hot Targets (1984). Dennis Lewiston.
Mr Wrong (1985). Gaylene Preston.
Bridge to Nowhere (1986). Ian Mune.
Dangerous Orphans (1987). John Laing.
Starlight Hotel (1987). Sam Pillsbury.
Mark II (1987). John Anderson.
Bad Taste (1988). Peter Jackson.
Chill Factor (1988). David McKenzie.
Send a Gorilla (1989). Melanie Read.
Zilch (1989) Richard Riddiford.
Flying Fox in a Freedom Tree (1989). Martyn Sanderson.
Meet the Feebles (1989). Peter Jackson.
Shrimp on the Barbie (1989). Michael Gottlieb.
An Angel at My Table (1990). Jane Campion
Crush (1992). Alison MacLean.
The Footstep Man (1992). Leon Narbey.
Braindead (1992). Peter Jackson.
Cops and Robbers (1993). Murray Reece.
Jack be Nimble (1993). Garth Maxwell.

Heavenly Creatures (1993). Peter Jackson.
The Last Tattoo (1944). John Reid.
Chicken (1995). Grant Lahood.
Broken English (1995). Gregor Nicholas.
The Frighteners (1996). Peter Jackson.
Abberation (1996). Mark Beesley
The Ugly (1996). Scott Reynolds.
The Lunatic's Ball (1998). Mark Beesley.
Savage Honeymoon (1998). Mark Beesley.
Hopeless (1998). Stephen Hickey.
Punitive Damage (1998). Annie Goldson.
Scarfies (1998). Robert Sarkies.
The Irrefutable Truth about Demons (1999). Glenn Standing.
Uncomfortable Comfortable (1999). Grant Campbell.
Shifter (2000). Campbell Walker.
Stickmen (2000). Hamish Rothwell.
Snakeskin (2000). Gillian Ashurst.
Tongan Ninja (2001). Jason Stutter.
The Maori Merchant of Venice (2001). Don Selwyn.

Sleeping Hot Dogs and the Buns of Navarone

Tongue-in-cheek film titles with a food theme

The Remains of the Date
Howards Endive
The King Prawn and I
Lord of the Ling
Asparaguspeare in Love
Souperman
Kung Food Fighting
Monty Piethon and the Lolly Grail
Grease

Guess Who's Coming to Dinner
The Fabulous Baker Boys
The Ten Condiments
The Last Supper
Braise Moi
Silence of the Lambs
The Man who Falafel to Earth
Bananas

Wallace and Vomit
Teddybears Picnic
The Colour of Honey
Catfish in Blackbean Sauce
Icecream
Smiling Fish and Goat on Fire
Diet Hard
The Big Cheese
Bean There

FILMS

Breadnobs and Broomsticks
Yellow Submarine Sandwich
Braising Arizona
Ace Tempura
State and Maincourse
Bar-b-cue ella
Blazing Saddles of Lamb
The Buns of Navarone
Sleeping Hotdogs
Canned By Me
The Pink Pantry
A Liver Runs Through it
Dead Calamari
Fried Green Tomatoes
The Sound of Muesli
Porky
101 Dahlmations
The Platterhorn
Goodbye Pork Pie
Magnum Force
MASH
Who Framed Roger Rabbit

Mr Bean
Nil by Mouth
Lord of the Fries
Honey, I Shrunk the Kids
Kelp!
The Maltesers Falcon
A Clockwork Orange
He Died with a Felafel in
   his Hand
Mushroom at the Top
Dessert Rat
Picnic at Hanging Rock
A Parfait Storm
Midnight Espresso
The Count of Monte Crispo
Chicken Run
Lentil
The Oat (Das Oat)
The Gladyouate
Vege Tales
Pheasantville
Never Say Fry

The Burps
I Sage
Mixed Nuts
Night of the Lettuce
Fish Finger
Life of Brain
Oliver Twisties
Gumbo
Much Ado about Nutting
The African Bean
Interview with the Ham Pie
First Wives Club Sandwich
Gone with the Wind
The Banger Sisters
Wayne's Newworld
Calender Grills
Frankenfurter
Goodbye Mr Chips
Tummy
Thelma and Louisecake
Rockyroad 11
Beetlejuice

Bug Houses, Flea Pits and Jaffa Alleys

New Zealand cinemas — then and now

Academy
Berkeley
Bridgeway
Brights
Cameo
Century
Cinerama
Civic
Coronation
Cosmos
Cosy
De Luxe
Embassy
Empire
Empress
Everybody's

Grand
His Majesty's
King George
Kings
Lido
Lyric
Majestic
Maoriland
Mercury
Mermaid
Movieland
Northside
Odeon
Palace
Paramount
Pavilion

People's
Plaza
Princess
Railway
Regent
Renown
Rialto
Roxy
Royal
Seaside
St James
Star
State
Tivoli
Victoria
Village 7

RADIO & TELEVISION

From a Shed in Newtown to 'Country Calendar'

'Chuckles with Jerry', a ventriloquist show, featured on New Zealand radio in the 1930s.

The short film *The woman at the store*, which was adapted from a Katherine Mansfield short story, was produced by Aardvark Films for screening on New Zealand television.

In 1975, TV 2, on its opening night, held New Zealand's first Telethon. Nearly $600,000 was raised for the St John's Ambulance Association. Subsequent Telethons were staged to raise funds for the Child Health Foundation, the Mental Health Foundation, the Arthritis and Rheumatism Foundation, the International Year of the Child, the International Year of Disabled Persons and the New Zealand Family Trust.

In 1975, a colour television licence cost $45, a black and white, $27.50.

New Zealand's first locally written television play, *All Earth to Love*, was written by Al Flett.

Professor Robert Jack of Otago University broadcast the first radio programme in New Zealand from his laboratory in 1921.

Clive Drummond was New Zealand's first radio personality.

In 1922, A McLay, R Apperly and A Simpson started radio broadcasts from a shed in Newtown, Wellington.

Culford Bell of 1YA, Auckland and Arch Curry of 3YA, Christchurch were two noted announcers of the early days of New Zealand radio.

Technically the first 'talkback' radio programme hit the airwaves as early as 1927 when announcer J Prentice of 1YA invited listeners to ring in and discuss international affairs.

In 1928, New Zealand listeners could hear the sustained single-note signal from the trans-Tasman flight of Hood and Moncrieff. Thousands of people gathered to welcome the pilots at Trentham but their plane apparently failed to make a landfall and sadly disappeared without trace.

New Zealand radio listeners were able to listen to the commentary direct from New York in 1928, when world champion heavyweight boxer Gene Tunney thwarted the New Zealand challenge from Tom Heeney.

'Dad and Dave from Snake Gully' was very popular with New Zealand radio listeners in the 1930s.

In 1935, an infamous incident occurred when a broadcast by Reverend LG Scrimgeour from 1ZB was jammed to prevent what the government feared would incite comment and jeopardise their chances in the upcoming election.

On 29 May 1926, the first rugby match was relayed via an outside broadcast (OB) by Alan Allardyce of 3YA, Christchurch.

In the same year, Allardyce presented coverage of the Canterbury Jockey Club's three-day race meeting, another first for New Zealand radio — and possibly the world. However, to satisfy the racing club's requirements, the commentator had to station himself on top of a haystack outside the actual course.

The introduction of a commercial radio network in New Zealand led to an increase in recorded serials. 'One Man's Family' was a local production that appeared in 1936. Others were overseas productions: 'Big Sister', 'Officer Crosby', 'Dr Mac', 'Dr Paul', 'The Lone Ranger', 'Fred and Maggie Everybody', 'Portia Faces Life' and 'Life with Dexter'. Many of them came from Australia.

'A Bicycle Built for Two' was the theme song for 'Aunt Daisy' Basham's weekday radio show.

'Rhythm on Record', a radio showcase for blues, jazz and swing music, ran for 40 years.

Lou Paul, Kingi Tahiwi, Te Ari Pitama and Airini Grennell were popular Maori radio announcers of the late 1930s.

In 1939, Station 5ZB operated using a converted railway carriage.

At the beginning of World War II a specially equipped mobile recording studio accompanied the New Zealand Army in the Middle East.

Dr HB Turbott, the radio doctor, started out with a brief to cover six weeks. His series of health talks ended in fact 40

years later when Dr Turbott retired.

In 1946, the National Broadcasting Service was renamed the New Zealand Broadcasting Service.

Auckland radio announcer Phil Shone caused panic when he announced on April Fool's Day that a huge swarm of wasps was approaching Auckland.

Selwyn Toogood and Jack Maybury, both quizmasters, dominated the New Zealand airwaves in the 1950s and 1960s. Toogood began with 'Posers, Penalties and Profits', but hit pay dirt with 'It's In the Bag'. Maybury started out with 'The Quiz Kids' and 'Money-go-Round', but was best remembered for 'The 64 Hundred Show'.

'The Lever Hit Parade', compered by Selwyn Toogood, was immensely popular.

DJ Neville Chamberlain was known as 'Cham the man'.

In 1952, Station ZL3XT at Canterbury University College transmitted New Zealand's first television signal.

In 1953, during the radio coverage of Queen Elizabeth's coronation ceremony, breaking news presented the heady news of Edmund Hillary's conquest of Everest.

A television licence fee of four pounds a year was introduced in 1960.

The first television drama produced by the NZBS was 'The Stranger', which, if nothing else, reflected New Zealand's 'Man Alone' ethos.

When Bruce Mason's play *The Evening Paper* was adapted for television, as New Zealand's first full-length dramatic production, it caused muttering in complacent, conservative suburbia because of its irreverent tone.

Television transmission hours were reduced in 1973–74 and in 1977.

In 1968, radio and television licences were combined, to the tune of $16 per annum.

The television coverage of the sinking of the *Wahine* won a World News Film award.

The power of television and sharp presenters was displayed when Brian Edwards, on the current affairs programme 'Gallery', was able to persuade the two warring factions in a Post Office dispute to come to a settlement.

In 1971, the radio licence fee was abolished, although the television licence fee was set at $20.

'Currant Affairs', a prospective light-hearted TV programme about 'berry fruit and other fruit' did not gain acceptance by the powers-that-were.

'Amazing Grapes', a similar attempt at sending up viticulture, failed to appeal to television producers.

'Green Gin Sunset', produced by Chris Thomson, was the first winner in the Best Arts section of the first Feltex Television Awards.

In 1971, 'Pukemanu', a TV series based on a North Island timber-milling town, hit the small screen. Most of its denouements developed in the Wairarapa town of Martinborough.

In 1973, colour television became a reality in New Zealand.

By 1977, the New Zealand drama series, 'Close To Home' attracted one million viewers every night. By the time it concluded its life cycle, 818 episodes had been made.

Joe Cote's documentary on the emerging independence of New Guinea won a Feltex Award.

'Country Calendar', the quintessential rural New Zealand documentary, was so popular that it won Feltex Awards in 1977, 1980, 1981, 1982 and 1983.

Jamie Higgins starred in the TV adaptation of Ian Cross's book *The God Boy*.

The television drama series 'The Governor' had a production budget of $1 million, a fact that displeased many New Zealanders.

In 1978, the satirical weekly 'A Week of It' first hit the TV sets of the nation. As a consequence, David McPhail received his first Feltex Award — for Light Entertainment, although the programme touched on some heavy topics.

'Gliding On' was declared Best Television Drama at the Feltex Awards in 1983.

Angela D'Audney was the first New Zealand woman to read the news on national TV.

More Than a Week of It

The top 20 New Zealand-made TV shows

Mortimer's Patch	The New Zealand Wars	Tangata Whenua
The Governor	Holmes	Gallipoli
Wild South	Pioneer Women	Close Up
Pukemanu	Letter to Blanchy	Hunter's Gold
The God Boy	Radio Times	Shark in the Park
A Week of It	Fair Go	Telethon '75
Country Calendar	Islands in the Gulf	

Rugby, Boxing and Netball

New Zealand's most popular TV programmes for year ending 30 September 2001

Rank	Programme	Channel	Percentage of potential audience
1	Tua v Lewis boxing	TV3	40
2	Tua v Lewis boxing build-up	TV3	26
3	60 Minutes Special	TV 1	24
4	Olympic Games closing	TV 1	24
5	Olympic Games weekend coverage	TV1	24
6	Fair Go Advertising Awards	TV1	22
7	Fight for Life boxing	TV3	21
8	NZ v England netball (2nd test)	TV1	21
9	Olympic Games review	TV1	21
10	NZ v England netball (1st test)	TV1	20
11	NZ v England netball preview (1st test)	TV1	20
12	Fair Go	TV1	20
13	Pioneer House	TV1	20
14	One News	TV1	20
15	Holmes: Attack on America	TV1	20
16	Coro Nation	TV1	19
17	Eye of the Storm	TV1	19
18	NZ v Australia rugby (1st test)	TV3	19
19	Coca-Cola Cup netball final	TV1	19
20	Changing Rooms: Revisit	TV1	18

MUSIC

Split Enz of the Earth

Rock and pop

Cathy and the Cucumbers, a New Zealand group, recorded a version of 'Day Trip To Bangor'.

Nash Chase sang 'Today I Killed A Man I Didn't Know'.

Hugh and the New Zealanders released 'What's Wrong with Huntly' in 1995.

'I Can't Sing Very Well', written by Steve Young, won the Australasian Performing Right Association (APRA) Silver Scroll for best New Zealand song of 1981/82.

In 1964, the year the Beatles toured New Zealand, Ray Columbus and the Invaders from Christchurch became the first Kiwi artists to hit the top both within and outside New Zealand.

Their recording of an obscure British song 'She's A Mod' topped the charts in Australia and New Zealand and is credited with kicking off the mod craze in both countries.

'Po Ata Rau', originally a Maori song, became a million-selling hit single for Bing Crosby as 'Now Is The Hour'.

Johnny Devlin's backing band was called the Devils.

One of Devlin's earlier hits was 'I Got A Rocket In My Pocket'.

'Blue Smoke', a landmark song in New Zealand popular music, was published in 1947.

In the same year, Dinah Lee, another product of Christchurch, became the first female artist to top the Australian charts with 'Don't You Know Yockomo?'.

Bogdan Kominowski was the real name of Mr Lee Grant, who had several hits in the 1960s.

Hogsnort Rupert won the 1970 Loxene Golden Disc Award with the song, 'Pretty Girl'.

Split Enz' record label for much of their career was Mushroom Records.

In 1981, Coup d'Etat won the single of the year title with, 'Doctor I Like Your Medicine'.

Cool Bananas by DD Smash was best album in 1982. The following year — 1983 — their album Deep In The Heart Of Taxes again won the title.

Expatriate New Zealand songwriter Reece Kirk had a number one country single in the USA with Crystal Gayle's version of 'Our Love Is On The Fault Line'.

In January 1985, Maori entertainer Prince Tui Teka died.

The Four Fours were a Tauranga rock'n'roll band.

In 1978, New Zealand singer Suzanne Lynch recorded a song — 'You Really Got A Hold On Me' — on Ringo Starr's Ring-O Records.

The band, The Rumours, who came from Huntly, recorded 'Holy Morning' backed by the Ladies of the St Mary's Cathedral Choir.

Throb and Pussyfoot were New Zealand bands from Dunedin.

Human Instinct were the most successful New Zealand group to visit Britain in the 1960s. At a time when the hippy movement was in full swing they wrote a song called 'Visions of Flowers'. It was never released.

Alistair Taylor formed Red Rat Records in the early 1970s.

Gutbucket, Killing Floor, Mad Dog Choir and Dog Breath were New Zealand bands.

New Zealand's first real stadium rock concert featured Elton John at Western Springs in 1971.

The Great Ngaruawahia Music Festival occurred in 1973. It was New Zealand's first three-day rock festival. Eighteen thousand fans attended, but there weren't enough toilets. Corben Simpson performed nude.

Gayle Garnett, who was born in New Zealand and moved to the US when she was nine, had a US Top 10 hit in 1964 with 'We'll Sing in the Sunshine'.

Chris Thompson, a Kiwi from Hamilton, became lead singer for Manfred Mann's Earth Band, who scored an international hit with 'Blinded by the Light'.

Alannah Currie of the Thompson Twins was the first New Zealander to score consecutive US Top 10 hits.

OMC (Otara Millionaires Club) hit the UK charts with 'How Bizarre' in 1996.

Reports have it that the first copy of the Beatles' landmark single 'Hey Jude' — the first on their own Apple label — was dropped into the sea near the Tiri, flagship of Radio Hauraki — and after being recovered, was played to a beguiled nation.

There was a one-day rock festival at the Gore racetrack in the early 1970s.

Tex Morton, the famous New Zealand country-and-western singer, added hypnotism to his shows.

Bodies of Work and Festive Overtures

Kiwi classical music

Kiri Te Kanawa won both the New Zealand Mobil Song Quest and the Melbourne Sun Aria in 1965.

In 1881, Pollards Lilliputian Opera Company began its first New Zealand tour in Invercargill.

Inia Te Wiata was the first Maori opera singer to gain an international reputation.

'Soundweb', a musical piece for trombone and electronic sounds, was composed by John Rimmer.

The New Zealand Symphony Orchestra was originally called the National Orchestra.

David Farquhar is one of New Zealand's most prolific composers. Included in his body of work are 'And one makes ten' and 'A unicorn for Christmas'.

'Nastasya', Edwin Carr's opera, featured a libretto by Edward Hill. The latter was based on Dostoyevsky's novel *The Idiot*.

'Earth and Sky', written by Jenny McLeod, was a music-dance drama based on the Maori legend of the creation.

Michael Houston, the Kiwi concert pianist, is regarded as one of the best in the world.

Douglas Lilburn was made Professor of Music and Director of Electronic Music Studies at Victoria University, Wellington, in 1970.

Amongst his body of work, Jack Body composed 'Turtle Time' for chamber ensemble and speakers.

Carl Fornes, a baritone, toured with the NSW State Orchestra to New Zealand in 1920.

Donald McIntyre, the New Zealand bass-baritone, made his Covent Garden debut in 1967 as Barak in *Die Frau Ohne Schatten*.

Henry Braithwaite, a New Zealander, conducted the Welsh National Orchestra.

New Zealand's first chamber music society was established in Wellington in 1945.

In 1960, Kiwi Records released an album featuring Douglas Lilburn's 'Sings Harry' and 'Landfall in Unknown Seas', the first New Zealand music, other than popular songs, to be recorded by a New Zealand recording company.

New Zealand's first pipe band was the Caledonian Pipe Band of Southland.

In 1856, the Auckland Choral society was formed.

New Zealand's first volunteer brass band was the band of the Taranaki Volunteer Rifles.

In 1893, the Nelson School of Music was founded by Michael Balling.

Alfred Hill composed the cantata *Hinemoa*, based on the Maori legend. He also composed the 'Maori' opera *Tapu*.

Dame Clara Butt made her first concert tour to New Zealand in 1908.

Pre-European Maori musical instruments included flutes (koauau, nguru and putorino), signalling instruments (the wooden war gong — pahu), the conch trumpet (putatara), the long wooden war trumpet (pukaea), flax trumpet (tetere), the bullroarer (purohohu) and the humming disc (kororohu).

Yehudi Menuhin, the famous violinist, was only 17 years of age when he toured New Zealand in 1935.

Douglas Lilburn composed 'Nine short pieces for piano' and 'Three Inscapes', amongst many others.

The New Zealand Opera Company was founded by Donald Munro.

What was advertised as the first New Zealand-produced LP record featured the National Orchestra playing *Festive Overtures*.

In 1964, 'Five Epigrams' for 12 solo strings was composed by Ronald Tremain.

Acclaimed Wagnerian tenor, Chris Doig, spent time in the 1980s as the Director of the New Zealand International Festival in Wellington. He also temporarily gave up singing from 1995–2001 to act as Director of the New Zealand Cricket Council.

New Zealand composer of Greek heritage, John Psathas, was chosen from more than 600 international composers to write and arrange 13 pieces of music for the 2004 Athens Olympics, including the official fanfares and ceremonial music during the opening and closing ceremonies.

Of Boy and Girl Sopranos

A brief history of recording and early music

The oldest published song to be found in New Zealand libraries is 'The Whalers of the Deep Blue Sea' which was composed by Te Heu Heu in 1857.

Charles Begg opened New Zealand's first music store in Dunedin in 1861.

In 1880, the Dresden Piano Company was established in New Zealand. Eventually the Company had agencies in 50 New Zealand towns.

EW Secker, a Palmerston North rugby player and accountant, wrote one of New Zealand's most notable songs — 'On the Ball' in 1887.

Shops called 'Talkeries' were established in Christchurch, Wellington, Auckland and New Plymouth where paying customers could go to hear recorded music played on gramophones.

Wax cylinders and phonographs were popular in New Zealand at the turn of the twentieth century.

In the early 1900s, songs from Gilbert and Sullivan's operettas were available on disc in New Zealand.

The Polish pianist Paderewski toured New Zealand in 1904.

The first New Zealander to release commercial recordings was a baritone called John Prouse, who recorded 12 songs for the Gramophone and Typewriter Company in 1905 while visiting Britain.

In 1910, Christchurch soprano Frances Alda made a record with Caruso on Victor Records.

Prime Minister WF Massey made a recording on the subject of the British Empire, which was released in New Zealand in 1913, with a version of 'God Defend New Zealand' by Australian Peter Dawson on the flip side.

In 1914, Rosina Buckman of Blenheim, New Zealand, recorded 'The Blackbird' and 'The Fairy Pipers' for Columbia Records in Britain. She later recorded for Pathé and HMV. One of her recordings for HMV, Britain, was 'Waiata Poi', which featured another Kiwi, Irene Ainsley, on the flip side.

Catherine Aulsebrook, a New Zealander, cut discs in Britain for the Winner, Columbia and Colliseum labels.

There were no radio broadcasts in New Zealand prior to World War I. After the war, New Zealand and the Falkland Islands were the only countries in the world where locals were banned from owning a radio receiver.

Miss Gladys Watkins travelled to Britain to record the sound of a carillon, bought by Wellington City at the end of the 1920s. The recording was made by the Gramophone Company and released in New Zealand on their Plum label.

New Zealand's first record labels were Minstrel and The Herald.

In 1925, most New Zealand homes had gramophones.

In 1926, the Australasian Performing Rights Association (APRA) was established in New Zealand.

A Maori welcome and duet by Ana Hato and Deane Waretini were recorded in 1927 during the visit of the Duke and Duchess of York.

In the 1930s, HMV (NZ) Ltd was the major importer of records into New Zealand.

Tex Morton, New Zealand's first significant country singer, made 20 recordings onto metal discs in 1932, to take with him when he set out to further his career overseas.

In 1932, Wellington boy soprano Lex MacDonald recorded in Australia for the Columbia subsidiary label, Regal.

Velvet Face was the name of one of the early record labels to surface in New Zealand.

Gracie Field's records were released in New Zealand on EMI's budget label, Regal Zonophone. She released a version of 'Now is the Hour', which she claims she learnt from a Maori taxi driver.

In 1948, HMV began the first New Zealand record-pressing plant in Kilbirnie, Wellington. The first record to be produced was 'Buttons and Bows' by Dinah Shore.

Pixie Williams, the vocalist on 'Blue Smoke', New Zealand's first locally recorded and produced disc, learnt to sing while milking cows.

'Blue Smoke', was released with a song called 'Senorita' on the flip side. It was later re-released with 'Let's Talk It Over' on the flip side.

The biggest-selling New Zealand 78 rpm recording was believed to be Johnny Cooper's 'One By One' (1955), for a one-off release, although the many reissues of 'Maple On the Hill' by Cole Wilson and the Tumbleweeds probably tipped the scales its way as the biggest one-off.

My Fair Lady is generally accepted as being the most successful album, in terms of sales, in New Zealand's recording history.

Allison Durbin's 'I Have Loved Me A Man', with official sales of 85,000 copies, is regarded as New Zealand's largest-selling single release.

The most successful singles in New Zealand by overseas acts were 'Snoopy's Christmas' by the Royal Guardsmen, 'Love Letters In The Sand', by Pat Boone and 'Release Me' coupled with 'Ten Guitars' by Englebert Humperdinck. Each sold over 100,000 copies.

Something to Do After Work

New Zealand bands, entertainers and their songs — a random selection

The Abel Tasmans sang 'Tired Sun'.
Alms for the Children put out a song
    called 'Alms, not arms'.
Bailterspace recorded 'Splat'.
Bamboo recorded 'Do What I Did',
    backed by a version of 'Ten Guitars'.
Gray Bartlett and Brendan Dugan sang
    'Ballad of Robbie Muldoon'.
Bill and Boyd sang 'Put Another Log On

The Fire'.

Bird Nest Roys sang 'Whack It All Down'.

Black Belt and the Silver Ferns sang 'Give 'Em A Taste Of Kiwi'.

Kevin Black sang 'The Fridge'.

Blam, Blam, Blam sang 'No Depression In New Zealand'.

Challenge sang 'La Dee Do Down Down'.

Chicago Smokeshop sang 'Mind On My Sleeve'.

The Chills sang 'I Love My Leather Jacket'.

The Clean sang 'Boodle, Boodle, Boodle'.

Coconut Rough sang 'Sierra Leone'.

Coup d'Etat sang 'Doctor I Like Your Medicine'.

Crocodiles sang 'Tears'.

Crowded House sang 'Chocolate Cake'.

Barry Crump and Scotty sang 'Side by Side'.

Fred Dagg sang 'Gumboots'.

Daggy and the Dickheads sang 'Brothers'.

Dave and the Dynamos sang 'Life Begins at Forty'.

Dead Flowers sang 'Plastic'.

Laurie Dee sang '(Rugby) Deck of Cards'.

Double J and Twice the T sang 'She's a Mod/Mod rap'.

Ebony sang 'Big Norm'.

Richard Eriwata sang 'Dewdrops and Robins'.

The Exponents sang 'Whatever Happened to Tracy?'.

Flight 67 sang 'I Lose Control'.

The Front Lawn sang 'Beautiful Things'.

Garageland sang 'Queer'.

Mister Lee Grant sang 'Bella Linda'.

The Gremlins sang 'You Gotta Believe It'.

Gumboots Orchestra and Chorus sang 'Fred Dagg and the Man from Taranaki'.

John Hanlon sang 'Damn the Dam'.

Headband sang 'Ballad of Jacques La Mere'.

Headless Chickens sang 'Gaskrankinstation'.

Hello Sailor sang 'New Tattoo'.

Jan Hellriegel sang 'Maniac (is a state of mind)'.

Herbs sang 'French Letter'.

Hi Revving Tongues sang 'Rain and Tears'.

Hogsnort Ruperts Original Flagon Band sang 'Pretty Girl'.

Holidaymakers sang 'Sweet Lovers'.

Holy Toledos sang 'Mistakes in Remembering'.

Hulamen sang 'Beer and Skittles'.

Igelese sang 'Groovalation'.

In Betweens sang 'Boom Sha La La La'.

Kal-Q-Lated Risk sang 'Angelina'.

Knobz sang 'Culture'.

Kulcha sang 'Shaka Jam'.

La De Da's sang 'I Love My Feet'.

Anna Leah sang 'Love Bug'.

Look Blue go Purple sang 'Bewitched'.

Eddie Low sang 'Sunday Daddy'.

Marvin and the Twisters sang 'Twist'.

MC, OJ and the Rhythm Slave sang 'Body Rhymes'.

Misex sang 'Computer Games'.

Moana and the Moahunters sang 'Black Pearl'.

Mockers sang 'My Girl Thinks She's Cleopatra'.

Monte Video sang 'Shoop Shoop Diddy Wop Cumma Cumma Wang Dang'.

Tex Pistol sang 'Game of Love'.

Mother Goose sang 'Baked Beans'.

Muttonbirds sang 'Dominion Road'.

Netherworld Dancing Toys sang 'American Dream'.

Newzy sang 'Accident Prone'.

Sharon O'Neill sang 'How Do You Talk To Boys?'.

Otara Philharmonic sang 'Drummer Boy'.

Past To Present sang 'Crazy'.

Ponsonby DCs sang 'G'day Mate'.

Pop Mechanix sang 'Celebration of the Skin'.

Pumpkin Head sang 'Nark'.

Push Push sang 'Song 27'.

Quick sang 'Hip Shake Jerk'.

Ragnarock sang 'Ferris'.

The Rumour sang 'L'Amour Est L'Enfant De La Liberté'.

Satellite Spies sang 'Living in a Minefield'.

Simple Image sang 'Little Bell That Cried' and 'Michael and the Slipper Tree'.

Sisters Underground sang 'In the Neighbourhood'.

South Side of Bombay sang 'What's the Time Mr Wolf?'.

Space Waltz sang 'Fraulein Love'.

Stark Naked and the Car Thieves sang 'Nice Legs, Shame About Her Face'.

Strawpeople sang 'Taller Than God'.

Supergroove sang 'Tractor'.

Suzy and the Sailors sang 'You Can't Beat A Plastic Fantastic'.

Tall Dwarfs sang 'Throw A Sickie'.

Three The Hard Way sang 'Hip Hop Holiday'.

Timberjack sang 'Dahli Mohammed'.

Toy Love sang 'Bride of Frankenstein'.

Track Daniel and the New Zealand Yamaha Youth Jazz Band sang 'Children'.

Triffids sang 'Bury Me Deep In Love'.

Troubled Minds sang 'I'm Good For You'.

Upper Hutt Posse sang 'Ragga Girl'.

Urban Cookie Collective sang 'High On a Happy Vibe'.

Bunny Walters sang 'Take the Money and Run'.

When the Cat's Away sang 'Melting Pot'.

Toni Williams sang 'Rose (Can I Share a Bed With You?)'.

Jo Jo Zep and the Falcons sang 'Shape I'm In'.

MUSEUMS & HISTORIC PLACES

600 Museums and 6 Million People

The Museum of New Zealand Te Papa Tongarewa, New Zealand's national museum, opened in February 1998. In its first four years of operation more than six million people visited the museum.

New Zealand has about 600 museums and art galleries.

The New Zealand Cartoon Archive was founded by Ian F Grant and was launched on April Fool's Day, 1992.

From Chicks to Styx

Some Historic New Zealand hotels

Brian Boru, Thames
Cape Broome Hotel, Fruitlands
Cardrona Hotel
Chicks Hotel, Port Chalmers
City Hotel, Ross
Criterion Hotel, Akaroa
Dansey Pass Hotel, Naseby
Duke of Marlborough Hotel, Russell
Eichardt's Tavern, Queenstown
Hardiman's Hotel, Rawene
Houhora Hotel
Hurunui Hotel
Lady Bowen Hotel, Thames
Northern Hotel, Oamaru
Port Chalmers Hotel
Provincial Hotel, Port Chalmers
Puhoi Hotel
Railway Hotel, Invercargill
Rangitaiki Hotel

Rawene Hotel
Red Lion Hotel, Rangiora
Shamrock Tavern, Wellington
Southern Cross Hotel, Dunedin
Stanley's Hotel, Macraes Flat
Styx Hotel, Paerau
Thistle Inn, Wellington
Tokaanu Hotel
Vulcan Hotel, St Bathans
Wains Hotel, Dunedin
Welcome Inn, Naseby

From Atene to Whangara

Some Historic marae and meeting houses

Atene, Wanganui Valley
Houngara, Pakipaki
Kikopiri, Ohau
Kokohinau Marae, Te Teko
Maketu Marae, Kawhia
Mangahanea
Mataatua, Otago Museum
Ngati Poneke Marae, Wellington
Otakou
Owae Marae, Waitara
Paku o te Rangi, Putiki
Papawai, Greytown
Parihaka
Poho o Kahungunu, Porangahau
Poho o Rawiri, Gisborne
Poho o Rukupo, Manutuke
Porourangi
Porowini Marae
Poutama, Koriniti
Puhaorangi meeting house, Tokaanu
Puniho Marae
Rongopai, Waituhi
Ruakawa, Otaki
Ruataupere, Te Teko
Tekapuwahia Marae, Porirua

Takitimu, Wairoa
Tamate Kapua, Ohinemutu
Te Hau ki Turanga, National Musuem
Te Ikoroa a Maui, Waitara
Te Koura Marae, Taumarunui
Te Mahua, Waihi
Te Mana o Turanga, Manutuke
Te Ore Ore Marae
Te Ti Marae, Waitangi
Te Tokanganui a Noho, Te Kuiti
Te Whai a te Motu, Mataatua
Thornton
Tiriti, Waitangi
Tukaki, Te Kaho
Tukorehe Marae, Ohau
Turangawaewae, Ngaruawahia
Tuwhakairiora, Hicks Bay
Waahi Marae, Huntly
Waitangi meeting house
Werewere, Morrinsville
Whangara

WOMEN'S AFFAIRS

Equality is a Many-lettered Word

The first Pakeha women to arrive in New Zealand in 1806 were Kathleen Hagerty and Charlotte Edgar, both escaped convicts from New South Wales.

The first Pakeha women settlers arrived in the Bay of Islands in 1814. They were June Kendall, Dinah Catherine Hall and Hannah King, whose husbands were missionaries.

The three Maori women who signed the Treaty of Waitangi in 1840 were Topeora and Kahe of Ngati Toa, and Erenora of Ngapuhi.

Before the 1860 Married Women's Property Act, women married under European law relinquished all property and earnings to their husbands. The 1860 act enabled women deserted by their husbands to retain their earnings and property.

In 1863, the Onehunga Ladies Benevolent Society was one of the first recorded organisations of Pakeha women.

Maori women fought at the Battle of Orakau, 1864.

In 1869, prostitutes had to register with the police and were examined regularly for contagious diseases.

Mary Colclough of Auckland became well known as a writer of feminist issues.

Kate Edger graduated with a Bachelor of Arts degree in 1877, the first woman to do so.

In 1887, Kate Wilson Sheppard was appointed national superintendent of the Women's Christian Temperance Union's Franchise Department.

The Atalanta Cycling Club, the first cycle club for women in

New Zealand, was formed in 1892, with Blanch Lough as captain.

Notes on Dress Reform was published in 1893, urging women to spurn restrictive and unhealthy clothing.

In 1893, Elizabeth Yates was appointed Mayor of Onehunga, the first woman mayor in New Zealand.

In 1893, Grace Neill was the first woman to be appointed as Inspector of Factories.

New Zealand was the first country to give women the vote — in 1893.

The first newspaper 'for women, by women, about women' — *Daybreak* — was published in 1895.

Grace Neill also became the first woman Inspector of Hospitals and Asylums, in 1895.

In 1896, 18 women were working as typists.

Mary Ann Bacon became New Zealand's first woman stockbroker in 1896.

Freda du Faur was the first woman to climb Mt Cook.

The Widow's Pension was introduced in 1911.

In 1913, Housewives Unions were formed in the main centres.

Ettie Rout started the Voluntary Sisterhood which inspected brothels in Paris and Egypt and counselled servicemen in the use of prophylactics.

In 1930, the Dunedin Housewives Association was formed.

A law change in 1934 enabled married women in New Zealand to choose between retaining their own nationality or opting for that of their husbands. Previously, women marrying foreigners lost their New Zealand nationality.

The Apprentices Act initially excluded women and only by special application to the Arbitration Court could an exception be made. Hairdressing was one of the trades excepted.

In 1942, the first policewomen took up station in the four main centres.

The first Maori woman to qualify as a doctor was Rina Winifred Moore, in 1949.

The contraceptive pill became available to New Zealand women in 1962.

In 1963, jury service was made compulsory for women.

The Society for Research on Women undertook social research on, among other features, women in unusual jobs.

Sisters of Homophile Equality was established in 1973.

Augusta Wallace became New Zealand's first woman stipendiary magistrate, in 1975.

Marilyn Waring, MP between 1975 and 1984, retired from Parliament at the age of 31.

In 1980, the Human Rights Commission charged the Ocean Beach Freezing Company with breaking the Human Rights Act when they refused to employ two women, Beryl Ross and Jessie Ruki, as slaughtermen.

Dame Sylvia Cartwright was New Zealand's first woman Chief District Court Judge.

Anne Barry and Elizabeth England became the first women firefighters in the New Zealand Fire Service, in 1981.

New Zealander Lorraine Downes was crowned Miss Universe in 1983.

Ann Hercus was appointed New Zealand's first Minister of Women's Affairs in 1984.

In 1984, Marilyn Waring, MP for Waipa, crossed the floor to vote against measures that could have adversely affected women's employment.

In 1985, Mary O'Regan was appointed the War Department's first permanent secretary.

Prime Minister Helen Clark is the eldest of four girls from a Waikato farming family.

FASHION & CLOTHING

Hat Pins, Steel Corsets and Bush Nighties

Walk shorts were closely associated with public servants of an earlier era, who were expected to wear ties, but in summer were allowed to don a more tailored kind of shorts.

Swanndris or swannies are coarse shirts made of waterproof woollen material, and popular with outdoor types.

Gumboots were imported into New Zealand until the middle of World War II. Then George Skellerup, who founded Para Rubber, travelled to the US, bought an old gumboot factory, and the New Zealand gumboot came into being.

Ladies were permitted to ride bicycles in 1901, but the attire for such a purpose dictated the wearing of sailor hat, tailormade habit, natty collar and tie, and natty gloves and shoes. The use of khaki garments was not recommended.

Bombay bloomers were loose and baggy military shorts able to be fastened below the knee.

A bush nightie is a humorous name for a bush-shirt or Swanndri.

A skivvy is a high-necked pullover of thin material.

Whalebone and steel corsets and heavy long dresses in the Victorian manner plagued New Zealand women in the early days of European settlement. Eventually, in the rough and tumble of life in the new colony, long dresses were seen as 'sweepers of filthy streets and station platforms' and a health hazard for women, given their propensity to trip the wearer.

Dip-front Adjusters made women's waists look smaller.

In 1901, a flat-fronted corset became fashionable which produced a pouter-pigeon mono-bosom above a flattened abdomen. A generous behind provided the lower curve on what became known as the S-bend. The hourglass ideal of Victorian times had been squeezed out of fashion consciousness.

At the turn of the twentieth century, New Zealand women were being warned about high-heeled shoes ('French heels'), which threatened to throw the spine out of alignment.

By 1910, New Zealand women were less likely to faint because their corsets were too tight. Corsets had become less constricting although, freed from the S-bend, the fashionable waist line rose in 1911 and dropped in 1913.

The sheath skirt of the 1900s was no longer full in the Victorian manner and, particularly if it had a split, women were now able to walk without difficulty.

The hobble skirt, a French aberration that narrowed at the ankles, brought new problems, for New Zealand fashion slaves found they could only effect a 'graceful mince'. Such a garment made it impossible for women to gather any pace while attempting to catch a train or tram.

Before being liberated from Victorian corsets, the ideal waist measurement for New Zealand women was a 22-inch (55-cm) constriction.

In 1901, no self-respecting New Zealand woman would reveal a glimpse of ankle. Yet low-cut evening dresses were considered respectable.

World War I swept away historical ideas of female elegance. Skirts were shorter and belts were worn low on the hips.

During World War I, when many New Zealand women were required to work in factories and other enterprises outside the home, dress style became more user-friendly. Waistlines, for a time, were permitted to settle at the position of the real human waist.

Dress style reflected the war years, with khaki coats, military overcoats and collars, and aeroplane hats becoming fashionable.

'Allotment coats', a wartime version of the trench coat, became synonymous with 'fast' young women.

Elaborate hats were fashionable in the early part of the twentieth century. On top of drifts of long, wound-up hair such hats often took on the appearance and contents of cuckoo nests. More commonly, flowers and fruit (enough to feed a military regiment) were arrayed on top of the hats, and to secure the menagerie, hatpins were required to be plunged into the mélange.

The hatpins, which protruded menacingly from these massive hats, became a public health hazard. In crowded streets and on public transport they could, and probably did, take an eye out. Eventually most councils banned hatpins on public transport.

In 1913, the Auckland City Council passed a by-law banning hatpins, but it was not until 1917 that council inspectors were able to enforce the edict.

One long-suffering victim of a 'decent hatpinning' likened walking down Queen Street, Auckland, to negotiating minefields in the battlefields of Flanders. While such a statement was sensationalist, it did highlight the extreme frivolousness of fashion that even caused injury to young children.

In the 1920s, the boyish look became fashionable, complete with bobbed hair and waistlessness.

By 1925, New Zealand skirts reached their highest point. By 1930, they had lengthened again to reach mid-calf.

Steel corsets were inclined to stain garments with rust.

In the 1920s and 1930s, New Zealand men's underwear was long and thick, despite the often warm weather.

Knickerbockers were the standard trousers for boys in the early 1900s.

Until the end of World War II, an essential item of clothing for New Zealand men was the hat, be it panama, tweed, felt, fedora, straw boater, cloth cap or the 'hard knocker'.

Oxford bags were trousers with 700-mm bottoms that enjoyed a brief period of favouritism with New Zealand males in the 1920s. Brightly coloured blazers augmented this brief 'look'.

Traditionally, New Zealand fathers and sons dressed identically, until the mid 1950s saw a discernible change in male dress habits.

American-style baseball caps became popular with some New Zealand males some time in the 1980s. The wearing of such caps became de rigueur even in conjunction with dinner suits.

The development of fibre technology during World War II gave a boost to the bra industry in the Western world, including New Zealand.

The bra-less look became fashionable in the 1960s in New Zealand, on the back of the women's liberation movement. However, some doctors — and bra companies of course — hinted at the emergence of a condition known as 'Cooper's Droop', the result of not wearing bras.

The boyish figure and styles associated with the 1920s were passed over in the 1930s for a return to luxurious fabrics, open-toed sandals and brightly coloured shoes. Elaborate hairstyles returned in place of the austere war-inspired bob or cropped styles.

After World War II, hemlines for dresses for New Zealand women dropped to a prescribed 170 mm above the ground.

'Knees are no longer naughty', announced New Zealand fashion magazines in the mid 1960s as the ground-breaking miniskirt was ushered in.

By 1967, the miniskirt was so well established in New Zealand that farmers' groups complained about the threat the mini represented to a declining wool market.

Some medical experts predicted a fattening of the thigh and knee as a result of the exposure granted by the wearing of miniskirts.

Women's bathing costumes in the early part of the twentieth century were voluminous apparitions of silk or taffeta. In 1913, the woollen Canadian costume hit New Zealand beaches, bringing a sleeker and less encumbered look.

The backless one-piece costume arrived in New Zealand in the 1930s.

Reports in New Zealand papers in 1947, alluding to riots in Australia provoked by the appearance of the two-piece bikini (the 'French' costume), were deemed to be a load of nonsense.

The topless bathing suit did not catch on in New Zealand.

Women's suits with shoulder pads were fashionable in the 1980s.

Hot pants were an item in the 1970s.

Stiletto heels on women's shoes damaged lino and other floor surfaces.

Paisley ties and platform shoes were the fashion statement for men of the 1970s.

Topless dresses caused a sensation when they emerged in the 1960s.

New Zealand Male Hairstyles

Hair of the dog
The mullet
The Beatle cut
The Tony Curtis cut
The flat-top
The crew cut
The Kojak look
The Mohawk
Short back and sides
Ponytail
The dag look
The Yul Brynner
Rat's tail with a crew cut
Dreadlocks

FOOD & DRINK

Eating Out and In; Drinking In and Out

Otago in 1871 was a boozer's paradise. It had no fewer than 17 breweries and produced more than 40 per cent of the nation's beer.

The cheerio, a small sausage, was not invented in New Zealand, but the name was.

Cervena is the trade name for New Zealand deer meat that has been raised on farms, rather than caught in the wild.

In 1989, New Zealanders spent $25 million on 382,000 litres of champagne — a 27 per cent increase on figures for 1988.

Pukeko was not unknown as a substitute for mutton in the early days, but it required at least two days' soaking in brine before it could be deemed palatable.

Colonial goose was not goose at all, but a boned leg of mutton stuffed with stuffing.

Bacon and eggs, and other mixed grill items, used to be cooked by railwaymen on a cleaned coal shovel on the firebox of a KA steam engine.

Lightning Rod was a combination of methylated spirits and raspberry.

Beer consumption in New Zealand peaked in 1975 at 132 litres per head per annum.

The first recorded brew of beer in New Zealand was the work of Captain James Cook and the crew of *Resolution* in Dusky Sound in 1773. It was used essentially as a cure against scurvy.

Prior to contact with Pakeha, Maori lived in one of the few corners of the world that had never developed alcoholic drinks, although there are some accounts by European travellers to the effect that the fermented juice of the tutu berry could be intoxicating.

Amongst Maori, liquor was called 'waipiro' (stinking water), or 'wai kaha' (strong water).

Early settlers made wine from the juice of wild turnips, makomako berries and peaches.

In 1879, a Taranaki settler was unfortunate enough to have 70 of his 100 bottles of home-made gooseberry wine explode.

One of the first illegal stills in Southland converted the sweet pulp of cabbage tree roots into a mixture not unlike brandy or rum.

Early New Zealand beer was also made from thistle juice, supplejack roots and matai sap, or from kohekohe bark and bush honey.

Matai beer was described as being like used machine oil.

Maori 'home brew' was called 'paikaka' and was made from maize, kumara and potatoes.

Pomare, a Ngapuhi chief, owned two pubs: the Sailor's Return and the Eagle Inn, in his Otiuha pa in the late 1830s.

'Whare karakia of Satan', was the ironic term for grog shops in the old days.

In 1879, there was one pub for every 287 people in New Zealand.

The average Pakeha man in the 1840s drank 45 litres of commercial spirits and 14 litres of beer a year.

During the six o'clock swill years, some enterprising men sold beer from telephone boxes.

Coconut oil is 89 per cent saturated fat.

Knitting burns 90 calories per hour; playing squash 840.

A deficiency of vitamin B can lead to beriberi. A lack of vitamin C can lead to bleeding gums.

A deficiency of sodium in your diet can lead to apathy.

Boiled asparagus has a 0.8 per cent fat content count.

From Rough to Ready

A brief history of New Zealand wine

Samuel Marsden planted grape vines at Kerikeri in 1819.

Charles Levet planted a vineyard on the Kaipara Harbour in 1863 and for 40 years made a living producing and selling wine.

Joseph Soler, a Spanish settler, grew grapes and made wine at Wanganui from 1869. Until his death in 1906 he dispatched 20,000-odd bottles of wine to customers throughout New Zealand.

In the early days of the colony, wine had a 'perception problem'. It was perceived by the new settlers as a drink for the elite and struggled as a consequence.

The Temperance Movement was a

significant threat to the wine industry in New Zealand, particularly between 1881 and 1918.

Assid Corban made his first recorded sale of wine in 1909. Corbans winery soon became the largest in New Zealand, and was to retain this status until the early 1960s.

Many New Zealand soldiers stationed in wine-growing areas during World War II had 'rough and ready' encounters with wine.

The 'Black Budget' of 1958, which applied high taxes on beer and spirits, helped the wine industry.

At the Connoisseurs Club Festival in 1966, 2000 Aucklanders consumed 5000

bottles of wine. In 1974, at the Kumeu event, 4000 people accounted for 8000 bottles of New Zealand wine.

Vintage acreage tripled between 1965 and 1970 as wine's image and access burgeoned. New, friendlier licensing laws and the fact that wine was no longer regarded as 'plonk' led to unprecedented industry growth.

The 1970s was regarded as the 'Cold Duck' era because of a cheap, famous sparkling wine of that name.

By 2002, the wine industry's local sales amounted to 32 million litres; exports accounted for 23 million litres.

Amazing Grapes

New Zealand grape varieties

Year 2004	Hectares	Percentage of total plantings
Sauvignon Blanc	4488	28.4
Chardonnay	3699	23.4
Pinot Noir	2743	17.3
Merlot	1276	8.1
Cabernet Sauvignon	816	5.2
Riesling	636	4.0
Pinot Gris	315	2.0
Müller-Thurgau	286	1.8
Sémillon	253	1.6
Gewürztraminer	202	1.3
Cabernet Franc	176	1.1
Malbec	158	1.0
Syrah	144	0.9
Chenin Blanc	129	0.8
Muscat varieties	129	0.8
Pinotage	88	0.6
Reichensteiner	56	0.4
Other/Unknown	235	1.3

The Blokes' Tipple

New Zealand beer

When Captain James Cook was looking for 'a tonic' for his weary crew in 1773, he came up with 'spruce beer' — a mixture of molasses, juice of wort, leaves of rimu and manuka. The concoction was considered to be New Zealand's first beer.

In 1835, Samuel Polack, using hops from Sydney and grain from Waimate North — and a brewer from Tasmania — produced regular supplies of beer.

Beer was very much the favoured beverage of the new colony of New Zealand, despite seemingly politically correct attempts to diminish its significance and highlight the glory of wine's development.

In 1865, there were 12 breweries in Auckland.

In 1867, 1.98 million litres of beer were brewed in Auckland province.

Auckland's Albert Brewery, named after Queen Victoria's consort, produced 30,000 litres of beer a day in 1870.

Richard Seccombe built a brewery in Taranaki, but later moved to Auckland where he set up a brewery at the White Hart Hotel in Queen Street.

In 1900, the first true New Zealand lager, 'Bismark' was brewed at Hancock's Brewery.

Drinking conditions in New Zealand remained less civilised than in other developed countries because of the extreme actions of the Temperance Movement.

'Teetotalitarianism' was the term given to the forces of the Temperance Movement.

Speight's was once the largest-selling beer in New Zealand and had a shareholding in a shipping company, which enabled it to ferry beer from Dunedin to Auckland, its largest market.

By 1984, just two New Zealand brewers, Lion and DB, dominated the scene.

Per capita beer consumption was lower in 2002 than it has been for over a century.

From Jack Mackerel to John Dory

New Zealand's eating-fish

Albacore Tuna
Barracouta
Bass
Bastard Red Cod
Big-Eye Tuna
Black Marlin
Blue Cod
Blue Mackerel
Blue Maomao
Blue Marlin
Blue Moki
Blue Warehou
Bluenose
Butterfish
Butterfly Perch
Common Sole
Elephant Fish
Gemfish
Goatfish
Greenback Flounder
Grey Mullet

Gurnard
Hapuku
Jack Mackerel
John Dory
Kahawai
King Tarakihi
Kingfish
Koheru
Leatherjacket
Lemon Sole
Ling
Mahimahi
Monkfish
Parore
Pilchard
Pink Maomao
Piper
Porae
Red Cod
Red Moki
Red Snapper

Rig
Salmon
Sand Flounder
Sea Perch
Sea-run trout
Silver Warehou
Skipjack Tuna
Snapper
Southern Bluefin Tuna
Spiny Dogfish
Sprat
Striped Marlin
Tarakihi
Trevally
Trumpeter
Turbot
Whitebait
Yellow-belly Flounder
Yellow-eyed Mullet
Yellowfin Tuna

Tastes a Bit Like Chicken

New Zealand wild foods

Chamois
Duck
Eel
Field mushrooms
Goat
Hare
Huhu grubs

Muttonbird
Pheasant
Possum
Puha
Pukeko
Quail
Rabbit

Thar
Venison
Wallaby
Watercress
Wild Pork

Play upon Food Words

Really 'wild' food

A good beef (braised argument)
A load of cobblers with side saddle
Baked Fiordland (a bit like baked Alaska)
Barbecued muscles and flesh (accidental)
Basilled Onions
Bat out of hell (pizza topping for the desperate)
Battered spinach and choked artichokes
Belly-buster burger
Borsch
Bosh
Brown-eye burger
Bull semen with a squeeze of lemon
Charred rump and testicles (accidental)
Chicken wings and scared centre three-quarters
Chilly con carne (iced)
Clay pigeon and buckshot salad
Cock and bull burgers
Cod pieces
Cooked goose
Corned watersider with horseradish dumplings
Couch potato chips
Cowradish with a Waikato salad
Crown roast of frankfurters
Curry-muncher casserole
Dead duck à l'orange
Deep sea gonad
Duffed plums
Fat belly boil up and over
Finger food and fondued thumbs
Goat's head soup with rolling bones
Ground nuts and lightly squeezed meatballs
Ham on the car
Herb dressing and the Kamo kumaras
Hindu krush (Asian dessert)
Hot curried chillis with sand-blasted red onions

Kina omelette with iodised salt
Lack of ram with roots
Lily liver and saved bacon
Mad cow and vegetables
Mincing on toast
Octopus clamp (tenderised)
Parsley, sage, Rosemary and Shirley
Pheasant under grass
Pickled Ginger and pissed Trevor
Pig's back
Pony shanks
Prune whip and lashed lentils
Red cods
Roast half-arse of hogget
Shaky Isles jelly
Short jabs to the ribs of beef, with broad beans and generalisations
Sitting duck on a bed of rice
Smoked mullet haircut
Squid tentacles with skyrocket salad
Steak and legs (frogs')
Stuffed pheasant and taxidermist soup
The bear essentials (Thai recipe)
Toasted melons and burnt bras
Tossed cabers, with capers
Tossed salad and boiled egg missiles
Warm roquefart tarts
Wedgie wedges
Well-hung stallion
Whitebait frittata and puha

Easy to Digest

Tongue-in-cheek tame food

Blenheim blancmange
Eltham junket
Fendalton flambé and fondue
Karori bread and butter pudding
Matamata milk soup
Remuera ratatouille

Beyond the Black Stump Beer

Little-known home-brew brands

Benneydale 15 per cent
Black Monday
Doctor Watson's rabies cure
Ellerslie elbow-bender
Methven foaming lager
Mokau mild lager
Paraparam slammer
Stout for stout men
Stratford-not-upon-Avon Stout
Te Kuiti Trenchmouth cure
The Black Plague Stout
Whangamomona whistle wetter

Lager Mentality and Pale Ale Attitudes

Bizzarre home brews

Len's Anaemic Pale Ale

A shy and retiring brew that loses its apparent passivity the more you get to know it. Has a kick like a shy, retiring mule. Best not to corner this number. Beloved of rugby goalkickers, this one should, like goalkickers, be handled very carefully. As goalkickers do, make sure you allow for the wind. A known cure for hay fever.

Burt Onion's Black Hole Solid Stout

Not so much a mid-winter stout, more a midnight offering. About as thick as four planks, with a similar woody taste, or as thick as four props and two hookers. Absolutely impenetrable, light is unable to escape from this bizarre brew, that doesn't so much pour or settle in the glass, but rather collapses in a heap at the bottom. Not your light, effervescent summer barbecue fare. More your standard cure for diarrhoea. Useful for repairing tyre punctures. A monument to the denseness of malt.

Twist and Shout Stout

A more accessible stout, this is to home brew as sump oil is to 96 octane. Knee-weakeningly tart, it also has the persuasiveness to get you gyrating on the dance floor, even when the band's not playing. Unashamedly non-commercial, it has a cult-following in areas west of a certain river. (Speaking of colts, young horses favour it as a tonic.) Don't attempt to douse the barbecue with this one. France would not have beaten the Springboks in 1958 had French Captain Lucien Mias drunk a bottle of this, rather than the rum he put away.

Desmond's Immaculate Lager

A characterless beer with the pulling and staying power of 'weezils'. No compensatory afterburn and no hidden agendas. As flat and lifeless as the Nullarbor Plains. Easy-drinking admittedly, but to what end? An ideal complement to a meal of curried onions and chilli pepper tornados. A favourite of non-tackling wingers.

Burt Onion's Brew 23

A refinement of the once commercial Brew 22, this is very heavy-going and explosive. Ideal as a barbecue accelerant. Features roasted caramel flavours, but not always. This is to Brew 22 what 'Six-up' used to be to 'Seven-up'. More a forward's drop.

Vic's Variable Bi-annual Lager

A delightfully unpredictable offering, no

two bottles behave the same. As lifeless as the Dead Sea on the one hand, it will lie disinterestedly in the glass. On the other hand, it can foam from the bottle for a fortnight out of control, as volatile as Chernobyl. On another hand, it can be a repository for suspended inanimate and animate objects, rather like science fair dissection samples. Then, out of the blue, a bottle will pour like DB Export, taste like Steinlager, arouse like Rheineck and leave you with a clear head. In these instances even the bottle seems to be self-cleaning.

Mick's Malty Muscle Bounder

This malevolent monster can clog you up inside five minutes. It will close down your systems despite a beguiling bouquet and a clear bubbly aspect. The palate remains coagulated, the nose basically blocked. An ideal anti-opposition weapon.

Jim's Nut-brown Beer

A wantonly yeasty, stroppy ale with blatant sedimentation. Not as bad as pre-50s Taranaki Ale, but no better than post-war West brew. A happy beer that makes you hop, combining elusiveness with unabashed drinkability. Much favoured of Welsh Flyhalves, who find they can go off either foot after a round or two of Jim's Nut-brown offering.

Pete's Light Placebo

For those special occasions when you're not having a beer, but need to be seen having a beer. Excellent hue (cold tea apparently), prominent head (detergent?), this revolutionary drop will enable you to survive any traffic blitz blow-up. And you'll have the most dazzling teeth on the block. Ideal for pre-match soirees.

Peewee's Malty Panacea

Has an undistinguished head, a nondescript hue, is pallid on the palate, non-eventful on the nose. Despite these factors and much more, this rollicking offering can cure anything from shingles to horse strangles. Much respected by rugby ale-tasters who find it possible to discard crash helmets and thigh pads when sampling this strain. A quiet, mutant drop which takes over its host by a form of osmosis. There are documented cases of even the most prudent tasters (those who prefer to use the spittoon), being pleasantly affected. It really does get in.

Boil-up and Dognuts

Kiwi tucker terms

A pair of bastards on a raft — poached eggs on toast

Afghan — a crunchy, chocolate-flavoured biscuit, named Afghan because it is dark

Anzac Day dinner — liquid lunch for old soldiers on Anzac Day

Awakino road kill — car-squashed

nightlife, usually opossum, known to be wrapped up in newspaper and auctioned off as legitimate food at local boozers

Barbecue — in which meat, and other food items, are cooked over a fire

Billy T James — outdoor tea, with reference to the famous comedian

Blowfly cake — wedge of fruit cake with lemon peel and raisins

Boil-over — a Pakeha variation on the boil-up, usually associated with heavy drinking and an attendant lack of attention to elementary matters in the kitchen

Boil-up — a collective dish, favoured by Maori, incorporating pork or brisket bones, potatoes, watercress and puha

Brazil sprouts — unusual spelling of 'Brussells sprouts' at a roadside stall

Bumpkin — unusual spelling of 'pumpkin' at a roadside stall

Cadger's fish — a bony variety of flounder saved by fishermen for human wharf scavengers on the lookout for free fish

Candy floss — a sugary, spun confection often procurable at A & P Shows — known as cotton candy in the USA — also a little-known name for a Kiwi call girl

Cauliflower and other flowers — confusion at a flower stall

Cheese and union sandwiches — cheese and onion sandwiches spelt incorrectly

Coliflour — more confusion at a roadside stall

Dognuts — poor spelling on billboard advertising doughnuts

Dressed pie (aka pea, pie and pud) — a late-night piecart sustainer: a mince pie with a blob of mashed potatoes and spoonful of peas perched precariously on top

Duck-shove — bushman's tucker. Duck shoved with little ceremony into the oven

Frogs' eggs — boiled sago or tapioca desserts

Gelly hangi — when a small amount of gelignite is used to create a hangi pit

Goodbye pork pies — an informal farewell spread

Goulash — a rough stew

Grease — rancid butter

Greasies — takeaway food, invariably fried

Grunter and chips — gurnard, which often makes a grunting noise when taken from the water, and chips, which don't

Half-pie and chips — unfulfilling piecart meal

Hash-house — an eating house

Hockey sticks — mutton chops

Honeymoon tucker — fine dining on gourmet food, thought to improve marital performance

Illegal Tegel — any protected bird taken illegally for food

Island chow mein — vermicelli and tinned corned beef

Knuckle sandwich — possibly a food item, but more commonly an expression for a punch in the face

Kummy kum — colloquial term for the Maori kamokamo, the stubby green marrow

Ladies a plate please — pre-feminism request for women to provide a food offering at a social function

Long John — a long, narrow loaf of bread

Long pig, baked warrior — human flesh. Something for the gourmet cannibal

Magpie pie — a desperate dish

Millionaire's salad — the edible heart of the nikau palm

Mountain mutton — venison

Mountain oysters — sheeps' testicles

Mousetrap — slices of bread with tomato relish, eggs, cheese and chopped onion

Nice one, Stew — a well-presented flatters' stew

Oranges and Lemings — unusual spelling of 'oranges and lemons' at a roadside stall

Paddy's apples — potatoes

Pairs — unusual spelling of 'pears' at a roadside stall

Pavlova — a distinctively Kiwi refinement: a meringue cake with a certain amount of snob value

Peachs — unusual spelling of 'peaches' at a roadside fruit stall

Pee and been — unusual spelling of 'peas and beans' at a roadside stall

Pigs in a blanket — oysters wrapped in bacon

Poorman's goose — a liver dish along the lines of pâté de foie gras

Poorman's whitebait — shredded skate wing

Pot luck — Similar to 'ladies a plate please', although nowadays it could be expanded to include 'blokes a plate too'

Rabbiter's breakfast — a trip to the toilet and a cigarette

Rat patties — dodgy hamburger patties

Scroggin — a concoction of dried fruit, nuts and chocolate

Scrotum burger — uncomplimentary term for certain down-country hamburgers

Shanghai ballast — boiled rice

Shark and 'taties — fish and chips

Shit-fish — parore or blackfish — often found near sewer outflows

Silva Beat — unusual spelling of 'silverbeet' at a roadside stall

Skim-dick — skim milk

Skull and cross-bones — macabre stew once found in the King Country

Snags — sausages

Snake sandwiches — sliced eel on bread

Snarlers — sausages

Spotted Tommy — raisin or current loaf

Spread — supper or 'eats' at a social function

Steelo pads — whitebait fritters

Twomatos — unusual spelling of 'tomatoes' at a roadside stall

Underground mutton — wild rabbit meat

Unions — unusual spelling of 'onions' at a roadside stall

Wet hen — boiled chicken

Plonk and Rooster's Blood

Kiwi booze terms

Amber liquid — beer

Barmaid's Blush — rum and raspberry

Blue Lady — meths as a drink — with bluish additive — for street alcoholics

Booze barns — huge public bars built in the 1960s, surrounded by large car parks — drink-driving issues were around at the time, so the assumption had to be made that only car passengers drank

BYOG — 'Bring your own grog' — a distinctly Kiwi way of providing your own alcohol at restaurants and other social functions

Half-G — half gallon jars of, invariably, beer

Henderson plonk — wine made mainly by Dalmation vintners in the Auckland suburb of Henderson

Henderson rough red — robust, unpretentious red wine from the days when New Zealanders' wine-drinking habits were underdeveloped

Hokonui — illicit distilled whiskey from the Hokonui Hills, Southland

Jessie's Dream — rhyming slang for steam: meths as a drink

Johnny Gee — an old name for meths as a drink

Jungle juice — strong liquor

Lunatic soup — alcoholic liquor

Maimai coffee — doctored coffee for duck shooters in maimais

Metho — methylated spirits as an alcoholic drink

Plonk– cheap or inferior wine

Port Craig cocktail — an egg, a spoonful of Worcester sauce and a dash of methylated spirits

Pub pet — a two-litre flagon of beer

Purple death — cheap red Italian wine

Rooster's blood — even cheaper red Italian wine

Shepherd's shandy — a sheep's dag in a glass of water

Six o'clock closers — an array of any number of jugs of draught beer waiting to be woofed before the pub closed during the era of six o'clock closing

Square gin — gin sold in a square-faced bottle

Sticky — a sweet dessert wine

Swill — beer, during the days of six o'clock closing

Titoki — beer, stout and raspberry cordial

Top-shelf tot — spirits as an alcoholic drink

White Lady — meths as a drink — based on the early colourless commercial vintage

Winebox inquiry — wine bingeing by more than one person

There's a Waiter in My Soup

Foreign objects found in New Zealand food

Bottle tops in bread.

Coins in Christmas puddings.

Fingernails in mince pies.

Glass in boiled lollies.

Lead in cornflour.

Mice in mixed vegetables.

Say Cheese

Cheeses made in New Zealand

Akarana
Amsterdam
Bleu de Bresse
Bleu de Montagne
Blue supreme
Blue vein
Brie
Camembert
Canestrato
Cassata
Cheddar
Cheese spreads
Cheshire
Chevrette
Colby
Cottage cheese
Cream cheese
Danbro
Edam
Egmont
Elsberg
Emmentaler

Farmhouse
Feta
Fior di latte
Flavoured cheddars
Fontina
Friesian clove
Gouda
Gruyère
Haloumi
Havarti
Joboe
Kapi-mana
Kapiti
Karnemelk
Leidse
Liptauer
Monterey Jack
Mozzarella
Parmesan
Poitevin
Port Salut
Provola

Provolone
Pyrenees
Quark
Raclette
Ricotta
Riverlea red
Romano
Ruapehu
Sage Derby
Sainte-Maure
Samsoe
Smoked cheese
St Paulin
St Pierre
Super crème
Tilsiter
Tupihi
Waitemata
Walnut cheese
Walnut red
Wensleydale

SPORT

What New Zealanders Do When They're Not Sleeping

Spike Milligan once attempted to crash-tackle All Black Ian Kirkpatrick in an Irish bar.

The first New Zealand rugby team to tour abroad to Australia in 1884 wore dark blue jerseys with a gold fern leaf on the left breast and dark-coloured knickerbockers and stockings.

Geoffrey Alley was an All Black in 1926 and 1928, and National Librarian between 1964 and 1967.

Former All Black first-five Earle Kirton weighed just seven stone at age 16. By contrast, fullback Don Clarke tipped the scales at 11 stone at age 11.

Terry Lineen, one of New Zealand's best performed second five-eighths, was forced to retire from all rugby because of a serious shoulder injury at the age of 24.

In 1982, the soccer All Whites made it to the World Cup finals as soccer enjoyed a surge of popularity in New Zealand.

Our greatest ever Olympian, in terms of gold medals won, was kayaker and canoeist Ian Ferguson who won three golds at the Los Angeles Olympics and one at the Seoul Olympics.

At the 1960 Rome Olympics, Peter Snell and Murray Halberg won gold medals on the same day.

All Black Cyril Brownlie was the first player to be sent off in an international.

The Bush Rugby Union was originally to be called 'The 70 Mile Bush Rugby Football Union'.

At the 1950 Auckland Empire Games, New Zealand won 10 gold medals. At the 1974 Christchurch Commonwealth Games, they won nine.

At the 1990 Commonwealth Games in Auckland, New Zealand won its largest haul of gold medals — 17.

Cricket is the oldest organised sport to be played in New Zealand. The first recorded match was between a Nelson team and the New Zealand Company surveyors at Nelson in 1844.

Curling, which is essentially bowls on ice, using a rounded granite stone instead of a bowling ball, has been a tradition in Central Otago simply because lakes freeze up to such an extent that human passage on the thick ice is possible.

Stewart Dempster was the first Kiwi to score a double-century for New Zealand in a first-class match. He was also the first New Zealander to score a test century.

New Zealand cricketer Martin Donnelly also played rugby for England while studying at Oxford University.

In 1989, a New Zealand horse called Horlicks won the Japan Cup, the world's richest horse race.

In 1989, Peter Blake won the Whitbread round-the-world yacht race in *Steinlager*.

The New Zealand cricket team went through the 1980s undefeated at home in a cricket series. They beat Australia, India, England, Pakistan, Sri Lanka and the West Indies.

'Agricultural sports' like wood chopping, ploughing, fencing and shearing are popular in New Zealand.

In 1923, Seacliff of Otago won the first Chatham Cup final, symbol of club supremacy in New Zealand soccer.

In 1931, an Auckland team known as Tramurewa beat Nomads of Canterbury to claim the Chatham Cup.

The Millerton All Blacks of Buller, a soccer team, made the finals of the Chatham Cup in successive years — 1932 and 1933. They lost both encounters.

In the 1934 Chatham Cup final, Thistle of Auckland beat Thistle of Canterbury 2–1.

In 1952, North Shore United and Western of Canterbury fought out a 1-all draw, and were declared joint winners of the Chatham Cup.

A team called Stop Out won the Chatham Cup in 1956.

The largest winning margin in Chatham Cup soccer finals is six goals. The largest number of goals scored in a single match was the eight scored in 1972 when Christchurch United and Mount Wellington of Auckland fought out a 4-all draw.

Tramways of Auckland beat Seacliff of Otago in the 1929 Chatham Cup final.

Waterside of Wellington have won the Chatham Cup four times.

When Technical Old Boys (Waikato) won the Chatham Cup in 1962 it was the first time a team outside the four main centres had been victorious.

In a high-scoring match in the 1997 national knockout final of New Zealand women's soccer, Three Kings United of Auckland beat Petone 7–5.

In 1937, W Wilson, an American, imported several softball bats into New Zealand and began coaching softball in Wellington and Hutt Valley.

The New Zealand women's softball team won the world title in 1982. The men have won the world title in 1976, 1984, 1996 and 2000.

In 1940, Jenkins Gym of Wellington became the first men's national softball club champion.

In 1946, Hinemoa of Wanganui won the first women's national softball championship.

In 2001, Christchurch United were both the men's and women's national champions.

G Kingscote was the first New Zealand men's squash champion in 1932. N New was the first women's champion in 1951.

Susan Devoy was the world women's squash champion in 1985, 1987, 1990 and 1992.

The Open Belt race is an event associated with surf lifesaving.

Water skiing is not a major New Zealand sport.

Nigel Avery holds several New Zealand weightlifting records in the snatch and the clean and jerk.

Women's wrestling became a national event in 1991.

In 1871, a yachting club was formed in Auckland.

In 1995, *Black Magic*, representing New Zealand, won the America's Cup.

Jim Barton, a champion New Zealand archer, is included in Ripley's *Believe it or Not* for his feat of scoring 238 consecutive bullseyes in 1957.

Neroli Fairhall won the archery gold medal at the Brisbane Commonwealth Games, despite being disabled.

K Uprichard won several New Zealand open target championship (recurve) titles.

In 1994, the New Zealand archery event the open clout championship (recurve) was abandoned.

L Murgatroyd won the initial open field championship (barebow) archery event in 1949.

Ann Shurrock of Ashburton won more than a dozen New Zealand archery titles.

Rod Heeps, an All Black winger, won three successive 100-metre athletics events in 1961, 1962 and 1963.

Tony Steel, another All Black winger, won the same event in 1965 and 1966.

Joe Leota, who played rugby for Canterbury, won the 100-metre event in 1984.

M Rae of Auckland won the New Zealand 220-yards title in 1955, 1956, 1957, 1958 and 1959.

R Oliphant won the New Zealand 440-yards title in 1898.

M Chamberlain won the New Zealand 440-yards title for women on seven successive occasions in the 1960s. She had earlier won the event for the first time in 1957.

P Boot of Canterbury won the New Zealand 880-yards title for men in 1936 and then in 1938–1940. D Earwaker won the same event in 1958.

Arthur Lydiard of Auckland won the New Zealand men's marathon in 1953 and 1955.

R Puckett of Auckland won five New Zealand marathons.

In 1995, C Dagg won the New Zealand men's half-marathon.

In 1994, there was no legal winner of the New Zealand men's 30-kilometre walk.

N Read, the gold medal winner in the 50-kilometre walk at the Melbourne Olympics, won his first New Zealand 50-kilometre walk in 1956, and his last in 1975.

T Upfill of Auckland won the New Zealand long jump title in 1891 and 1892.

D Norris won the New Zealand triple jump title 15 years in a row from 1957 to 1971. Later, for good measure, he added further New Zealand titles in 1974, 1975 and 1977.

Simon Poelman was three-time pole vault champion of New Zealand.

M Cheater was a 10-time hammer throwing champion of New Zealand.

Peter Snell broke the world mile record at Cooks Garden, Wanganui, in 1962.

John Walker set a new world mile record at Gothenburg, Sweden, in 1975.

A Strong of Waikato has been a leading light in the relatively new sport of men's mountain running.

Billy Savidan won a gold medal in the six-mile running event at the 1930 Empire Games in Hamilton, Canada.

The New Zealand women's steeple chase event was extended from 2000 metres to 3000 metres in 2001.

P Munro of Wellington was New Zealand's first national discus champion in 1920.

The first New Zealand national championships in badminton were held at Wanganui in 1927.

The Whyte Cup is a badminton trophy for competition between Australia and New Zealand.

Tim He and Chan Oi Ni won the New Zealand badminton mixed doubles title in 1995.

A women's basketball team called Wellington Swish won the New Zealand National League in 2001.

The game of basketball became popular in New Zealand as Kiwi servicemen returned from the Pacific after the war.

In 2001, the New Zealand men's basketball team beat Australia to qualify for the 2002 world championships in the USA.

Clark McConachy was New Zealand's most famous billiards player.

A Bowie of Te Kuiti was the 1928 New Zealand billiards champion.

D Meredith of Canterbury won the New Zealand billiards title 15 times.

S Wilkie of Hawke's Bay won the first two New Zealand women's billiards titles — in 1999 and 2000.

Lawn bowls was first played in New Zealand in 1860.

Three generations of the Skoglund family from Palmerston North have featured prominently in New Zealand lawn bowls.

New Zealander Elsie Wilkie won the women's bowls world singles title in 1973 and 1977.

Peter Belliss won three world bowls championships: the singles in Aberdeen (1984), the pairs in Auckland (1988), and the triples in Johannesburg (2000).

The first men's national bowling championships were held in Dunedin in 1914. J Kilgour of the Carlton Club won the initial title.

Battling Lavassa was a well-known New Zealand boxer.

New Zealand boxing championships have been fought out in the following graduated grades: Super heavyweight, Heavyweight, Light heavyweight, Middleweight, Light middleweight, Welterweight, Light Welterweight, Lightweight, Featherweight, Bantamweight, Flyweight and Light flyweight.

The Jamieson Belt is a New Zealand boxing award, given annually to the 'Most Scientific Senior'.

Ted Morgan of New Zealand won a welterweight gold medal at the Amsterdam Olympics in 1928.

Kevin Barry of New Zealand won a light heavyweight silver medal at the Los Angeles Olympics in 1984.

David Tua of New Zealand won a heavyweight bronze medal at the Barcelona Olympics in 1992.

New Zealand boxer Bob Fitzsimmons challenged three times for the world professional heavyweight boxing title — in 1897, 1899 and 1902.

David Tua lost on points to Lennox Lewis in a 2000 challenge for the world professional heavyweight boxing title.

Canoeing has developed a high profile in New Zealand, largely through the efforts of New Zealand Olympic competitors like Ian Ferguson, Paul McDonald, Alan Thompson and Grant Bramwell.

The first record of a cricket match being played in New Zealand was when Charles Darwin wrote of a match in the Bay of Islands in 1835.

New Zealand played its first cricket test at Christchurch in 1930.

The New Zealand women's cricket team became world champions in 2000.

New Zealand's first cricket test victory occurred in 1956 against the West Indies.

Martin Crowe has scored New Zealand's highest test innings, 299, against Sri Lanka in 1991.

Several years later, in 1997, Bryan Young scored 267 not out against the same opponents.

Glenn Turner, Matthew Sinclair and Stephen Fleming have each scored two double-centuries in test cricket.

The highest partnership in New Zealand test cricket was compiled by Andrew Jones and Martin Crowe against Sri Lanka in 1991 for the third wicket. The partnership total was 467.

Andrew Jones, Nathan Astle and Richard Hadlee have each featured in two record partnerships in New Zealand test cricket.

S Dempster, the New Zealand batsman, had a test batting average of 65.73.

Dick Motz, the New Zealand fast bowler, took exactly 100 test wickets.

Left-arm spin bowlers Stephen Boock and Daniel Vettori, although from different eras, both had best bowling figures in a test innings of seven for 87.

Bruce Taylor and Lance Cairns both had best bowling figures in a test innings of seven for 74.

Adam Parore, the former New Zealand wicketkeeper, holds the record for the most fielding dismissals in test cricket.

Murray Chapple, John Parker and Ian Smith each captained the New Zealand cricket test team once.

Gavin Larsen played in 121 one-day cricket internationals for New Zealand.

Glenn Turner averaged 47 in one-day cricket internationals for New Zealand. He scored three one-day centuries, including 171 not out against East Africa in 1975 — New Zealand's highest score in one-day cricket.

Dipak Patel, an off-spin bowler, had a one-day cricket economy rate of 4.17 runs per over.

Ewen Chatfield achieved the most economical bowling rate in one-day cricket for New Zealand, when he enjoyed figures of one for eight off 10 overs against Sri Lanka in 1982–83.

New Zealand have played one-day cricket internationals against Holland, Scotland and the United Arab Emirates.

A Moss of Canterbury took 10 wickets for 28 while playing against Wellington in 1889–90.

Bert Sutcliffe, while playing for Otago, knocked up the two highest scores in New Zealand first-class cricket: 385 against Canterbury, and 355 against Auckland.

Glenn Turner scored 103 centuries during his first-class career.

Richard Hadlee took 1490 wickets in first-class cricket, at an average 18.11.

Jack Alabaster took exactly 500 first-class wickets, at an average of 25.37.

Bert Sutcliffe won the Redpath Cup for best New Zealand batsman in a season, from 1947 to 1951, an unprecedented five successive seasons. He won the cup again in 1954.

Richard Hadlee won the Winsor Cup for best New Zealand bowler in a season, from 1977 to 1987, an unprecedented 11 successive times. He won the cup again in 1989 and 1990.

Chris Cairns has won both the Redpath Cup for batting and the Winsor Cup for bowling. John R Reid achieved the same feat.

The Plunket Shield was the symbol of New Zealand provincial cricketing prowess from 1907 to 1975. It was replaced by the Shell Trophy in 1976.

The New Zealand national women's cricket competition was first contested in 1933.

Wicketkeeper Ian Smith once scored 173 off 136 deliveries in a test innings for New Zealand against India.

The Burkner Medal is awarded each year to the New Zealand Dressage champion.

A horse named 'Landrover', ridden by E Uprichard, won the New Zealand show-jumping horse of the year title in both 1959 and 1960.

J Cottle rode a horse called 'Jeep Watch Me' while winning the show-jumping horse of the year award in 1997. The following year J Cottle won the same award on a horse called 'Jeep Super Moth'.

Fencing was introduced to New Zealand in 1916 by Major T Brown of the Indian Army who showed Auckland Territorial Army officers the rudiments of the game.

New Zealand's most notable fencer was

Dot Coleman who won the women's foil gold medal at the Perth Empire Games in 1962.

Between 1996 and 1999, R de Abaffy was the New Zealand men's épée fencing champion.

Brian Pickworth was the New Zealand men's foil champion on 10 occasions.

In 1987, N Nutt was the New Zealand men's foil champion.

Z Apathy was the New Zealand men's sabre champion in 1975. A Fake won in 1999.

The New Zealand men's amateur golf team won the Eisenhower Trophy in 1992.

Scottish settlers brought the game of golf to New Zealand.

New Zealand won the Asia-Pacific Amateur Golf Championship in 1995.

The Four Nations golf championship is a contest played off between Australia, New Zealand, Canada and Japan.

A Duncan was the first winner of the New Zealand Open Golf Championship — in 1907.

In 1893, J Somerville of Otago won the first New Zealand Amateur Golf Championship.

Until 1983, the New Zealand inter-provincial golf championship was known as the Freyberg Rosebowl.

New Zealand came third in the Women's World Amateur Golf Championship of 1992. In 1982 and 1990 they came second.

New Zealand has won the Women's Asia-Pacific amateur golfing championship title on three occasions.

O Kay of Otago won the New Zealand Women's Amateur Strokeplay Championship on nine successive occasions, from 1926 to 1934.

K Strong of Christchurch was the New Zealand national women's gymnastics champion in 1988 and 1989.

C Brownlee of Waikato was the first men's gymnastic champion — in 1955.

Arlene Thomas was a New Zealand and world aerobics champion in 1999.

The first hockey club in New Zealand was formed at Kaiapoi.

J Smith won 160 caps as a New Zealand hockey rep.

Bob Jackson has won over 20 New Zealand croquet titles.

The first national mountain bike championships were held in 1994.

Tino Tabak, a leading New Zealand cyclist of the 1970s, competed in four Tour de France races.

In 1995, K Giddy was the New Zealand men's national BMX champion. In the same year, D Head was the BMX women's champion.

New Zealand Hockey's Challenge Shield was first held by Auckland in 1908–1909.

Between 1931 and 1945, Auckland held off 23 challenges for the hockey Challenge Shield, by far the most successful reign in the Shield's history.

Women's hockey in New Zealand has featured some interesting national champions. Hawke's Bay were the first, in 1908, but Wairarapa, Poverty Bay, Ruahine, Eastern Southland, Canterbury A, Auckland Town, Maniatoto and North Shore A have all had their time in the spotlight.

New Zealand men won a hockey gold medal in 1976.

Lyall Creek, Petite Evander, Nigel Craig and David Moss were all horses — leading trotters that tasted fame since World War II.

Ice hockey in New Zealand experienced its first national championship in 1990.

B Tufnail was New Zealand's second senior men's figure ice skating champion. The first was A Robertson in 1939. J Walkingshaw dominated the event between 1977 and 1982, and then C Blong took over. Between 1986 and 1991, he won the event six years running, equalling Walkingshaw's run on ice.

H Hubbard won the first New Zealand men's indoor bowls singles title in 1950.

In 1981, G Pash, M Pash, I Pash and J Barr won the New Zealand Fours indoor bowling title. In 1983, it was the turn of K Goodgame, K Just, C Just and R Just.

Judo in New Zealand was first contested nationally in 1956, the same year the All

Blacks, using a fair bit of judo, defeated the Springboks.

H Dash won a New Zealand women's judo title in both 1984 and 1985.

Women's marching became established as a sport in Otago in the 1920s.

In 1947, Shaws Kilties of Hastings became New Zealand's second champion marching team. The year before, Manahuna of Timaru became the first.

Acme Pioneers and Uniflex Pioneers were successful marching teams from Canterbury.

In 1950, the Sargettes of Wellington were New Zealand marching champions.

New Zealand has produced three world-class speedway champions: Ronnie Moore, Barry Briggs and Ivan Mauger.

The Sidecar Grand Prix is a popular event in New Zealand motorcycling. The team of A Scrivener and C Meads won the event in 1996 and in the following year repeated the dose.

I Ffitch won the 0–750 cc 'All terrain' motocross in 2000.

Bruce McLaren was the first New Zealander to win the New Zealand Grand Prix in 1964.

Chris Amon won the New Zealand Grand Prix in 1968 and 1969.

Dennis Hulme of New Zealand won the World Formula One Championship in 1967. In all, he won eight grand prix events.

Bruce McLaren, in 1959, was the youngest driver to win a championship grand prix.

M Brick, a man, won the first New Zealand Ironman title in 1989. F McKee, a woman, won the first women's event, technically and politically correctly, the New Zealand Ironwoman title.

The first half-ironman championship was contested in 1989 as well. And the first half-ironwoman.

The Coast to Coast run in the South Island has become an integral part of the New Zealand sporting scene.

A demonstration match between Eden and Epsom in Auckland in 1907, was the means whereby women's basketball was introduced to New Zealanders. Many years later it became netball and, on the back of the women's movement, is now one of New Zealand's leading sports.

The first national club netball championship

was won by Verdettes of Hamilton in 1982.

The Southern Sting of Invercargill is a champion netball team.

New Zealand have been world championship winners in netball in 1967, 1979, 1987 and 2003.

S Langrope was captain of the New Zealand netball team in 1974 and 1975.

Yvonne Willering's playing position on the netball court was goal defence. Rita Fatialofa was wing attack.

Waimarama Taumaunu was an excellent New Zealand netball defender.

Irene van Dyk played netball for South Africa before becoming a crucial cog in New Zealand netball.

Lois Muir coached the New Zealand netball team for 15 years, during which time the team won two world titles.

Pétanque has been described as deck coits on dry ground. National championships in New Zealand started in 1996, giving credibility to a sport that started out as an adjunct to latte, power shopping and the yuppie lifestyle.

N Ruta was the first winner of the New Zealand Pétanque Championship.

Polo in New Zealand has always had an elitist base: invariably played by landed gentry and well-heeled farmers.

The Saville Cup is New Zealand polo's major inter-club supremacy event.

Christchurch were the first winners of the Saville Cup — in 1890.

In 1948, the Saville Cup was not contested.

The Kihikihi polo club first won the Saville Cup in 1952. Their team was L Kay, E Kay, T Kay and A Elliott. When Kihikihi won the cup in 1991 their team was P Kay, S Kay, E Kay and A Parrott.

The first roller skating championships in New Zealand were held in Christchurch in 1937.

New Zealander Karen Yorke has been the world speed skating champion on two occasions — 1975 and 1980.

W Heap of Napier won the New Zealand Men's Figure Roller Skating Championship in 1968.

J Ballerini, M Pickles, R Flatt, C Beets, R Legge, D Crum, G Hollows, A Lobb, L Raffles, W Mudford, C Boyes-Hunter, C Over, T Jubilee and L Wiig have been prominent names in New Zealand roller skating.

'A Major Effort' won the precision team roller skating title in 1993.

In rowing, the champion New Zealand men's eights team in 1937, 1938 and 1939, was Union of Wanganui.

In 1940, another Wanganui combination won the title — Aramoho.

Rob Waddell won two world rowing championships and an Olympic gold medal.

Since 1971, the sport of rowing has provided eight winners of the annual Halberg Award, to underline its prominent position in New Zealand sport.

Since 1978 the men's national rowing eights competition has been dominated by Waikato, who have managed to win 18 out of 19 tournaments.

Rowing competitions in New Zealand were severely curtailed by the two world wars.

In 1958, 1959 and 1960, the Mercer rowing club were winners of the New Zealand coxless pairs title.

The Wairewa Club, Little River, south of Christchurch, won the New Zealand double sculls in 1896 and 1897.

M Watkinson won nine New Zealand single sculls rowing titles.

The Te Awamutu Rowing Club was very strong in women's rowing in the late 1970s and early 1980s. They won the national eights in 1980 and 1981; the fours in 1979, 1980, 1981 and 1982; the coxless pairs in 1980, 1981 and 1982; and the quadruple sculls in 1982.

The sport of rugby league was established in New Zealand by Bert Baskiville.

Alphonsus Carroll was one of many New Zealanders who have played both rugby union and rugby league for New Zealand.

The New Zealand Women's Rugby League team won the World Cup in 2000.

Philip Orchard scored 40 tries for the New Zealand league team in all matches.

Jock Butterfield just missed out on playing a century of league matches for New Zealand, being stuck on 99 when he retired.

Tony 'Butch' Coll and Graeme 'Tex' West were among the toughest New Zealand rugby league players.

The 'Carlaw handshake or clothesline' was a league figure of speech for a head-high tackle.

The 'Te Kuiti tickler' was another league definition for the same sort of tackle, although rugby league never became established in Te Kuiti.

The New Zealand men's rugby league team have never won the World Cup, although they have come second on two occasions — in 1988 and in 1999.

New Zealand have played test league against Lebanon.

Hugh McGahan, a forward, once scored six tries in a league test against Papua New Guinea.

Matthew Ridge scored 168 points while playing rugby league for New Zealand.

Stacey Jones once scored 20 points against Lebanon.

Craddock Dufty scored 224 rugby league points for New Zealand.

A House of Wellington was a test match league referee who used to play test match league for New Zealand.

Dennis Williams scored a try in a league test match for New Zealand, the first time he touched the ball.

David Fagan of Te Kuiti has on four occasions won the world shearing competition.

The first winner of the Golden Shears event, symbol of sheering supremacy in New Zealand, was I Bowen of Te Puke. The same shearer won the initial New Zealand Shearing Championships in 1946.

Edsel Forde of Orepuki, won the 1989 Golden Shears.

David Fagan of Te Kuiti won 13 Golden Shears between 1986 and 2001.

The New Zealand Merino Shearing Championships used to be known as the National Fine Wool Championship.

In 1953, M Smiler of Gisborne was adjudged to be New Zealand Shearing Champion.

The sport of shooting in New Zealand is made up of the following events: rifle, target, pistol, shotgun and deer stalking.

The Ballinger Belt is the most highly sought after prize in New Zealand rifle shooting.

A Lieutenant Brighton of Auckland was the initial winner of the Ballinger Belt in 1861.

Bandmaster W King of Oamaru Rifles won the Ballinger Belt in 1899.

D Roots of Taranaki was a four-time winner of the Ballinger Belt.

B Clinch was the New Zealand skeet shooting champion in 1965. C Gunn won in 1975.

Annelise Coberger won New Zealand's only medal at a Winter Olympics when she secured silver in 1992.

S Wi Rutene has won seven New Zealand National Combined Alpine championships.

S Moses was the first New Zealander to win the New Zealand billiards and snooker competitions.

Women's soccer in New Zealand began in the early 1970s.

In the 1982 World Cup campaign, the New Zealand soccer team the All Whites needed to win 5–nil away to Saudi Arabia to continue. At halftime the All Whites led 5–nil, which was also the final score.

The All Whites lost 2–nil and 4–nil to Iraq in a 1974 World Cup qualifying match.

At the other end of the political spectrum, the All Whites lost 4–nil and 2–nil to Israel in a 1970 World Cup qualifier.

During their 1982 World Cup qualifying campaign, the All Whites beat Fiji 13–nil.

The New Zealand women's soccer team have enjoyed some emphatic victories during World Cup qualifying matches. In 1991, they beat Papua New Guinea 16–nil and 11–nil; In 1999, they beat Samoa 21–nil and Fiji 14–nil.

Three New Zealanders were among the Australasian team of 30 that competed at the 1908 Olympics in London.

Olympic champion Jack Lovelock was presented with an oak seedling by Adolf Hitler at the 1936 Berlin Olympic Games. The seedling became the oak tree that now stands in the grounds of Timaru Boys High School, Lovelock's old school.

New Zealand cricketer Glenn Turner achieved a very English cricketing milestone in 1973, that of scoring 1000 runs before the end of May.

Anthony Wilding, a New Zealander, helped Australia win the Davis Cup from the US in 1914.

George Nepia, who had never played fullback, took the field in the position in every one of the 38 matches played by the 1924 All Blacks.

Yvette Williams won the Olympic gold medal in the long jump after having fouled all but the last of her qualifying jumps.

Anthony Wilding won the All-England title four times at Wimbledon.

Danyon Loader, winner of Olympic golds in the 200 and 400 freestyle swimming events at Atlanta, was previously a champion butterfly swimmer in New Zealand.

Bert Cooke scored 27 tries for the 1924 All Blacks, from 29 appearances.

Squash champion Susan Devoy walked 1600 kilometres through New Zealand to raise funds for muscular dystrophy sufferers.

The first motor races on Muriwai Beach were run in 1921.

The first national yearling sales were held at Trentham in 1927.

Racing driver Bruce McLaren was killed in a crash in 1970.

The One Ton yacht 'Smackwater Jack' disappeared in 1980.

Trevor Chappell, on the instruction of his brother, skipper Greg, bowled underarm in a one-day cricket international between Australia and New Zealand.

Allison Roe won the New York marathon in 1981.

When Alinghi, the Swiss syndicate, beat New Zealand 5–nil to win the America's Cup, their skipper was New Zealander Russell Coutts.

The first New Zealand national chess championship was held in 1879, the winner being Harry Hookhan. The 'Silver Rook', also known as the Robert Jones Championship Chess Trophy, is the oldest national chess trophy being contested anywhere in the world.

Murray Chandler became a chess Grand Master, a first for a New Zealander.

Chess by correspondence has been played in New Zealand since the mid 1930s.

Ortvin Sarapu, an Estonian by birth, won the New Zealand chess title in 1951–52.

New Zealand's first golf course was established at Dunedin.

Miss DR Foote of Otago, a gymnast, failed to qualify for the 1972 Munich Olympic Games.

Table tennis used to be called ping pong in New Zealand.

Good as Gold

Olympic gold medal winners

1912 Stockholm: M Champion, Australasian 800 metres swim relay team.

1928 Amsterdam: T Morgan, welterweight boxing.

1936 Berlin: J Lovelock, 1500 metres.

1952 Helsinki: Y Williams, women's long jump.

1956 Melbourne: N Read, 50-metre walk. P Mander, J Cropp, yachting.

1960 Rome: P Snell, 800 metres. M Halberg, 5000 metres.

1964 Tokyo: P Snell, 800 metres and 1500 metres. H Pedersen, E Wells, yachting.

1968 Mexico City: D Joyce, D Storey, R Collinge, W Cole, S Dickie (cox), rowing coxed four.

1972 Munich: T Hurt, W Veldman, D Joyce, J Hunter, L Wilson, A Earl, T Coker, G Robertson, S Dickie (cox), rowing eight.

1976 Montreal: J Walker, 1500 metres. P Ackerley, J Archibald, T Borren, A Chesney, J Christiensen, G Dayman, T Ineson, A McIntyre, B Maister, S Maister, T Manning, A Parkin, M Patel, R Patel, J Gillespie, hockey.

1984 Los Angeles: I Ferguson, canoeing — K1 500 m, K2 500 m, K4 1000 m. P MacDonald, canoeing — K2 500 m, K4 1000 m. A Thompson, canoeing — K1 1000 m, K4 1000 m. G Bramwell, canoeing — K4 1000 m. M Todd, equestrian — 3-day event. R Coutts, yachting. R Sellers, C Timms, yachting. C Robertson, S O'Brien, K Trask and L O'Connell, rowing — coxless four.

1988 Seoul: M Todd, equestrian — 3-day event. B Kendall, board sailing. I Ferguson and P MacDonald, canoeing — K2 500 m.

1992 Barcelona: B Kendall, board sailing.

1996 Atlanta: D Loader, swimming — 200 m and 400 m freestyle. B Tait, equestrian — 3-day event.

2000 Sydney: R Waddell, rowing.

2004 Athens: G and C Evers-Swindell, rowing. S Ulmer, cycling. H Carter, triathlon.

She'll (and He'll) be Coming Round the Wicket

Cricketing terms and their possible alternatives

Absent hurt A player is unable to bat because of injury.
A player refused to bat because someone has hurt his feelings.

Agricultural shot A typically down-country New Zealand shot where the batsman — sometimes a farmer — throws caution to the wind, and the bat at the ball.
Sniper fire from the bush, designed to run a batsman out.

Allow a single The bowler concedes a run to get the batsmen to change ends, thus exposing a new or tentative batsman to the bowling.
To allow a single person to attend the end-of-season marrieds-only social function, particularly if the single person is well endowed, in terms of free booze and other enhancements.

Back lift The raising of the bat before the batsman executes a shot.
Little-known escape route from a high-rise building.

Backward point A fielding position just behind the batsmen on the off-side.
A fielder who is 'one ball short of an over'.

Bad light When it gets too dark to play.
Suggestive silhouettes played on thin curtains at a strip joint.

Beamer A dangerous delivery that passes the batsman above chest height.
An affectionate name for the Club captain's BMW motor car.

Beaten in flight A batsman flummoxed by the ball deceiving him in some way before it even bounces.
A rowdy all-rounder, having had one too many, incurring the wrath of a fellow passenger on an airline flight.

Bottom hand The hand on the bat that imparts most of the power.
A rowdy all-rounder making unwelcome advances to the air hostess.

Carry one's bat An opening batsman batting throughout an innings and remaining not out.
Having made a pet of a most unlikely animal, the owner carries it wherever they go.

Caught behind Caught out by the wicketkeeper.
Discovered crapping behind the sight screen.

Change bowler A bowler who bowls a couple of overs to enable regular bowlers to change ends.
A bi-polar bowler.

Coming off a long run A bowler with a long run-up to the crease.
An inebriated, locked-out player attempting to gain access to his house at a late hour.

Cover drive An elegant batting shot.
Doing wheelies in the president's BMW on the wicket covers.

Cow corner Unusual fielding position between 'long on' and 'deep mid-wicket'.
That part of the pub bar where the wives and girlfriends gather.

Cross bat An ugly, unsafe shot by a batsman usually desperate for runs.
An angry pet bat.

Dancing on the crease Moving too much while batting.
Dancing on one's trousers.

Dead ball After the ball lands in the wicketkeeper's hands, the ball is declared dead and the batsman cannot be out until the next ball is bowled.
What happens after the vasectomy.

Dead bat A very defensive shot, in which the bat is held still, allowing the ball to hit it.
A deceased pet bat.

Deep mid-wicket A fielding position on the leg side.
A highly intelligent person fielding at mid-wicket.

Delivery stride The final step a bowler takes before delivering the ball.
Cricket trousers delivered by courier.

Dot ball A ball from which no runs are scored.
Affectionate name for Dorothy Ball, barmaid at the 'Shoulder Arms'.

Face of the bat The flat, front portion of the bat.
Ugly dial of an unlikely pet mammal.

False stroke Where the ball ricochets into areas not intended by the batsman.
Fabricated symptoms, like a purported loss of sensation in the left arm, excusing a player from acting as night watchman against hostile bowling.

Fine leg A fielding position on the leg side.
Deflecting spectacle provided by a shapely girlfriend, to confound opposing batsman.

Flat bat A shot played with the bat horizontal when it hits the ball.
Road kill in the Awakino Gorge.

Fly slip A fielding position. A deep third slip.
An oversight after visiting the clubrooms' urinal.

Force off back foot An attacking shot played with the weight on the back foot.
Policemen playfully tackled by drunk cricketers.

French cut A false shot that narrowly misses the leg stump.
A kind of frog haircut.

Full toss A ball reaching the batsman without pitching.
A total regurgitation of lunch.

Get one's eye in To bat carefully until the vagaries of the pitch are understood.
A critical move for a one-eyed batsman who used to open the batting for 'Old Opticians'.

Get one's head over the ball A batting survival technique.
A basic sexual technique.

Give the ball air To lob the ball so that it takes a while to reach the batsman.
To open a few windows at the end-of-season ball.

Golden duck An innings in which the batsman is out for nought on the first ball he faces.
An increasingly popular dish at Chinese restaurants.

Ground one's bat To make sure one's bat is touching ground within the crease, to avoid being run out or stumped.
To destroy one's bat in a grinding machine after scoring a golden duck.
To destroy one's pet in frustration at scoring a golden duck.

Gully A fielding position on the off side.
'Lost ball' area at many country cricket grounds.

Handled the ball An unusual way for a batsman to be given out.
Unfortunate mannerism by a losing captain.

Hat trick When a bowler takes three wickets with successive deliveries.
When a bowler once bowled his cricket cap instead of the ball and the batsman tried to hit it out of the ground.

Heavy roller A large roller used to flatten the pitch.

A 20-stone fielder rolling into the gully while looking for a 'lost ball'.

Hold one's end up When a batsman battles to remain not out while his partner at the other end goes for the runs.

A disgusting piece of behaviour during a social game in the agricultural belt.

Kill the spin To negate the effects of a spinning delivery.

To deny the spin put on a political conundrum by shooting the 'spin doctor'.

Leg glance A batting shot played subtly down the leg side.

To be distracted, while fielding on the fence, by scantily clad female cricket watchers.

Long hop A delivery that bounces half-way down the wicket.

An excellent ingredient in home-brewed beer.

Late cut A batting shot played behind the wicket on the off side.

Visiting the barber's at 4.55 p.m.

Leg before wicket One of the ways a batsman can be out.

Getting one's priorities right.

Leg bye A run to the total when the ball deflects off the pads.

Showing a bit of leg when saying goodbye to her favourite batsman.

Leg slip A fielding position on the leg side.

An item of female apparel no longer in polite usage.

Leg spin The art of bowling leg breaks.

Horrific outcome of a serious motorbike accident.

Leg stump The stump behind the batsman nearest the leg side.

Eventual even more horrific outcome of a serious motorbike accident.

Loose ball A ball that is unlikely to take a wicket.

The result of an inadequate box.

Loosener A bowler's first and often inaccurate delivery.

A shot of rum, vodka, whisky and vermouth.

Loose delivery About the same as loose ball.

When the baby falls on the maternity unit floor.

Maiden over An over from which no runs are taken.

When a sure thing turns over in bed in disinterest.

Medium pacers Bowlers who are faster than slow but slower than fast.

No-so-rare horse steaks on a Mongolian barbecue.

Non striker The batsman who stands at the bowler's end.

A very poor cigarette lighter.

Nagging length Consistently testing bowling.

A long horse.

Orthodox bowler Usually means the left-arm equivalent of an off-spinner.

A little known Caucasian religious cult.

Outside edge A false stroke where the ball deflects from the outside edge of the bat.

What inebriated players have to be aware of when urinating under the stars in elevated settings.

Overthrows Runs scored when a fielder throws wildly to the wicketkeeper.

Projectile vomiting.

Pick one's spot To hit the ball accurately through the field.

Unfortunate habit of acne-ravaged country player.

Pick up runs To score runs steadily, without fuss.

To become a victim of highly contagious 'Delhi belly'.

Play back Batsman moving back towards his stumps to play a slot.

Tape-recorded evidence of groping in the back of the president's BMW.

Quick single A run taken in a situation where a run didn't appear likely.
An unmarried lower-order batsman streaking across the pitch after one too many late in the day.

Recognised batsman A competent batsman. Not a bowler.
An escaped prisoner hiding out as opening batsman, recognised by the local cop, fielding at silly square leg.

Retired hurt Temporary end to an innings because of injury.
Retired elderly gentleman in the crowd receiving a direct hit from a Lance Cairns smash into the crowd.

Reverse sweep Reasonably new batting shot.
Sweeping the floor with the wrong side of the broom.

Saving the single A fielder making it hard for the batsman to steal a single.
Rescuing a damsel (unmarried) in distress.

Seeing the ball early A batsman in really good form.
Unsecured pyjamas at 5.00 a.m.

Shoulder arms To deliberately avoid hitting the ball by lifting the bat and arms above the head.
What most people have dangling from their shoulder region.

Silly square leg A fielding position close to the bat.
A fielder at square leg standing on his head, making animal noises and in other ways being silly.

Six runs Achieved by hitting the ball over the boundary.
An attack of the trots by a diarrhoea victim, necessitating his frequent attendance in the toilets.

Slow bowlers Not as fast as fast bowlers, or even medium pacers.
Bowlers who think Tequila is the capital city of Mexico.

Square cut A batting shot on the off side.

A very unfashionable haircut.

Stock bowler A bowler who bowls a lot of overs.
A powerfully built bowler in country cricket who, having been confronted by straggling sheep and other stock, carries on his run-up and bowls them over.

Straight bat An orthodox way of playing shots with the bat.
A heterosexual pet bat.

Streaky runs Runs scored in a fortuitous fashion.
Something 'Out of India'.

Strokeplayer A batsman known for playing elegant, fruitful shots.
A player who has no feeling down his left side. Often has to bat one-handed.

Sundries Extra runs, like byes and leg-byes.
How touring players dry their flannels and smalls while touring India.

Swing the bat To go for as many runs as possible.
Exuberant gesture, involving a pet bat, following a famous cricketing victory.

Take guard To prepare to face the first ball.
To playfully kidnap the guard on the homeward-bound train following an excellent away win and subsequent beers.

Throat ball Dangerous bouncer that rears at the batman's throat.
What can accumulate after a nasty throat infection.

Tickle around the corner A subtle leg-side shot.
Traditional Friday-night activity in Te Kuiti.

Tight bowling Accurate bowling.
Drunken bowling, with eventual full toss creating a sticky wicket.

Top hand Batsman's hand that's furthest from the main part of the bat.
A very good chef's aide.

Twelfth man Reserve player. The main substitute fielder.
Little known Johnny Mathis song from the 1950s.

Slips of the Tongue

Quotations from the 2004 Athens Olympics

Weightlifting commentator: 'This is Gregoriava from Bulgaria. I saw her snatch this morning during her warm-up and it was amazing.'

Dressage commentator: 'This is really a lovely horse and I speak from personal experience since I once mounted her mother.'

Gymnast: 'I owe a lot to my parents, especially my mother and father.'

Boxing analyst: 'Sure there have been injuries, and even some deaths in boxing, but none of them really serious.'

Softball announcer: 'If history repeats itself, I should think we can expect the same again.'

Basketball analyst: 'He dribbles a lot and the opposition doesn't like it. In fact, you can see it all over their faces.'

At the rowing medal ceremony: 'Ah, isn't that nice? The wife of the IOC president is hugging the cox of the British crew.'

Soccer commentator: 'Julian Dicks is everywhere. It's like they've got 11 Dicks on the field.'

Tennis commentator: 'One of the reasons Andy is playing so well is that before the final round, his wife takes out his balls and kisses them . . . Oh my God, what have I just said?'

From Parsley Cutters to Pebble Pickers

Sundry sporting terms

In lawn bowls, 'to kill the end' is to play a shot that knocks the jack out of bounds, with the end then being replayed.

'Kneebangers' are very long baggy shorts worn by surfers.

A 'kneeknocker' in golf is a reasonably short putt, enough to cause consternation.

The kneeroll is the horizontal padding on a cricket batsman's pads.

In trampolining, a 'kaboom' is a backward somersault.

In surfing, the term kamikaze relates to a planned wipeout.

'Backside off the Lip' is a surfing term.

In yachting, 'baggywrinkle' is padding material made of old rope or foam rubber, used to wrap around stays to prevent chafing.

Ball abuse is a tennis term referring to hitting the ball out of court.

A 'parsley cutter' is a canoeing term denoting a tool used in building a fibreglass canoe.

A 'peach basket' is a move on the parallel bars in gymnastics.

A 'peanut bag' is a small training bag used in boxing.

'Peanut brittle', in golf, relates to an uneven, bouncy green.

In baseball, a 'pebble picker' is a player who blames bad hops for poor fielding.

'Faucet nose' is a surfing term referring to water up the nose and sinuses.

'Favouring a leg' occurs during equestrian events.

Weak surfing conditions are known as 'feebletosis'.

'Fat-out' in surfing refers to a wave that becomes less hollow and larger because of the deepening of the ocean floor.

In boating, abaft means towards the stern of the vessel, and abeam means at right angles to a vessel.

In surfing, an 'acid drop' is a fall into a wave that suddenly bottoms out.

A 'dry bounce' in diving occurs when you land on the springboard after taking off.

'Dry fly' is a fly-casting term.

In surfing parlance, 'duck feet' are flippers.

'Dweed' is a surfing term for dork.

Dwichook is associated with taekwondo.

A 'dying cockroach' is a surfer who waves his arms and legs, in seeking help, at the slightest hint of danger.

'Eccentric contraction' is a term associated with sports physiology.

'Ebi garami' is a jujitsu term meaning 'lobster entanglement'. It is a type of strangulation technique.

An 'early shower' is a rugby term associated with a player being sent from the field.

In skiing, an 'eggbeater' is a bad fall.

An 'eggroll' is an inexperienced surfer.

An 'eggshell blonde' is a surfing term for a bald surfer.

In horse racing, 'elephant juice' is the banned drug etrophine.

An 'emperor pair' in cricket occurs when an opening batsman is dismissed first ball in both innings of the same match.

The term 'stiff' is often used in cricket when a batsman is run out without facing a ball. 'Absolutely stiff' is when a batsman is run out twice in one match without facing a ball.

In gymnastics, the 'English position' is a handstand with the hands close together.

A narrow bowl in lawn bowls is known as an 'Errol Flynn'.

An 'extended spider' is associated with billiards, pool and snooker. It is a shaft with a raised metal frame.

'Eye gouge' is a croquet term. Unfortunately, it can be rugby-related as well.

'Face hold' is an illegal hold in wrestling.

'Face plant' is an alternative to 'wipeout' in surfing.

'Fake bunt' is a softball and baseball term.

A 'false keel' is associated with yachting when an extra keel is built onto the main keel to provide a yacht with more draught. (This doesn't mean that the yacht is then capable of carrying more beer.)

An 'absence of blades' occurs in fencing when the fencers' blades are not in contact.

An 'academic assault' refers to a fencing bout when hits are not usually counted.

In trampolining, an 'Adolph' is three and a half twisting somersaults.

In aerobatics, 'adverse yaw' occurs when the force resulting from the downward ailerons have more drag than the upward ailerons.

'Aerodynamic drag' occurs in cycling, thanks to the slowing-down effect of the air upon the body.

In sports physiology, 'agates' refer to the testicles.

An 'agetsuki' is an uppercut in karate.

All Blacks and The Rest

Rugby

Nickey Allen, who played two tests for the All Blacks, died while playing rugby in Australia.

Mark Richard Allen was commonly known as 'Bull'.

Brent Anderson of Wairarapa played one test for New Zealand, although he continued to give yeoman service for Waikato in later years.

The 45 points scored by Simon Culhane against Japan in 1995 is the highest total by an individual All Black in a test match. It is also the highest total by an All Black playing in his first test. The 20 conversions included in the total is the highest number of conversions in a single test.

David Lloyd Ashby of Southland played one test for the All Blacks as a fullback in 1958, deputising for Don Clarke when the latter was injured.

Two players named Ashworth played for the All Blacks: Barry Graeme and John Colin.

Arthur Bullock-Douglas of Wanganui scored a try in his first test.

Dennis Young, the Canterbury hooker, failed to score any points in his 22 tests for New Zealand.

John and Malcolm Dick, a father-and-son combination, both played for New Zealand as wing three-quarters.

George Aitken, Colin Gilray, David Kirk and Chris Laidlaw were all All Black backs and Rhodes scholars.

Ben Couch, Bill Glenn, Chris Laidlaw, Tony Steel and Grahame Thorne were all All Blacks who served time as Members of Parliament. Only Bill Glenn was a forward.

At 40 years, 123 days, Ned Hughes of Auckland was the oldest All Black — against South Africa in 1921.

Graham and Murray Mexted, father and son, both played for New Zealand as No. 8s.

Brian and Sean Fitzpatrick, father and son, both played for New Zealand, one as a second five-eighth, the other as a long-serving hooker.

Ivan Vodanovitch, better known as an All Black coach in the 1970s, was also an All Black prop forward who scored a try in his first test match against Australia in 1955.

Troy Flavell scored three tries against Tonga on the occasion of his test debut.

Ten new All Blacks took the field when New Zealand played France in a one-off test in Christchurch in 1986.

Marc Ellis, with six, holds the New Zealand record for the most tries in a single test — against Japan at the 1995 World Cup.

Four test matches involving the All Blacks have been played on a Monday.

In 1903, Albert Arapeha Asher played one test for New Zealand.

Two players with the surname Batty played for the All Blacks: Grant Bernard and Walter.

George Beatty of Taranaki played one test as a first five-eighth against the 1950 British Lions.

Bill Birtwistle represented New Zealand from two provinces — Canterbury and Waikato.

Robert Stanley Black played one test for New Zealand as a first five-eighth while representing the lowly Buller province. He was one of only two Buller All Blacks. The other was William John Mumm.

Todd Blackadder was an All Black captain. 'Blackadder' was also the name of a popular British TV comedy series.

Richard Guy Bowers became an All Black while playing for Wellington. He carried that mantle and continued to play in All Black trials while representing the tiny Golden Bay-Motueka rugby union, which has since been amalgamated with Nelson.

Taranaki provided two All Black fullbacks in the early 1950s — NJG Bowden and MC Cockerill.

Selwyn George Bremner, an All Black five-eighth, was known as 'Mick'.

Taranaki provided the two halfbacks during the All Blacks' campaign against the 1959 British Lions — Roger Urbahn and Kevin Briscoe.

Zinzan Brooke's second Christian name is Valentine.

Mark Brooke-Cowden (Auckland) was one of only two test match All Blacks with hyphenated names. The other was GAH Bullock-Douglas of Wanganui.

Four Browns have played tests for New Zealand: Charles Brown (Taranaki), Olo Max Brown (Auckland), Ross Handley Brown (Taranaki), and Tony Eion Brown (Otago).

During the period 1960–1965, the Auckland province provided five different first five-eighths who played test rugby: Adrian Clarke, Steve Nesbit, Tony Davies, Mac Herewini and Peter Murdoch.

Des Connor, who played 12 tests as a halfback for New Zealand, had already played a similar number for Australia.

Albert Edward Cooke played test match rugby while representing four different unions: Auckland, Hawke's Bay, Wairarapa and Wellington.

MSB Cooksley, who played 11 tests between 1992–2001, was the tallest man to play for the All Blacks. His third Christian name was Bill.

Pat Walsh played test rugby in four different backline positions: fullback, wing, centre and second five-eighth.

RR Cossey of Counties played one test for the All Blacks in 1958. TD Coughlan of South Canterbury also played one test in the same year.

Two props with the surname Dowd played test rugby: Craig William Dowd of Auckland, who played 60 tests, and Graham William Dowd of North Harbour, who played one.

Tom Lynch, Christian Cullen, Jeff Wilson and Frank Mitchinson all scored three tries when making their debut in test rugby.

Bob Scott kicked five conversions while making his debut in test rugby — against Australia. Carlos Spencer kicked 10 conversions on his debut against Argentina — and added two tries and a penalty goal for a points haul of 33.

Kieran Crowley of Taranaki kicked six penalty goals on the occasion of his test debut against England in 1985.

Frano Botica kicked two dropped goals against France, while playing in his first test match in 1986.

Sean Fitzpatrick played 63 successive tests during the course of his 92-test career.

All Blacks Frano Botica and Matthew Cooper also played test rugby for Croatia.

Sean Fitzpatrick scored 11 test match tries.

In 1913, against Australia, 13 new All Blacks were selected for the test match at Wellington.

Andrew Mehrtens has twice kicked nine penalty goals in a test match, once against

Australia in Auckland, the other against France in Paris. Mehrtens has also kicked seven penalty goals against South Africa in Pretoria and on four separate occasions has managed six penalty goals in a test.

Grant Fox kicked six penalty goals on three separate occasions in tests, and once kicked seven penalty goals against Samoa.

Don McKay of Auckland not only scored a try on his test debut against France in 1960, he did so inside the first two minutes of the game.

When the 1991 All Blacks played 10 tests it was the first time the number of tests a year entered double figures. In 1995, 1997 and 1999 they played 12 in each year.

The All Blacks once played a test against Australia at the Epsom Showgrounds.

All Black prop Ian Clarke also played test rugby as a No. 8.

Phil Gard was the only native North Otago All Black test player.

Three Dunns have played tests for New Zealand: brothers Eddie and Ian, and John Markham Dunn, an Auckland wing.

Two All Black players named Harvey, from Wairarapa, have represented New Zealand in tests: Ian Hamilton Harvey, in 1928, as a lock and Brett Andrew Harvey, in 1986, as a loose forward.

The longest rugby match in the history of the game took place at Turangi in 1987, between Tongariro High School and Taupo College. It lasted 24 hours and is listed in the *Guinness Book of Records*.

A long dropout is not a kind of outside toilet, but a long drop kick taken from the 22 to restart play.

A long dropout from the long drop was a prankish kick, following a certain amount of inebriation on the West Coast.

Former All Black wing Bernie Fraser's daughter is Brooke Fraser, a very popular New Zealand singer and recording artist.

Duncan Hales once scored a try for the All Blacks in Britain that few people were able to see, given that thick fog reduced visibility.

A virtual night test without floodlights occurred in the final quarter of the New Zealand-Scotland test in 1978. During this time, Bruce Robertson scored an apparent try that sealed the match and an All Black Grand Slam.

Perry Harris, a one-test All Black replacement, was forced to mark Springbok hardman Johan Strauss. Some scribes suggested he would have been better off marking Mozart.

Former All Black Jock Hobbs' real name is Michael James Bowie Hobbs.

Allan Hewson scored 201 points for New Zealand.

A John Hore played rugby for New Zealand but it was not the country-and-western

singer who later became known as John Grenell.

John Hotop was an All Black five-eighth.

Shane Howarth played test rugby for New Zealand and Wales, although his eligibility to play for the latter was somewhat clouded.

When Andy Jefferd played for New Zealand in 1981 he was representing the tiny East Coast union.

Lancelot Johnson was an All Black in 1928.

Gerald Kember was a second five-eighth who played mainly as a fullback for New Zealand.

Charles Napoleon Kingstone was an All Black fullback in 1921.

Kent Lambert, a prop forward, once kicked a sideline conversion for New Zealand.

Jules Le Lievre was one of the few players with a French name to play for New Zealand.

Terry Lineen, a prominent tryscorer for New Zealand in provincial games, was unable to break his duck in 12 test matches.

Two players named Thomas William Lynch played test rugby for New Zealand.

Ian Neven MacEwan played test rugby at No. 8, lock and prop.

Atholstan Mahoney was the only All Black to come out of the Bush rugby union.

Two McCaws have played test rugby for New Zealand: William Alexander of Southland and Richard Hugh of Canterbury.

Ex-All Black prop Kees Meeuws' second Christian name is Junior.

Nelson Bays have produced just one All Black: Trevor Morris in 1972–73.

Gerald Kember played one test — and scored 14 points in that test for New Zealand.

Jon Paul Preston played test match rugby for New Zealand at halfback and first five-eighth. As did Ian Neal Stevens. Both players were from Wellington.

Three players with the surname Purdue played internationals for New Zealand. All represented the Southland province.

Sana Torium Reid played nine tests for New Zealand.

Norm Maxwell has received two yellow cards (temporary suspension) in test matches for New Zealand.

W Fright, a policeman, refereed two All Black tests in 1956.

Three referees with the surname Thomas have refereed test matches involving the All Blacks.

Referee Pat Murphy pulled a hamstring during a test match between New Zealand and South Africa in 1965 and was replaced by Alan Taylor. David McHugh, an Irish referee, suffered a serious shoulder injury during a 2002 test match between South Africa and New Zealand, and was replaced by Chris White. McHugh had been the victim of a pitch invasion and crash tackle by Pieter van Zyl, a disgruntled South African supporter.

Frank, Victor and Thomas Hewitt, three Irish brothers, played in test matches against New Zealand.

Hugo Porta, the champion Argentina flyhalf, kicked four field goals against New Zealand during his career.

Owen Bridle, an Australian, scored four tries in seven tests against New Zealand.

Owen Stephens played one test for the All Blacks in 1968, before playing one test for Australia against the All Blacks, again in 1968.

Len Clode, an All Black coach, had a 100 per cent record. Mind you, he was coach for one season only, during which New Zealand played Australia three times and came away with three wins.

John Hart, All Black coach between 1996 and 1999, oversaw the playing of 41 tests.

Marc Ellis, the record holder for number of tries in a test for New Zealand — six against Japan — while playing as a wing, also scored two tries on his All Black debut — as a first five-eighth against Scotland.

Murray Davie and Dave Hewitt were both Canterbury prop forwards who scored tries on debut for New Zealand in test matches.

Duncan Robertson, a first five-eighth from Otago, played two tests as a fullback against South Africa.

Nesetorio Johnny Schuster played 10 tests for New Zealand. He also played test rugby for Western Samoa.

Gary Seear of Otago and Neville Thornton of Auckland were both No. 8 forwards who kicked long-range penalty goals in test matches for New Zealand, Seear against France and Thornton against Australia.

Eight players with the surname Smith have played test match rugby for New Zealand: Alan Edward Smith, Bruce Warwick Smith, George William Smith, Ian Stanley Talbot Smith, John Burns Smith, Ross Mervyn Smith, Wayne Ross Smith, and William Ernest Smith.

Augustine Spillane from South Canterbury played two tests for New Zealand in 1913.

Eight players with the surname Wilson have played test match rugby for New Zealand: Bevin William Wilson, Douglas Dawson Wilson, Hector William Wilson, Jeffrey William Wilson, Nathaniel Arthur Wilson, Norman Leslie Wilson, Richard George Wilson, and Stuart Sinclair Wilson.

Neil William Thimbleby, a Hawke's Bay prop, played one test match for New Zealand.

Va'aiga Lealuga Tuigamala played 19 tests for New Zealand and also turned out for Samoa.

John Creighton of Canterbury, Des Webb of North Auckland, Daniel Udy of Wairarapa, Ernest Dodd of Wellington and Ian Hammond of Marlborough were all hookers who played just one test match for New Zealand.

The only All Black to have been born in the Chatham Islands is Robert Mathieson.

A total of 109,878 rugby fans watched New Zealand beat Australia 39–35 at Stadium Australia, Sydney in 2000.

All Black Skinny Humphries weighed only 59.40 kilograms, but Ginger Nicholls, Merv Corner and Ponty Reid weighed less — 58.93 kilograms each. They were the lightest-ever All Blacks.

The All Blacks played their first test in 1903.

All Black Billy Wallace occasionally played in a sunhat, most notably when he scored 28 points for the 1905 All Blacks against Devonshire.

John Spencer, a Wellington loose forward, was the first All Black replacement in a test match — in 1907.

In 1905, New Zealand beat Australia 14–3, at Tahuna Park, Dunedin.

The 1905 All Blacks, in successive tests, beat Ireland and Wales by the margin of 15 to nil.

A team known as the Anglo-Welsh toured New Zealand in 1908. As the name suggests, neither Irishmen nor Scotsmen were included.

In 1913, the All Blacks undertook a full-scale tour of the Pacific Coast of the USA. They scored 156 tries and conceded one.

Because of the outbreak of World War I, a test match between New Zealand and Australia at Sydney commenced an hour early.

Only 3000 spectators watched the All Blacks play Australia at Dunedin in 1905 — the lowest turnout for a test match involving the All Blacks.

Favoured All Black songs from their 1928 South African tour included 'Old MacDonald Had a Farm'.

When the 1928 All Blacks played Griqualand West, six local Springboks did not take the field for their province. Work commitments were cited as the reason.

The All Blacks last used the 2-3-2 scrum configuration against Australia in 1931.

The All Blacks were due to tour South Africa in 1940, but the outbreak of World War II saw the cancellation of the tour.

On 3 September 1949, New Zealand lost two test matches — against South Africa and Australia.

During the test match between New Zealand and France at a storm-lashed Wellington in 1961, the winds reached 130 kilometres per hour.

The All Blacks' test success rate was 71.6% at the start of the twenty-first century.

The New Zealand Native team of 1888–89 included five Europeans.

Queensland toured New Zealand in 1896, losing all six games.

The first official All Black team — the 1903 tourists to Australia — won all 10 of their games.

Opai Asher of the 1903 All Blacks scored 17 tries during the Australian tour.

Bob Deans, who claimed he scored against Wales in 1905, was a devout Christian.

The 1905 All Black tourists to Great Britain scored 976 points, and had only 59 scored against them.

Of the 24 games the 1949 All Blacks played in South Africa, they managed to win only 14. Seven were lost and three drawn.

In 1976, the All Blacks in South Africa played 24 games for a return of 18 wins and six losses.

During the 1905 All Black tour to Great Britain, Billy Wallace played in all five test matches. On three occasions he played as a winger, once at fullback and once at centre.

Billy Wallace scored 246 points on the 1905 tour to Great Britain, France and North America, a record for any touring team.

George Dixon, manager of the 1905 All Blacks, wrote a book about the tour. The captain, Dave Gallaher and vice-captain Billy Stead wrote a coaching manual – *The complete rugby footballer*.

George Smith of the 1905 All Blacks set a world record for the 440-yard hurdles in 1904.

Lui Paewai played only seven games on the 1924–25 All Black tour to Great Britain.

There were seven All Black selectors at the time the 1924–25 All Black team was chosen.

Mark Nicholls, who starred for the 1928 All Blacks in their series-equalling game against the Springboks in the fourth test, was omitted from the first three tests.

The first two test series between the All Blacks and the Springboks — in 1921 and 1928 — produced two drawn series.

In the 1930 test series between New Zealand and Great Britain in New Zealand, the home side played in white jerseys to avoid a clash with the dark blue jerseys worn by Great Britain.

Vinny Meredith, manager of the 1935–36 All Black tourists to Great Britain, was Crown Prosecutor in Auckland for 31 years.

Prince Alexander Obolensky, the star of England's win over the 1935–36 All Blacks, was killed soon after World War II broke out, as a pilot in the RAF.

Gerry Brand of the 1937 Springbok touring team to New Zealand, scored exactly 100 points on tour.

The 1949 All Blacks who toured South Africa were involved in a train crash.

The 1949 All Blacks conceded only eight tries.

Ron Elvidge became captain of the All Blacks in the final two tests against the Springboks after Fred Allen, the designated tour captain, was injured.

In 1950, Peter Henderson, the All Black winger, was a finalist in the Empire Games 100 yards.

Kevin Skinner, the All Black prop, was a former New Zealand heavyweight boxing champion.

Colin Meads was playing No. 8 when he scored New Zealand's crucial try in their 11–3 victory over the Springboks in the second test of the 1960 series.

The 1963–64 All Black touring team to Britain lost just one game — to Newport, 3–nil.

Kelvin Tremain, the All Black flanker, scored tries in three of the four tests played between New Zealand and South Africa in 1965.

Two Manawatu lock forwards became test players in the 1960s and 1970s — Sam Strahan and John Callesen.

The All Black selectors, in error, selected 31 players for the 1967 tour to Great Britain. The player subsequently culled was Mick Williment, the Wellington fullback.

English midfielder Danny Hearn broke his neck while playing for Midland Counties against the 1967 All Blacks.

The 1970 All Blacks in South Africa used 27 players in the four-match test series.

Bryan (BG) Williams, the All Black winger, scored for New Zealand the first time he received the ball.

Eleven new All Blacks were introduced to the team during the 1971 series against the British Lions.

Phil Gard, All Black second-five for the fourth test against the 1971 British Lions, hailed from North Otago province.

Colin Meads captained the All Blacks in the 1971 series between New Zealand and the British Lions.

Colin Meads played for New Zealand for 15 seasons.

Loose forward Ken Stewart was 19 years of age when selected for the 1972–73 All Blacks.

All Black second five-eighths scored New Zealand's only tries in the first two tests of the 1976 series between New Zealand and South Africa. Lyn Jaffray touched down in the first test and Joe Morgan in the second.

Bryan (BG) Williams was the first back to play 100 games for the All Blacks.

Andy Dalton, John Ashworth and Gary Knight, long-serving All Black front-rowers of the late 1970s and early 1980s, were known as the 'Geriatrics'. All three were farmers.

Ian Dunn and Eddie Dunn both played for New Zealand as first-fives.

Michael Jones, the All Black flanker, was the first player to score a try in a rugby World Cup tournament.

'Buck' Shelford, at the time of his dropping from the All Blacks, had led New Zealand through 14 unbeaten tests.

When the All Blacks became victims of food poisoning during the 1995 World Cup campaign, Robin Brooke, the lock, was one of the few players unaffected.

The most successful decade of All Black rugby was the 1960s, when 83.4 per cent of games were won.

Several 'Bucks' and 'Bulls'

All Black nicknames

Abe	HG Munro	Copper	CRB Speight
Ack	AJ Soper	Cowboy	MW Shaw
Angry	T Cross	Curley	ML Page
Angus	BE McLeod	Dad	WG Lindsay
Axle	GA Knight	Darby	T Ryan
Baker	WD Cottrell	Dick	D Stewart
Balfour	KW Stewart	Dick	RW McGregor
Bam Bam	TT Koteka	Did	FH Vorrath
Barney	AM Armit	Diesel	IB Deans
Barney	BC O'Dowda	Doc	HC Burry
Beau	AI Cottrell	Doddy	GD Gray
Ben	JH Geddes	Doolan	AJ Downing
Bluey	DA Arnold	Dougie	AJ McGregor
Bolla	ARH Francis	Farmer	MJ Dick
Bronco	CE Seeling	Fox	JF McCullough
Brownie	NP Cherrington	Fritz	EM Snow
Brushy	NA Mitchell	Froggy	AG Dalton
Bubs	A Knight	General	EE Booth
Bubs	MA Mayerhofler	Ginge	PW Henderson
Bubs	G Tyler	Ginger	JTH Colman
Buck	BL Anderson	Ginger	HE Nicholls
Buck	WT Shelford	Goldie	JW Wilson
Buff	HP Milner	Goss	GNK Mourie
Bull	MR Allen	Grim	GTM Bachop
Bull	WR Irvine	Grizz	AJ Wyllie
Bullett	MW Donaldson	Harry	H Jacob
Bunk	HR Pollock	Hayburner	KA Eveleigh
Bunny	HL Abbott	Herb	KJ Schuler
Bunny	I Findlayson	Hud	HA Rickit
Bunny	KR Tremain	Jack	L Stohr
Buster	J Barrett	Jake	JF Burns
Camel	DB Clarke	Jazz	BL Muller
Carbine	WJ Wallace	Jimmy	RGB Sinclair
Chester	CS Davis	Jock	MJB Hobbs
Chutney	IJ Clarke	Jock	RJ McKenzie
Circus	HO Hayward	Jock	J Richardson
Clock	JF Karam	Jock	JC Ross
Cocky	W Roberts	Jockey	WA Ford
Colt	KJ Crowley	Joey	BS Sadler
Colt	BJ McKechnie	Jum	HS Turtill
Conch	EW Kirton	Kamo	ID Jones

Kelly	N Ball	Red	GW Delamore
Kipper	JA Gallagher	Rigger	MSB Cooksley
Kit	CL Fawcett	Robin	WR Archer
Kiwi	AW Blake	Sandy	A Kerr
Kuza	JR Watt	Sandy	ALR McNicol
Lammy	BP Larson	Sandy	AM Paterson
Legs	IM Eliason	Scobie	WE Hay-MacKenzie
Massa	W Johnston	Scotty	DL Baird
Mick	SG Bremner	Scrum	CE Evans
Mick	RR Cossey	Sharky	MD Robinson
Mickey	HAD Kiernan	Simon	HJ Mynott
Mike	GDM Gilbert	Skinny	AL Humphries
Moke	EA Bellis	Snip	L Allen
Mona	HD Thomson	Snow	HL White
Monkey	KC Briscoe	Snowy	KS Svenson
Moose	RM Brooke	Spider	RJ Urbahn
Moose	GJ Whiting	Spock	LG Knight
Nap	CN Kingstone	Spooky	IST Smith
Nectar	IN Stevens	Stainless	AG Steel
Nibs	SD Culhane	Stormy	SJ McLeod
Norkey	H Dewar	Tabby	WT Wynyard
Nugget	A Pringle	Tana	JF Umaga
Nut	EW Hasell	Tiger	PFH Jones
Nutcracker	NH Thornton	Tiger	TW Lynch
Offside Mac	W McKenzie	Tiny	SF Hill
Opai	AA Asher	Tiny	RA White
Paddy	AJ Long	Toby	HH Macdonald
Paddy	FA McMinn	Toby	HV Murray
Pascoe	RH Brown	Toby	JT Robinson
Pat	THC Caughey	Toby	TR Sheen
Pat	WA Harris	Tonk	A Mahoney
Pat	E Purdue	Trapper	DS Loveridge
Pat	EP Wood	Trout	JLB Salmon
Peg	AEG Elsom	Tubby	AW Holden
Pinetree	CE Meads	Tumbles	KJ Tanner
Pole	PJ Whiting	Tuppy	ES Diack
Ponty	AR Reid	Twig	M Sayers
Postie	CR Innes	Wampy	JR Bell
Ranji	NA Wilson	Wishbone	JC Ashworth
Razor	SM Robertson	Worzel	AT Earl
Red	RJ Conway	Yoda	GM Somerville

Lifting the Log

The Ranfurly Shield

John Kirwan of Auckland once scored eight tries in a shield match against North Otago.

North Otago suffered again at the hands of an individual from a shield-holding province when Bruce Reihana of Waikato scored 35 points against them.

A total of 52,000 spectators watched the 1985 shield challenge between Canterbury and Auckland.

Auckland once beat challengers North Otago 139–5 in a shield match.

When Auckland challenged Canterbury for the shield in 1995, they won easily 35–0 — the largest winning margin by a successful challenger.

When Bay of Plenty beat holders Auckland in 2004, it was the first time Bay of Plenty had held the shield.

King Country, now struggling to thrive in the third division of the NPC competition, once beat shield holders Canterbury 48–28 in Te Kuiti. Luckily for Canterbury they hadn't brought the shield north from Christchurch.

Zinzan Brooke of Auckland scored 46 tries in Ranfurly Shield rugby.

Dave Trevathan of Otago dropkicked 14 field goals in shield games.

Ross Brown of Taranaki, twice kicked three dropped goals in a single Ranfurly Shield match against Wanganui and North Auckland, both in 1964.

Two Canterbury first-fives, Greg Coffey and Andrew Mehrtens, kicked three dropped goals in a single match. Coffey notched his hat trick against Auckland in 1990 and Mehrtens against Southland in 1995.

SL Watt, a goal-kicking Auckland prop, kicked 75 points in Ranfurly Shield matches.

GK Cocks, a goal-kicking lock from Marlborough, kicked 59 points in shield games.

SBT Fitzpatrick, the Auckland hooker, scored 12 Ranfurly Shield match tries.

In 1907, at Alexandra Park, Auckland, Wanganui pushed Auckland, the shield holders, to a 6–5 scoreline.

South Auckland challenged Auckland for the shield in 1911.

The first shield match was played on 6 August 1904, when Wellington beat Auckland 6–3. The first successful challenge for the shield occurred the following year when the same teams fought out a 10–6 margin, with Auckland being the victors.

Buller first challenged for the shield in 1907, when they lost 21–0 to Auckland.

In 1911, there were only two shield matches, with Auckland beating South Auckland 21–5 and Poverty Bay 29–10.

Taranaki first won the shield in 1913 when they downed Auckland 14–11.

In 1920, there were 11 shield matches, the largest number in a season since the competition began.

Hawke's Bay beat Wairarapa 77–14 in 1926, an unusually high score for the times. JM Blake alone, scored five tries for the holders. Later in the same season, Hawke's Bay repulsed the challenge of Wellington 58–8 and this time BA Grenside scored five tries for the holders.

Manawatu and Horowhenua, as a fleeting combined union called Manawhenua, challenged for the shield against Wairarapa in 1927. The final score was 18–16 to Manawhenua.

The 100th shield match was staged at the Showgrounds Oval in Carterton in 1928 when the holders, Wairarapa, lost the shield 19–16 to Southland.

Wairarapa beat Canterbury 8–7 at Lancaster Park to lift the shield in 1928.

BA Grenside scored 30 Ranfurly Shield tries for Hawke's Bay.

BG (Bryan) Williams of Auckland played in successfully-challenging sides four times.

King Country scored no points when they first challenged for the shield in 1933.

Albert de Clifton of Wellington refereed the shield match between Hawke's Bay and Taranaki in 1934.

Horace Deavoll scored a try and kicked two conversions in Canterbury's successful shield match against Auckland in 1935.

HW Southern scored a try for Southland against Canterbury in 1935.

BM Craies, playing for Auckland and Waikato, scored 59 Ranfurly Shield points in only three outings. MJ Carrington of Auckland scored 57 in the same number of games.

CI Green scored 25 tries in 25 shield games for Canterbury.

Wellington, in 1919, were the first shield-holding team to take the shield on tour.

Southland won the shield for the first time in 1937, when they beat Otago.

Otago beat Hawke's Bay 4–0 in 1938, a dropped goal by D Trevathan being the only points.

When World War II broke out in 1939, Southland held the shield. Following the cessation of hostilities and the resumption of shield rugby in 1946, Southland continued to hold the shield. In all, they repulsed challengers 11 times — six before the war and five after. Technically their tenure lasted eight years.

JH North of Southland refereed the 1946 shield match between Southland and North Otago.

GH Spittle scored a try for Southland when they finally lost the shield to Otago in 1947.

Dr MN Paewai scored North Auckland's only try against Otago in 1947.

AS Fong, from the West Coast, refereed the 1948 shield match between Otago and Southland.

RH Giddy scored one of Thames Valley's two tries in their unsuccessful challenge against Canterbury in 1955.

RQ Randle of Waikato scored 27 tries in only 17 Ranfurly Shield games.

MC Wills, an All Black flanker from Taranaki, and not a recognised goalkicker, kicked a conversion in a shield defence against Buller in 1964.

In successive shield challenges for Wanganui against Taranaki in 1963 and 1964, CL Pierce kicked eight penalty goals and scored a try. They were the only points scored by Wanganui.

When Taranaki beat North Auckland in a 1964 shield match, all of Taranaki's 12 points came from dropped goals. RH Brown kicked three and TPA O'Sullivan one.

KR Tremain scored 12 tries during Hawke's Bay's shield reign of 1967–69.

Dropped goals played a big part in Hawke's Bay retaining the shield 12-all against Wellington in 1967. M Blackburn kicked two for Wellington, and BDM Furlong one for Hawke's Bay. Furlong's came in the last minute of the game.

All Black IR MacRae scored four tries for holders Hawke's Bay against Waikato in a shield match in 1967. Two years later, when Waikato challenged again, another All Black midfielder, WL Davis, scored another four tries for Hawke's Bay.

D Panther, a North Auckland wing, scored three tries in a shield game against Buller.

When Marlborough beat holders Canterbury in 1973, it was the first time Marlborough had held the shield.

Waikato challenged for the shield twice in 1974 and once the following year. They lost all three games.

When Counties went close to lifting the shield from Manawatu in 1977, P Clotworthy scored the challengers' only try.

D Hill of Southland once scored 26 points for his side in a shield challenge against Waikato, yet his team were unable to lift the shield.

The longest tenure in Ranfurly Shield history was that of Auckland between 1985 and 1993, when they repulsed 61 challenges.

King Country have never held the Ranfurly Shield.

The shortest tenure in shield history was that of Wellington in 1963, who held the Log of Wood for seven days.

Buller once drew 6-all with Otago in a shield game.

In 1932, West Coast pushed the holders Canterbury to a scoreline of 5–3.

Ashburton County (later Mid-Canterbury), first challenged for the shield in 1933.

CK Cakabou scored a try in Wanganui's total of 16 points, when the latter lost 39–16 to holders Hawke's Bay.

CM Le Quesne kicked a goal from a mark for Hawke's Bay in an unsuccessful challenge against Auckland in 1934.

WJ Hardham, VC, scored Wellington's only try in their 3-all draw with Wairarapa in 1905.

247

During the 1906 Ranfurly Shield season, JH Dufty of Auckland kicked three goals from a mark (then worth four points).

E Coote scored two tries in Auckland's successful defence against first-time challenger Marlborough in 1908.

Ernest Dive kicked a conversion for Taranaki in their 1909 challenge against Auckland.

When MJ O'Leary of Auckland kicked a goal from a mark in the 1910 shield game between Auckland and Wellington, the goal was only worth three points. However, it was enough to enable Auckland to hold the shield in a drawn game, 3-all.

The first draw in shield rugby occurred in 1905 when Wellington and Wairarapa fought out a 3-all draw.

Erekana Pewhairangi kicked a dropped goal during the course of Poverty Bay's challenge against Auckland in 1911. The following season Poverty Bay had another challenge and this time William Tate kicked a goal from a mark.

Poverty Bay have never held the Ranfurly Shield.

CF Young of Taranaki was the second player to score four tries in a shield game. The first was JV Macky of Auckland in 1912. Remarkably, Macky's tries were the only points in the game.

When Wellington lifted the shield from Taranaki in 1914, a five-eighth called Beethoven Algar scored a try and kicked a four-point dropped goal, critical components of a 12–6 win.

The Reverend Paul Markham scored a try for holders Wellington in their 28–13 win over Southland.

GL Owles scored two tries for Otago in a shield game in 1921.

Bay of Plenty nearly won the shield from Hawke's Bay in 1922. Both sides scored four tries but the holders held out 17–16.

The famous George Nepia scored tries in three successive shield defences for Hawke's Bay in 1923.

Edward Single scored one try for Hawke's Bay in their 58–8 triumph over Wellington in 1926.

In 1928–29, Wairarapa defended the shield on eight occasions.

The shield went into recess during World War I.

H McSkimming scored a try and R McSkimming converted it when Otago went close to lifting the shield from Canterbury in 1933.

John Boys scored a try for South Canterbury in their narrow 6–3 loss to shield holders Canterbury in 1933.

In successive seasons, 1981 and 1982, Counties challenged for the shield against Waikato and Canterbury, respectively. Both games were drawn, and as a consequence Counties came away empty-handed.

In the 1987 shield campaign, Zinzan Brooke scored 11 tries for Auckland. In the 1990 season, he scored 12.

In 1988, Auckland took the shield on the road and played challenge matches in Te Kuiti, New Plymouth and Napier.

Against Mid-Canterbury in 1989, V Tuigamala scored five tries for Auckland in a shield defence.

The only time the outstanding Auckland shield team, who held the shield from 1985 to 1993, were seriously troubled was in struggling to beat Counties 12–9 in their second defence, and Canterbury 33–30 in 1990. Otago on a couple of occasions, and North Harbour, got within cooee, but for most of their 61 successful defences Auckland were in a class of their own.

During Auckland's record reign, eight challenging teams were unable to score points.

Carlos Spencer scored a try for Horowhenua in their 1993 challenge against Auckland.

A whopping 120 match points were scored when Waikato repulsed South Canterbury's challenge in 1994. The final score was 98–22.

Andrew Mehrtens scored in four different ways when Canterbury beat Counties in 1994. He scored two tries, two conversions, four penalty goals and two dropped goals in a 42–16 win.

In 1998, Waikato beat Poverty Bay 121–nil.

In 1950, the shield changed hands four times. Canterbury initially lifted it from Otago, before promptly losing it to Wairarapa. South Canterbury claimed it from Wairarapa before North Auckland lifted it for the first time in their history.

When Waikato won the shield for the first time in 1951, DB Clarke, a 17-year-old fullback, kicked two penalty goals.

In 1952, Waikato lost the shield to Auckland on 9 August. On 23 August, Waikato promptly won the shield back.

RA Jarden scored six tries in a shield match between the holders Wellington and East Coast.

DP Mumm kicked a penalty for Buller in their unsuccessful shield challenge against Canterbury in 1953.

CR Skates, a winger, scored West Coast's only try in their unsuccessful challenge against Manawatu in 1978.

MD Nutting was one of the tryscorers for Horowhenua when they were beaten 42–14 by Manawatu in a 1978 shield game.

SK Henderson, a goal-kicking centre from Canterbury, scored 163 points in 15 Ranfurly Shield games.

All Black halfback, Kevin Briscoe, who was not a recognised goalkicker during the early part of his All Black career, later kicked 24 conversions and 14 penalty goals in Ranfurly Shield rugby.

TJ Wright of Auckland scored 53 tries in 52 Ranfurly Shield matches, the highest number of tries in shield history.

When Waikato took the shield from Auckland in 1980, the opposing halfbacks — D Phillips for Waikato and R Dunn for Auckland — both kicked penalty goals.

When Waikato repulsed East Coast's challenge in 1981, the home wingers G Major with five and B Smith (four), scored all but two of Waikato's tries.

HORSE RACING

The Bit that Goes with Rugby and Beer

Jockey Roy Reed would have been the first man to ride 1000 winners had he not died in a fall at Trentham in 1936.

The most successful run by a New Zealand owner was that of Bill Hazlett at the three-day Riverton Easter meeting in 1968. He won all five steeplechases and his jumpers recorded four seconds and two thirds.

At Tuapeka, South Otago, in 1890, a horse called Metford won the race, without the judge being in his box. It was necessary to re-run the race and Metford won again.

In 1931, in Taranaki, a jockey was thrown out of his saddle, but had the good fortune to land on his feet on the running rail, from where he leapt back into the saddle and completed the race.

In 1947, at Tauherenikau, a jockey's saddle slipped just short of the winning post and, although the jockey was seen to be clinging to the horse's neck as it crossed the line, it was still deemed to be 'contact' with the horse. The win was declared good.

During World War II, some racing clubs grew vegetables to help ease food shortages. Hastings grew peas for the local cannery, Pukekohe grew all sorts and Takapuna produced big onion crops.

In 1891, at Kurow, W Sharp became the first New Zealand jockey to ride six winners in a day.

Three of the four starters fell in a race in Hawke's Bay. Two were remounted by spectators, who completed the race to fill the minor placings.

An illegal race meeting was held on Matakana Island in 1922, but the portable tote was concealed and so little official action was taken.

In 1985, Trudy Archer was the first woman to ride in the Great Northern Steeplechase.

When the Taieri Amateur Turf Club went into recess, their funds were donated to the local fire brigade, municipal band and poultry society.

Auckland racing fans used to travel by steamer to the Thames races.

Jockey JW Dooley rode all six winners on the first day of a race meeting at Beaumont in 1931, and six seconds on the second day.

The first winning trifecta in New Zealand featured the combination of Saddleback, Bretwelda and Sanctify.

The biggest field to contest a race in New Zealand was the 42-horse line-up at Ellerslie in 1921.

The first jockey to fly to the races was George Clark, who flew from Carterton to Wellington in 1921 for the Sylvia Park Handicap.

In 1877, the Canterbury Jockey Club built their own railway siding from the main south trunk line to Riccarton, which was quite a distance from Christchurch in those days.

The first live racing telecast in New Zealand occurred at Ellerslie in 1966.

In 1868, a racehorse named Ladybird swam ashore from a boat moored in the Manukau Harbour, walked all the way to Ellerslie racecourse and duly won its race.

Incredible won two races in a row at Marlborough in 1955. It was the last time a horse achieved the feat.

Waipapakauri was the most northern racing club in New Zealand, until it was forced to close in 1933.

Saint Hippo was regarded as such a certainty in the Great Northern Derby of 1893 that the club paid out the winning dividend on the second horse.

During wartime in New Zealand, racehorses were often ridden to racecourses, because of travel restrictions relating to trains and the lack of horse floats.

In 1980, Rex Cochrane of Gore was the first trainer to train 1000 galloping winners.

Jim Tomkinson was 17 years of age when he trained his first winner — Arcade — which won at Washdyke in 1934.

'Granny' Maher was the first woman trainer licensed in New Zealand. She trained Melbourne Cup winner Catalogue, although at the time the credit went to her husband Alan McDonald because women trainers were not permitted in Australia.

In 1933, Miss D Bray was appointed secretary of the Wellington Racing Club, the first woman secretary of a racing club in New Zealand.

In 1924, at Devonport, there was a dead heat for first and a dead heat for third in the same race.

During the days of the Central Otago gold rush, the Blacks and Drybread Jockey Clubs amalgamated.

Three horses died in a training accident at Washdyke in 1970.

The only fatality involving a spectator at a New Zealand race meeting occurred at

Otautau in 1897, when a horse swerved off the course into the crowd.

A 17-year-old horse called Donald won a race in Hawke's Bay in 1907. The jockey was several years younger than the horse.

Alf Banks was one of New Zealand's lightest jockeys. When he began his career at age 12 he weighed only 21.5 kilograms.

Sue Day was the first New Zealand woman rider to win a race when she came home on Jaws at the South Canterbury Hunt Club meeting in 1984.

Jockeys used to play in an annual North Island–South Island rugby match. When they staged their 1924 encounter on a Sunday, the Presbyterian Church complained.

Steve Malone was only 11 years of age when he rode his first winner at Gisborne in 1901.

In 1913, when trains were the primary means of travel, 11 full trains carried Aucklanders to the Avondale races.

When the Waikato Racing Club moved from Claudelands to Te Rapa in 1925 there were punters who thought the racecourse had moved too far out of Hamilton.

Phar Lap never raced in New Zealand, the country where he was foaled.

Mercian Queen is believed to be the oldest brood mare ever in New Zealand. She died in 1968 at the age of 39, after having produced her last foal at 34.

In 1922, the Wingatui Racecourse was declared a sanctuary for native game.

In 1947, there were three dead heats at Wingatui, a New Zealand record.

The Chatham Islands have enjoyed horse racing since 1873.

The famous racehorse Carbine didn't like getting his ears wet. On one wet occasion his trainer held an umbrella over the horse's head all the way to the starting post.

In 1911, a jockey broke his leg when he hit a spectator leaning over the inside rail on the straight.

The Ann and Ken Browne partnership holds the record for the most jumps winners in a season, with 28 in 1992–93 and the same number in 1999–2000.

This Time . . .

New Zealand galloping tracks

Arawa Park, Rotorua
Ascot Park, Invercargill
Ashburton
Avondale
Awapuni
Cromwell
Dargaville
Egmont, Hawera
Ellerslie
Foxton
Gate Pa, Tauranga
Gore
Hastings
Kumara
Kurow
Makaraka, Gisborne
Matamata
Motukarara

New Plymouth
Oamaru
Omakau
Omoto, Greymouth
Otaki
Paeroa
Patterson Park, Westport
Pukekohe
Rangiora
Reefton
Riccarton
Richmond, Nelson
Riverton
Ruakaka, Whangarei
Stratford
Tapanui
Tauherenikau
Taupo

Te Aroha
Te Awamutu
Te Rapa
Te Teko
Thames
Trentham
Waikouaiti
Waimate
Waipukurau
Wairoa
Wanganui
Washdyke
Waterlea, Blenheim
Waverley
Westland, Hokitika
Wingatui
Woodville
Wyndham

You Little Beauty

Jockeys with more than 1000 winners

WD Skelton	2156
DA Peake	2079
LA O'Sullivan	1862
DM Walsh	1747
RJ Skelton	1739
NG Harris	1618
JC Collett	1525
WJ Broughton	1446
GF Hughes	1276
CW Johnson	1228
GA Phillips	1176
PD Johnson	1138
LJ Ellis	1062
MR Campbell	1060

Horse Whisperers and Shouters

Trainers with more than 1000 winners (partnership wins in brackets)

DJ O'Sullivan	(1366)	1877
RJ Cochrane	(34)	1520
PD O'Sullivan	(1306)	1402
GA Rogerson	(329)	1361
ND Eales		1275
WA Winsloe		1200
TJ McKee	(852)	1167
CM Jillings	(529)	1156
RC Verner	(236)	1079
E Temperton	(4)	1004
W Sanders	(500)	1002

From Saint Hippo to Spring Rain

Top New Zealand stake-earners

1892–93	Saint Hippo	2801	1915–16	Desert Gold	8350
1893–94	Blue Fire	2082	1916–17	The Toff	4255
1894–95	Mahaki	1434	1917–18	Estland	3815
1895–96	Euroclydon	2090	1918–19	Gloaming	6765
1896–97	Multiform	2761	1919–20	Amythas	7695
1897–98	Multiform	2144	1920–21	Gloaming	5630
1898–99	Screw Gun	1782	1921–22	Gloaming	5765
1899–1900	Advance	3251	1922–23	Enthusiasm	5942
1900–01	Renown	3185	1923–24	Ballymena	5665
1901–02	Nonette	3960	1924–25	Count Cavour	5577
1902–03	Achilles	2865	1925–26	Rapine	4930
1903–04	Gladstone	2665	1926–27	Commendation	6187
1904–05	Mahutonga	2970	1927–28	Star Stranger	4630
1905–06	Noctuiform	3747	1928–29	Gay Ballerina	3950
1906–07	Master Delaval	2365	1929–30	Hunting Cry	4985
1907–08	Zimmerman	3375	1930–31	Karapoti	5007
1908–09	All Red	3230	1931–32	Bronze Eagle	3840
1909–10	Formby	2610	1932–33	Silver Scorn	4310
1910–11	Danube	3185	1933–34	Red Manfred	2280
1911–12	Counterfeit	3547	1934–35	Sporting Blood	2345
1912–13	Bon Reve	3742	1935–36	Cuddle	2985
1913–14	Merry Roe	3130	1936–37	Wild Chase	3210
1914–15	Warstep	6360	1937–38	Stretto	3540

1938–39	Defaulter	4515
1939–40	Beau Vite	5365
1940–41	Kindergarten	7330
1941–42	Happy Ending	3765
1942–43	Rakanui	4480
1943–44	Lord Chancellor	5350
1944–45	First In	5682
1945–46	Golden Souvenir	10,545
1946–47	Bruce	8030
1947–48	Signal Officer	11,780
1948–49	Tauloch	13,475
1949–50	Beaumaris	15,881
1950–51	Main Brace	21,590
1951–52	Dalray	14,582
1952–53	Mt Denby	11,045
1953–54	Coaltown	12,450
1954–55	Somerset Fair	13,715
1955–56	Syntax	19,105
1956–57	Passive	14,915
1957–58	Red Eagle	12,265
1958–59	Froth	12,405
1959–60	Fair Filou	8690
1960–61	Ruato	9160
1961–62	Otematata	10,490
1962–63	Stipulate	16,110
1963–64	Gay Filou	9976
1964–65	Empyreus	11,680
1965–66	Apa	12,600
1966–67	Star Belle	16,340
1967–68	Bright Chief	34,330
1968–69	City Court	29,980
1969–70	Il Tempo	59,590
1970–71	Kirrama	38,655
1971–72	Sailing Home	60,780
1972–73	Duty Free	41,535
1973–74	Battle Heights	76,895
1974–75	Kia Maia	67,765
1975–76	Balmarino	85,075
1976–77	Royal Cadenza	78,775
	Grey Way	78,775

1977–78	Uncle Remus	130,100
1978–79	La Mer	76,675
1979–80	Blue Denim	112,075
1980–81	Drum	137,150
1981–82	Altitude	128,335
1982–83	Our Flight	205,175
1983–84	I'm Henry	208,300
1984–85	Secured Deposit	169,850
1985–86	Bonecrusher	379,675
1986–87	Tidal Light	397,150
1987–88	Daria's Fun	399,750
1988–89	Horlicks	696,625
1989–90	Horlicks	712,750
1990–91	Rua Rukuna	574,500
1991–92	Castletown	455,250
1992–93	The Phantom Chance	269,800
1993–94	Miltak	257,500
1994–95	Avedon	266,125
1995–96	Roysyn	331,850
1996–97	Great Command	361,450
1997–98	Tycoon Lil	344,575
1998–99	So Casual	315,250
1999–2000	Spring Rain	347,625

NB: Earnings in £ until 1967, and $ thereafter.

HUNTING

Stalkers and Shooters

Prior to Captain James Cook's first voyage to New Zealand, the only animals to be successfully introduced into New Zealand were the Polynesian rat and the kuri or Polynesian dog.

The pig was the first real game animal in New Zealand.

In 1876, the rabbit was seen to be increasing in vast numbers. In the same year, the first rabbit legislation was introduced, which led to the introduction of ferrets, stoats and weasels to keep rabbit numbers down.

Feral animals in the 1870s thrived and they

were often a ready source of fresh meat for New Zealanders.

Between 1851 and 1923, red deer were released into New Zealand. The Wairarapa herd was established by one stag and two hinds from the Royal Park at Windsor. The Prince Consort presented them to the people of New Zealand and they were liberated near Taratahi, Carterton.

The highland stags of Otago were the only pure Scottish-bred red deer in New Zealand, and within a few years they were growing large antlers — far bigger than their Scottish counterparts.

By 1900, only red and fallow deer had increased in number to allow hunting, although there were also herds of axis and Ceylon elk (sambar).

The 1920s were among the golden years of deerstalking in New Zealand. The Otago herd, with their impressive antlers, had become world famous.

In 1930, all protection was removed from deer, chamois and thar.

The early settlers snared the abundant wood pigeon and brown parrot.

Wild cattle roamed the Manapouri region in the 1890s.

In 1839, EJ Wakefield saw wild cattle near the entrance of Pelorus Sound.

In 1841, cattle were introduced to the Chatham Islands. Many of them became wild in a short space of time.

In 1866, the Otago Acclimatisation Society liberated 60 rabbits. By 1878, rabbits had reached Lake Wakatipu, leaving devastation behind them, and a few years later the greater part of Otago and all of Southland were feeling the pinch of rabbit-ravaged pastures.

It is believed that the blame for importing the very first rabbits into New Zealand belongs to a private individual who released a pair near Invercargill.

The introduced sika deer failed to establish themselves in Otago in the 1890s.

Five species of deer failed to establish themselves after being introduced to New Zealand before 1890.

In one year (1892–93), 503,546 rabbit skins were paid for on a single estate — the K-Station in Central Otago, which covers 206,695 acres. One hundred hunters were employed all year just to trap and poison rabbits.

Falconer Larkworthy was responsible for the establishment of fallow deer in several parts of the North Island.

The names of Conrad and Harold Hodgkinson were well known in the early days of hunting in Otago.

Frank Newport was described as one of the great stalkers of Nelson Province.

President Theodore Roosevelt of the United States played an important part in introducing wapiti, the large North American deer, into New Zealand, when he presented a herd of wapiti to the colony in 1904.

In 1904, five thar or Caucasian mountain goats were presented to New Zealand by the Duke of Bedford. They arrived from London on board the SS *Corinthic*. Originally, six were presented, but one was lost overboard during the journey.

In 1906, a number of red deer were presented to New Zealand by Miss Audrey Chirnside of Werribee Park, Victoria, Australia, and liberated near Lake Kaniere.

The first open season on sambar deer in the Marton district was held in 1906.

In 1906, Japanese red deer were liberated near Rangitaiki in the Northern Kaimanawas and, according to reports, acclimatised successfully.

In 1906, a good year for animal liberation, three pairs of Tasmanian black-and-grey opossums were set free on Mr Benn's run and seven on the northern shores of Lake Rotoiti. A further 10 pairs were let loose near Kumara on the West Coast, and on the slopes of Mount Tuhua.

Four hundred and ten pheasants were reared and liberated during 1907.

The Department of Tourist and Health Resorts was responsible for the introduction of various game animals from abroad. In 1905, they purchased five blacktail deer from the US and liberated them at Tarawera, Hawke's Bay. In the same year, 18 elk and 19 Virginian deer were either purchased from or were presented by the USA; and in 1907, eight chamois were presented by the Emperor of Austria.

In 1909, three bharal sheep were liberated in the Mount Cook District.

The two sambar deer that were purchased in Noumea, New Caledonia and liberated at Galatea, near Rotorua, were in fact risa deer.

SOCIAL CHANGES

What Happens When You're Not Looking

Early houses in New Zealand had outside toilets.

In 1901, 40 per cent of New Zealanders declared themselves to be Anglican, 22 per cent Presbyterian, 14 per cent Catholic and 10 per cent Methodist. In recent years, the largest category has been that of 'no denomination'.

In 1915, a crowd in Wanganui attacked shops operated by Germans, following the sinking of the *Lusitania*.

Until 1917, New Zealand pubs and bars closed at 10 p.m.

As a wartime measure, hotel bars began closing at six o'clock in 1917.

Soldiers returning from the war in 1919 reversed the vote for New Zealand to go dry.

In 1920, the Anzac Day Act declared Anzac Day to be a public holiday.

In 1923, it became possible to get a divorce after three years' separation.

Daylight saving was tried for one year in 1927.

During the Great Depression, Gordon Coates, the Minister of Finance, was reputed to have told a delegation of hungry unemployed to 'eat grass'.

In 1935, English coins ceased being legal tender in New Zealand.

The school-leaving age was set at 15 in 1944.

Friday-night shopping became a regular event in New Zealand in the 1950s and 1960s.

New Zealand's population passed the two million mark in 1952.

In 1954, a Special Committee on Moral Delinquency in Children and Adolescents was set up, in response to teenage delinquency, teddy boys, bodgies and widgies.

Invercargill experienced a book-burning episode in 1955, as police came down hard on pornography. At the same time, New Zealand libraries banned books by US writer Mickey Spillane.

In 1962, Auckland had seven licensed restaurants.

There has been a declining trend in the number of marriages in New Zealand in recent years. In 1971, there were 27,199. In 2000, the number had dropped to 20,655.

Since the early 1970s, the average age of those getting married has risen.

An Auckland jury, in 1972, declared the musical *Hair* was not indecent.

The Domestic Purposes Benefit (DPB) was introduced in New Zealand in 1973. The number of solo parents receiving this benefit has increased by 10 per cent for every year since its introduction.

In 1973, New Zealand's population crested three million and our overseas debt was recorded as being one billion dollars.

In September 1977, over 10,000 New Zealanders were waiting for a new phone connection, such was the incompetence of the government-operated phone company.

Saturday shopping commenced in New Zealand in 1980.

In the 1980s, personal growth seminars and 'workshops' became popular for the affluent middle classes. Shamanism, alternative health, reincarnation, inner awareness, rebirthing, self-actualisation, neurolinguistic programming, aliveness training and actual realisation were just some of the 'products' peddled.

Gym culture also emerged in the 1980s.

In 1981, Tania Harris, a 22-year-old Auckland sales representative, organised a protest march bemoaning the frequent industrial stoppages bedevilling the country.

The arrival in New Zealand waters of the nuclear-powered USS *Texas* in 1983 triggered off a 20,000-strong protest march down Queen Street, Auckland.

In 1984, *Metro* magazine published an article entitled 'From feminism to Fascism — Is this what wimmin want?' Among the sundry acts of retribution from outraged feminists was to send the editor used sanitary pads in the mail.

New Zealand's unemployment rate hit 80,000 in 1984, which was comparable with Great Depression levels.

During the 1988 Telethon for victims of child sexual abuse, the claim was made, based on statistics supplied by the Mental Health Foundation, that one in four girls had experienced sexual abuse, half of them by their own fathers. The figures were palpably overstated.

In 1989, the first experiment in Sunday trading in supermarkets was undertaken.

The minimum age to be able to marry in New Zealand is 16.

Solo parent families made up 18 per cent of all New Zealand families in 1996.

The Department of Work and Income was established in 1998, combining the Department of Social Welfare's income support unit, the New Zealand Employment Service and the Community Employment Group.

On average, New Zealanders spend about two hours a day watching TV, DVDs or videos.

In New Zealand, there are over 300 food banks providing food parcels to needy New Zealanders.

In 2001, 63 per cent of all solo parents receiving the DPB were those whose marriages or long-term de facto relationships had ended in separation or divorce.

In 2001, 22.9 per cent of New Zealand households were one-person arrangements.

One-family households in New Zealand in 2001 accounted for 60.7 per cent of the total.

In 2001, over 11,000 households consisted of eight or more people.

In 2001, there were over 21,000 inquiries to the Human Rights Commission in New Zealand. A couple of years earlier that figure was closer to 10,000.

In 1906, there were 151 divorces in New Zealand. In 2001, the number had escalated to 9700.

Prostitution was decriminalised in New Zealand in 2003 and licensed brothels became permissible.

A Growth Industry

Divorce rates

Year	Number of divorces	Divorce rate (% of total marriages)
1991	9152	12.0
1992	9114	11.9
1993	9193	12.0
1994	9213	11.9
1995	9574	12.3
1996	10,009	12.7
1997	9754	12.3
1998	10,067	12.7
1999	9931	12.6
2000	9699	12.3

Feel the Benefit

Special needs grants

Number of payments and amount paid for the year ended 30 June 2001:

Main Benefit	Number	Amount ($)
Domestic Purposes Benefit	131,572	15,690,992
Community Wage (job seeker)	125,094	14,730,966
Low income earner	43,329	6,557,391
Community Wage (sickness)	34,751	3,760,171
Community Wage (invalid's)	3740	3,884,328
New Zealand Superannuation	6183	751,064
Community Wage (training)	3482	374,292
Widow's Benefit	3175	347,444
Transitional Retirement Benefit	1013	107,013
Orphan's/Unsupported Child Benefit	290	36,866
Veteran's Pension	75	10,876
TOTAL	**352,704**	**46,251,403**

Special needs grants paid by reason for grant:

	Number	Amount ($)
Food	273,186	24,423,094
Medical, in rest home	45,173	10,783,222
Other	28,158	3,669,210
Released prisoner	11,847	3,747,938
School uniform	10,410	1,747,211
Striking worker	6778	548,468
Emergency travel	3685	226,339
Accommodation	2305	714,655
Clothing	833	114,407
Electricity and gas	707	157,872
Beds, tables, chairs	237	71,645
Funeral and tangihanga	221	23,047
Fire loss and burglary	158	19,748
Rural sector	6	4848
TOTAL	**383,704**	**46,251,704**

KIWI THINGS

From the 'Long Drop' to the 'Lost Tribe'

Aftermatch function — a gathering convened after a game, featuring beer and bravado

Anorak — a hip-length waterproof jacket, often with a hood

Artic — an articulated truck

Bach — a holiday home

Bare-bottom haka — a haka featuring the baring of buttocks as a mark of contempt

Barracouta — a loaf of bread with a raised crust

Belly-buster — an awkward or failed dive into water

Big smoke — the city

Bitser — something made up of bits and pieces

Boilover — an unexpected result

Boob — prison

Bowser — a pump for dispensing petrol, or beer

Brown eye — the baring of the buttocks to cause outrage or surprise

Brumby — a wild horse usually associated with the central North Island

Buckshee — something free

Buzzy bee — iconic Kiwi wooden toy

Cab Sav —abbreviation of Cabernet Sauvignon

Cabbage train — the overnight Picton–Christchurch express goods train carrying vegetables for the Christchurch market

Chrissie pressie — Christmas present

Chuddy — chewing gum

Cow gravy — fresh or liquid cow muck

Cuppa — a cup of tea or coffee

Cuz — cousin

Dag — an amusing Kiwi

De facto — a permanent, live-in extramarital relationship

Dog tucker — in a no-win situation

Donkey lick — to beat decisively

Dry horrors — alcoholic dehydration

Dunny budgie — blowfly

Early shower — having been sent off in a game of rugby

Electric puha — marijuana

Ensuite — a bathroom attached to a bedroom

Ex — former partner

Fart sack — sleeping bag

Flat — a dwelling originally

characterised by a single storey, hence its 'flat' aspect

Fly cemetery — a fruit square full of currants and raisins

Flying fox — a means of conveying materials or people on a cable

Foxie — a fox terrier

Foyer — open arrival area at a hotel (more commonly known as the entry or lobby in other countries)

Garage sales — the selling of unwanted household goods

Gib board — abbreviation of Gibraltar Board™

Golden Shears — a national championship for competitive shearing

Goob — a lump of phlegm

Goolies — testicles

'Granny Herald' — nickname of Auckland's daily newspaper

Gurgler — as in 'down the gurgler', lost, irretrievable

Gutser — to make a mistake

Hash house — a cheap boarding house

Head sherang — the boss

Heaps — lots

Hiding to nothing — an impossible task or project

Hissy fit — losing one's cool

Hokey pokey ice cream — vanilla ice cream containing lumps and shards of hokey pokey made from golden syrup and sugar

Homebake — home-made illicit drugs

Hoodickey — variation on thingamabob

Hoondom — collective universe of hoons

Hospital pass — rugby term for a pass to a player about to be tackled heavily

House of Pain — Carisbrook Rugby Grounds, Dunedin

Jack-up — an underhand deal

Jandals — rubber sandals known as flip-flops and thongs in other countries (the word is believed to have derived from 'Japanese Sandals')

Janola — bleach

'Jap' imports — more affordable Japanese cars which flooded the market in the 1990s

Joint — prison

Judder bars — speed bumps for Kiwis

Jumping spider — a cave weta

Kai — food

Kaingaroa Forest — planted in the 1930s' Depression, this expanse of *Pinus radiata* is reputedly the largest man-made forest in the world

Kaimanawa horses — wild horses that feed off the tussocklands in the foothills of the Kaimanawa Ranges — the herds are believed to have originated from unwanted domestic and military horses released from the nearby Waiouru Army Camp

Kindling — thin wood to start a fire

King Country spanner — a Te Kuiti bottle opener

Kingie — a kingfish

Kiwiana — collectibles celebrating New Zealand's uniqueness

Kohanga reo — language nest

Lager phone — a broom handle with beer-bottle tops attached, used as a percussion instrument

Laughing gear — mouth

Leaner — a small, high table found in pubs

Lemon & Paeroa — a fizzy mixture of lemon flavouring and mineral water from the town of Paeroa (affectionately known as L & P)

Loosie — a loose forward in rugby

Maori bread — rewena bread, usually made with fermented potato yeast

Maori strum — a particular way of strumming a guitar

Mates' rates — reduced rates for friends or acquaintances

Milkbars — where young folk of the 1950s used to hang out, to listen to the jukebox, drink milkshakes and generally escape the cloying conservatism of the average Kiwi home

Moko — Maori tattoo

Molesworth Station — New Zealand's largest sheep and cattle station, covering 1800 square kilometres of high country between Marlborough and Canterbury

Monkey oyster — an Auckland rock oyster

Mooloo — the cow mascot of the Waikato rugby team

Morepork — a small, brown native owl

Mutton birds — oily seabirds regarded as traditional delicacies for Maori and other New Zealanders

Nappy valley — dormitory suburbs where young couples with children lived

Nibbles — small food items

Nippon clipon — Japanese-made extension to the Auckland Harbour Bridge

No. 8 wire — heavy-guage steel wire that has been used for manifold purposes

Octopus clamp — a wrestling hold and a more generalised 'strong-hold'

Ohu — state-sponsored communes instigated by the Labour Government in 1973

Op shop — second-hand shop

Overseas Experience ('OE') — young adults undergoing international travel, usually to the other side of the world

Oz — Australia

Paddock — a playing field

Palmy — abbreviation for Palmerston North

Pav — short for pavlova cake

Perk — work-related gift or advantage

Pet Day — when kids take their pets to school

Piecart — a mobile eating place

Piece of piss — something easy to accomplish

Pig's back — a successful venture

Pigeon post — the sending of messages tied to the legs of homing pigeons was the basis of what is believed to be the first airmail service in the world — between Great Barrier Island and Auckland

Pisser — a pub

Pokie — a poker machine

Puku — stomach

Pygmy pine — the world's smallest pine tree which grows in alpine regions of New Zealand

Railway pies — overnight sustenance once associated with railway refreshment rooms

Remittance men — English 'settlers' who received a regular 'remittance' from the home country on the understanding that they would never return — bounders, ne'er-do-wells and outcasts who were as unpopular in New Zealand bush camps and goldfields as they were in England — or from whence they came

Republic of Whangamomona Day — tongue-in-cheek 'breakaway' state in inland Taranaki that celebrates its 'republican' status once a year

Rugby, racing and beer — at one time regarded as traditional New Zealand culture, all three aspects of the 'holy trinity' have been under threat in recent decades — fewer people attend rugby matches, racing is having financial difficulties and wine drinking has made inroads

Rural delivery — contractors delivering mail and parcels to country areas of New Zealand

Scarfies — university students from Otago University, where the cold winters dictate the wearing of scarves

Semple's Tank — during World War II, the Minister of Public Works, Robert Semple, had his new Caterpillar tractor encased in armour plating and added a gun turret, in an endeavor to help the war effort — it didn't

Service cars — before buses, large American cars were used to ferry passengers, and surprising amounts of freight, down New Zealand country roads

Sharemilking — a typically Kiwi arrangement where a dairy farm owner allows an unpaid worker to take a share of the gross profits instead of paying wages or a salary

Smoko — a Kiwi tea or coffee break, based on the fact that smoking a cigarette at the same time was once an everyday occurrence

South of the Bombay Hills — a saying based on Auckland's pre-eminence in terms of population — first comes Auckland ('North of the Bombay Hills'), and then comes the rest of New Zealand

Stephens Island wren — a species of wren that used to be found on this small, lighthouse island in Cook Strait — the rare bird was found in 1894 when the lighthouse keeper's cat caught several wren specimens; after several more cat catches the wren vanished altogether

Suffragettes— New Zealand women who fought for the right to vote for all women

Sugarbags — versatile hessian bags that were often used for functions other than carrying sugar — during the Great Depression they were converted into shirts and girls' dresses

Sunbathing — ritualistic pastime in the New Zealand summer, although with the discovery of a hole in the ozone layer and its attendant skin cancer risks, such hedonistic habits have lost some of their allure

Tamarillos — a subtropical fruit from Brazil and Peru, once known as tree tomatoes

Tane Mahuta — the largest New Zealand kauri tree, located in Waipoua Forest Sanctuary

Tangi — Maori funeral

Taniwha — a Maori spirit, seen as a guardian of waterways

Taranaki gate — an immensely practical, if unglamorous way of building a gate, using barbed wire and fence stakes

'Taranaki wool' — tongue-in-cheek name for the ear fungus found in the bush and harvested and exported as a delicacy to China in the 1880s and 1890s

Tea tree — colloquial name for manuka and kanuka trees

Ten-acre blocks — rural lifestyle living, often close to cities

The Auks — the Auckland rugby team

The Great Fleet — the trek of 12 canoes long believed to have brought the Maori to New Zealand

The haka — traditional Maori war dance

The hangi — traditional Maori method of cooking food

The Hawera Republic — settlers of the Hawera district declared their 'Independence' in 1879 when the government refused to help them in their fight against the Maori

The Honourable Roddy — the largest nugget of gold discovered in New Zealand, weighing 99 ounces, 12 pennyweights and 12 grains

The hui — a Maori custom that has become part of the wider Kiwi community; a meeting to discuss issues and hopefully reach resolutions

The jet boat — invented by Sir William Hamilton, this work of Kiwi ingenuity has been adopted worldwide

The largest Polynesian city in the world (Auckland) — with the immigration of thousands of Maori to Auckland from rural areas and the influx of Pacific Islanders from Polynesia, the number of people of Polynesian descent living in Auckland amounted to over 280,000 in the year 2001

The log of wood — rugby's Ranfurly Shield, a unique aspect of New Zealand's sporting life

The long drop — an outside toilet featuring a deep hole designed to thwart flies

The longest place name in the world — located in Hawke's Bay near Porangahau is Taumatawhaka-tangihangakoauauotamateapokai-whenuakitanatahu, which just pips a Welsh name in its claim as the longest place name in the world — a basic translation is 'the summit where Tamatea Pokai Whenua played his flute to his beloved'

The lost tribe — a romantic notion of a tribe or group of Maori living in the wilderness of Fiordland

The Mainland — an affectionate reference to the South Island, which was once known as the 'Middle' island

The murder house — schoolchildren's name for the school dental clinic

The New Zealand Christmas tree — the pohutukawa, which flowers in the three or four weeks leading up to Christmas

The oldest hotel in New Zealand — the Duke of Marlborough Hotel in Russell, Bay of Islands, claims the oldest liquor licence in the land

The Pigroot — an old miners' route into Central Otago, which turns off at Palmerston and meanders through to the site of the Old Maniatoto goldfields

The Pohutu Geyser — largest of the surviving geysers at Whakarewarewa, Rotorua

The quarter-acre section — cornerstone of the baby-boomer generation when family homes were placed uniformly on quarter-acre sections

The Queen Street Riots — the first riots occurred in 1932 in the depths of the Great Depression, when protesting Post and Telegraph workers were joined by hundreds of unemployed, who turned on police and ran amuck — in 1984, a free concert in Aotea Square got out of hand, with similar results

The Queen's chain — although mischievous types have suggested that this is something to do with royal toilet-flushing systems, it is generally accepted as relating to public access along river banks, lake shores and the seafront

The Riverside Community — New Zealand's longest-surviving alternative community; having been established in 1938, it achieved a measure of notoriety by being anti-war during World War II

The Shaky Isles — a laconic reference to New Zealand, with its high incidence of earthquakes

The silver fern — the official New Zealand plant, often used as a symbol by New Zealand sporting teams

The Slump — the Great Depression, the most serious civil event in twentieth-century New Zealand history; following the Wall Street crash in the US, massive unemployment and social misery descended on New Zealand

The Wairau Massacre — the death of 22 Nelson settlers following a dispute with Maori in Marlborough — these days it is more commonly known as the Wairau Affray

Tohunga — the Maori priest class

Ute — a small utility vehicle

Vegetable caterpillar — This strange specimen begins life as a porina moth caterpillar which then becomes the host of a type of fungus; the fungus produces a rhyzome that protrudes above ground

Wop wops — the back of beyond

Working dogs — New Zealand's specially-bred sheep dogs, traditionally bred from border collies

KIWI TYPES & STEREOTYPES

Ankle Biters and Boguns

A right Joe — a fool

Amber gamblers — drivers who run the amber traffic light

Ankle biters — small children

Arseholes — unpleasant types

Backdoor man — married woman's fancy Dan who sneaks in when the husband's out

Bandicoot — eccentric

Battler — tenacious tryer

Big noter — person who tries to impress

Blatherskite — a boaster

Blockie — someone who lives on a lifestyle block

Bloke — an 'ordinary' Kiwi male, down-to-earth, unpretentious, often hard-working

Bludger — a loafer

Bodgie — a male member of a street gang of the 1950s

Bogun — an uncouth or stupid young male

Bone wearer — a middle-class liberal Pakeha

Boobhead — a prison inmate

Boofhead — a stupid person

Boxhead — a fool

Boy racer — a young male car driver who uses the highway as the school playground

Broken arse — someone with the lowest status in a prison population

Bunrunner — a person who ferries ready-to-eat food around offices

Bush Baptist — a religious person, not a member of an official church

Cardigan brigade — older public servants

Chardonnay socialist — a liberal-left politician usually associated with Helen Clark's government

Chunder bunny — a student unable to hold down a lot of booze

Cocky — a farmer

Commo — a member of the Communist Party

Conchies — conscientious objectors, usually to war service

Cookaroos — unusual high-country cooks, with strange culinary habits and debatable claims to fame

Couch kumara — a New Zealander who watches a lot of TV while lying on the couch

Cowspanker — a dairy farmer

Cuba Street Yank — a Kiwi who parades the main street with the dressy confidence of an American

Deadbeat — a person down on his luck

Dero — a down-and-outer

Dickhead — a stupid person

Dinkum Kiwi — a 'real' Kiwi

Dirt tracker — a mid-week rugby-playing tourist

Dirty dirty — a rugby player not required, not even as a reserve

Do-gooders — overzealous volunteers, who are perceived to be 'serving the community' for self-serving reasons, one of which is the hope that someone will nominate them for the New Zealand honours list

Dole bludger — a loafer, living on the dole

Doolan — a person of the Roman Catholic faith

Double yoker — a stupid person within a prison population; occasional name for a set of twins

Drip whisker — an unkind term for a woman

Drongo — a stupid person

Drop kick — a stupid person

Dropper — an obsolete term for sly-groggers

Dweeb — an undynamic young male

Egg — an idiot

Feminazi — a radical feminist

Fernrooter — humorous term for a New Zealander

Flax bag terrorist — a Maori activist

Folkie — a folk singer

Foodie — a food seller or restaurant owner

Fuck knuckle — a stupid fool

Fuckwit — another stupid fool

Fundie — a fundamentalist Protestant Christian

Gal Blacks — unaccepted name for the New Zealand women's rugby team

Geri — as in geriatric

Goose — a difficult customer

Grasshopper — a prison informer

Greenie — a conservationist or environmentalist

Gripper — a male masturbator

Guppy — young upwardly-mobile professional gay

Hippy — a member of the 'dropout' counter-culture of the 1970s

Ho — a prostitute

Homie — a peer of a group or gang, mainly Polynesian, who tend to wear baseball caps backwards, baggy trousers and like rap music

Hoonchaser — a traffic cop

Huckery mole — an unpleasant or promiscuous woman

Jack Nohi — a nosey person

Jafa — an acronym for 'just another fucking Aucklander'

Joe Hop — rhyming slang for a cop

Journo — a journalist

Kakapo cuddler — an overzealous conservationist of native species

Kerosene cowboy — a jet pilot

Larrikin — a lively adolescent

Left-footer — a Roman Catholic

Littlie — an infant

Lolly boy — a boy who sold confectionery off a tray at the movies

Loosie — a loose forward in rugby

Mainlander — a South Islander

Mickey Doolan — an Irish Roman Catholic

Milkbar cowboy — a motorbike-riding youth associated with milkbars of the 1950s

Milko — an early name for a milkman

Moll — a prostitute

Mongie — a member of the Mongrel Mob

Monkey man — bank manager

Munter — a fool

Music Nazi — a politically correct person who decides the type of music everyone must enjoy

Muso — a musician

Musterer's dog — a tall thin man

Nat — a member of the National Party

Nerd — bookish, computer-age 'square'

New chum — a novice

New Enzedder — a new immigrant

Ngati Pakeha — a New Zealander of European origin

Ning-nong — a fool

No-hoper — a down-and-outer

Nong — a fool

Numbskull — a fool

Off-sider — a sidekick, assistant or, some would say, your average openside flanker

Ordinary blokess — a New Zealand woman unfettered by extreme feminism and political correctness

Pakeha — initially a pale-skinned, non-Polynesian New Zealander; nowadays, whatever you want it to mean

Pillion pussy — a girl riding pillion for a milkbar cowboy

Pisshead — a heavy drinker or alcoholic

Pollie — a politician

Pom — a British immigrant

Poofter — a blowhard, or male homesexual

Pro — a prostitute

Probie — a probation officer

Prody hopper — an unkind name for a Protestant

Quack — a doctor, or a medical charlatan

Queen Street farmer — a city businessperson owning a farm as an investment

Ratbag — a right bastard

Red lady — a prostitute

Rellie — a relation or relative

Ridie — a show person who arranges rides on merry-go-rounds and Ferris wheels

Ring barker — a circumcised male

Road hopper — a hitch-hiker

Rob's mob — supporters of divisive Prime Minister, Robert Muldoon

Rogernomes — believers in Rogernomics, the economic policies of Roger Douglas

Rough guts — an uncouth person

Sausage jockey — a prostitute

Scarfie — a student from Dunedin

Screw — a prison officer

Shagnasty — an unpleasant Kiwi

Sheep shaggers — unpleasant term for New Zealanders

Ship girl — an on-board prostitute

Sicko — a mentally ill person

Six-day bike rider — a Seventh-Day Adventist

Skatie — a skateboard rider

Skinboy — an uncircumcised male

Skinheads — shaven-headed white supremacists

Skite — a boaster

Slob — an untidy person

Sly-grogger — a purveyor of illegal grog in the days of booze prohibition

Smart arse — a show-off, skite

Snag — a sensitive new age guy

Snork — a baby

Snott — a fool

Sparkie — an electrician

Stairdancer — a thief who specialises in stealing from people in high-rise buildings

Stickybeak — a nosy parker; a curtain jerker

Subbie — a subcontractor

Swatty blouse — a person of unmanly intellect

Tall halfback — a person of average height

Tall poppy — a successful Kiwi, often inciting envy

Tin arse — a lucky person

Tin bum — a lucky person

Tonk — an effeminate person

Town bike — a promiscuous small-town woman

Truckie — a truck driver

Tussock jumper — a South Island high-country musterer

Tyre kicker — a time-waster; a person who looks but never buys

Vollie — a voluntary worker

Water burner — a shearers' cook

Westie — a person from West Auckland

Wet hen — a stupid person

Whaka blonde — a Maori woman

Wharfie — a watersider

Whingeing Poms — a stereotype of British immigrants

Widgie — the female counterpart of Bodgie

Wimmin' — women — in politically correct terms, a sarcastic way of emphasising, through misspelling, how some women, often overzealously, wanted 'women' to sound

Woolly woofter — poofter

Word Nazi — a politically correct person who decides what words are inappropriate

Word police — similar to Word Nazi but they are often sanctioned by the state

Wowzer — an anti-booze person

Yahoo — a loud lout

Yuppy — young upwardly-mobile professional

Zambuck — a St John's ambulance attendant at sporting functions

BIZARRE KIWI BEHAVIOUR & MORE 'NORMAL STUFF'

Don't Try This at Home

Streaking

In 2004, a scantily clad young woman streaked during an All Black practice session in Rangiora. It continued the proud tradition of streaking in New Zealand which has included:

The cricket fan wearing nothing but sneakers and a smile who ran across the one-day pitch at Eden Park. After being chased by security types he hurdled the picket fence, narrowly failing to leave his manhood behind, before being bundled up and processed.

The rugby spectator who provided the extra, unwanted man in a backline move on a perishingly cold day. Although he was stark naked, his bluish tinge, brought on by the snow-flecked southerly, almost matched the light-blue jerseys of his 'team-mates', and he escaped detection for a minute or two.

The two male student streakers who raced through a crowded conference hall with the intention of shocking conference-goers before escaping out the back entrance. Unfortunately someone had locked the rear exit and the two streakers were obliged to retrace their steps back through the chortling conference crowd where, rather than slink away cowering and shamed, they circulated freely amongst the guests, chatting amiably and drinking champagne.

Bungy jumping

Out of the 'don't try this at home' basket, bungy jumping has become about as Kiwi as *Lord of the Rings* and Colin Meads. The idea is for tourists to jump from a high point, like a bridge or a building, while attached by a piece of elastic rubber which prevents them from being dashed to death on whatever lies below. AJ Hackett is credited with developing and commercialising the idea which has certainly gained cult status in New Zealand with young tourists. The idea is said to be based on a tradition practised by inhabitants of Pentecost Island who, to prove their manhood, leap from high towers with fibrous ropes around their ankles. And, of course, an Irish-Kiwi postured the notion of Irish bungy jumping — jumping with no attachments at all!

Gumboot throwing

An activity that has become associated with the township of Taihape, in which gumboots are hurled down the main street once a year and the winner is obviously the thrower who is able to throw the gumboot the furthest.

Pie-eating contests

Based on New Zealand's traditional affection for meat pies, this phenomenon involves contestants attempting to eat as many pies as they can in one sitting — or standing. A popular pastime with university students, who have been known to incorporate beer drinking and sprinting into the contest, with often disastrous effects on the digestive systems of the contestants.

Knicker twisting

A little-known and barely legal activity associated with drunken student parties, in which mainly willing participants subject themselves to unorthodox wrenching of the undergarments.

Skulling

Another activity often associated with students and traditional rugby teams, in which glasses of beer are dispatched by

the contestants in the twinkling of an eye and an opening of the throat. The winner is invariably the person who can account for as much beer in the shortest time.

Beer sitting

This activity probably evolved as a reaction to the excesses of beer skulling. Participants in this minority activity see how long they can confine themselves to a single glass of beer, during the course of the activity's duration. The latter have been known to continue for days.

Projectile vomiting

Often convened in conjunction with pie-eating marathons and drinking contests, this often disgusting activity requires contestants to vomit over as great a distance as they can manage. The New Zealand record is believed to be held by a former Otago University student.

Rural shock treatment

A laddish prank in which inebriated sons of cockies urinate on electric fences, following functions at the local community hall.

Geek Olympics

A variation on the 'Nerd International Games', this series of competitions coincided with the 2004 Greek Olympics. Events in the Geek Olympics held at Waikato University included CD-Rom throwing and motherboard assembly.

Cat swinging

Thankfully this little-practised activity was only once included as an event in the Students' Olympics. More a shocking, throwaway line than a serious intention, it was obviously based on the Kiwi saying, when confronted by a pokie living area — like some student flats — that 'there wasn't even room to swing a cat'.

Do it yourself (DIY) for someone else

There have been reports of well-intentioned Kiwis painting other people's houses, or making over barbecue areas without their knowledge, as a gesture of goodwill and reward for outstanding service to the community. Unfortunately, on more than one occasion the 'do-gooders' have gone to the wrong address, with mixed results and reactions.

Corrugated ironing

'As Kiwi as corrugated iron', became a well-known and much-used term in New Zealand. Corrugated ironing was the practice of using corrugated iron for everything from roofs and fences to outdoor toilets and compost bins.

Backyard shedding

A distinctly Kiwi-male activity, involving backyard sheds where men can secrete themselves away from the aggravations of the household. All manner of blokish activities can be indulged in, including stripping cars, making home brew and entertaining your mates, while generally kicking tyres and gutting fish. Sheds have also been used for more bizarre pastimes like smoking acrid substances, both legal and not so, and showing socket-wrench collections to nubile neighbours.

Coming out

The process whereby girls became young women in days gone by. A ball would be held, during which the girls, or debutantes as they were called, found themselves 'presented' to some dignitary, whereupon they became young women. The term 'coming out' later became associated with the process of 'coming out of the closet', where gay men and women made their sexual orientation publicly known.

Night carting

In pre-sewer — and septic tank — days, a council truck (the 'night cart'), used to empty toilet tins, often in the depths of the night. The night cart, and often its driver, took on a macabre aspect as it did its dirty deed. There have been reports of citizens undergoing their lawful business at night, only to have the toilet tin whisked out from under them by overzealous nightcarters. The mischievous suggestion was made, during the halcyon days of Rogernomics, that had night carts still been in existence, they too would have been subjected to market forces — night carts would have been opened up to competition.

Sheep tackling

A recently introduced pastime in areas of the King Country and the Volcanic Plateau, where supplies of sheep are plentiful. A useful adjunct to rugby training if you have to travel 300 kilometres to training. The sheep can also be used for rucking and mauling practice. Many sheep were released in the streets of Te Kuiti in recent times, in an attempt to give the town an identity, but unlike the bulls of Pamplona, the sheep refused to abide with a pre-arranged route of passage, and much applied sheep-tackling was required — including the input of famous All Black Colin Meads, before a semblance of common sense was restored.

Underwater snooker

A relatively rare and genuinely dangerous activity, particulary for those without gills, this underwater sport has, nevertheless, retained a toehold in more silly university centres.

Nude skydiving

Not for the faint-hearted, or the shambolic-of-buttock, this elitist activity requires at least one aeroplane, parachutes, and no clothes to speak of. A very liberating experience apparently, it is essentially perpendicular streaking.

Cricket in the rain

Given New Zealand's blotchy summers, this aberration was bound to gain favour, what with global warming and weather bombs. Reduced bowlers' run-ups and batting in raincoats have been features of this more manly form of cricket, where formerly the first friendly drift of an isolated shower would see chaps sprinting — faster than they had in the field — for the watertight, beer-welcoming pavilion.

Body contact bridge

A result of the increased levels of violence in society, even such a sit-down, stay-down activity as bridge has evolved to a point where contentious moves can expect to be accompanied by half-charges, a finger in the eye, and a general overturning of tables.

Crap shooting

A development on traditional crap shooting, this mutant has shooters poised in sheep paddocks with guns trained on the dag-ends of grazing sheep. The object of the activity is to take out sheep pellets before they hit the ground, and endeavouring at all times to leave the grazing sheep intact.

Tupperware parties

Gatherings, usually of Kiwi women, where purchases and procurements of plastic receptacles are made, along with a round of Chardonnay and gossip thrown in.

Amway mystique

In which complete strangers and occasional friends are invited to in-house gatherings to be inducted into a mysterious, apparently lucrative method of making big money, with promises of having that private dream come true: a new car, a bigger house, a trip to Europe. At no stage is it admitted that the fountain of new fortune is in fact 'Amway', until it becomes necessary to reveal the fact.

THE KIWI LANGUAGE

The Flightless Tongue

Sons of 'Crapper' — alternative terms for toilets
Bog
Bomb disposer
Can
Clanger
Dike
Dunny
John
Little house
Long drop
Loo
Outhouse
Shithouse
Shitter

Barking mad — alternative terms for vomiting
Barking
Chucking
Chucking up
Chundering
Coughing one's cud
Driving the porcelain bus
Gargling
Parking your lunch
Ralph
Spitting
Taking a load off
Technicolour yawning
Yodelling

Full as — alternative terms for drunkenness
Boozed
Cut
Drunk as a fish
Drunk as a lord
Drunk as a skunk
Fonged
Full as a boot
Full as a bull
Full as a butcher's dog
Full as a fart
Full as a lord
Legless
Nicely
Out of it
Out of one's tree
Out the monk

Pissed
Pissed as a fart
Plastered
Shickered
Sloshed
Tanked
Tiddly

The morning after — alternative terms for hangover
Alky's flu
Brewer's asthma
Dry horrors
DTs
The Joe Blakes
The shakes

Day tripper — falling over or coming undone
Arse over kite
Head over heels
Head over turkey

Underdone — not too bright
A sandwich short of a picnic
A sausage short of a barbeque
Not all the lights are on in the auditorium
Not the brightest crayon in the box
The lift doesn't go to the top floor
The scrum's down but no one's pushing
The wheel's still turning but the hamster's dead
To have the brains of a chocolate fish
Two kumara short of a hangi

Boots and All and a Box of Birds

Sundry Kiwi slang terms

A bit of how's-your-father — a punch-up on the rugby paddock

Angel gear — driving your car with the ignition turned off

Anzac shandy — champagne and beer

Away laughing — something that is easily managed

Away with the fairies — someone who is not focused

Back of beyond — a really remote place

Backbone of the country — farmers

Bang on — precisely correct

Beat about the bush — to prevaricate

Been there, done that — knowing all there is to know about a subject

Big ask — a difficult assignment

Big girl's blouse — a weak, timid male

Blue-rinse brigade — middle-class, elderly New Zealand women

Booboo — a mistake

Boots and all — wholehearted attempt

Box of birds — fit and happy

Bugger off — go away

Cockey's string — No. 8 fencing wire

Could eat a horse and chase its rider — very hungry

Couldn't lie straight in bed — a liar

Cunning as a shithouse rat — very cunning

Dag — a funny person (dag derives from 'daglock', an eighteenth century British word)

Dig deep — make a huge effort

Do it yourself — Kiwi home handyman's tradition of doing house repairs and renovations

Do one's block — to lose one's temper

Don't bust your boiler — don't overdo things

Don't get off your bike — don't lose your temper

Down the gurgler — a complete failure

Down the road — losing your job

Down to the wire — a very close finish in a sporting event

Duck's disease — being a short person

Dumb cluck — a stupid person

Educated boot — rugby player with an ability to kick the ball cleverly

Every man and his dog — a large crowd

Fat show — no chance

Feel like a spare prick at a wedding — feeling out-of-place

Fit as a buck rat — very fit

Flat to the boards — making maximum effort

Get in behind — do as you're told

Get off the grass! — exclamation of disbelief

Give it a bash — have a go

Goneburger — something or someone with no chance

Good night, nurse! — no way back

Gutless wonder — a useless person

Half-pie — not properly done

Hard cheese — bad luck

Head down, arse up — working hard

Hit the sack — to go to bed

Hit the spot — when something has exactly the desired effect

Home and hosed — safe and sound

Hosed off — upset

Huckery — unpleasant, undesirable, rough and ready

Humdinger — something outstanding

Humungous — huge

I didn't come down in the last shower — I'm not a fool

If you can't be good, be careful — advice to take precautions

In the dogbox — in disgrace

Judder bars — haemorrhoids

Just a tick — in a moment

Just quietly — a confidential remark

Kick it in the guts — to become more assertive

Knock it on the head — stop, complete a job

Let her rip — get something started

Lift your game — play better

Like a dog's dinner — a mess

Like a robber's dog — very keenly

Like a stunned mullet — stupid or dazed

Like balls on a ballerina — inappropriate

Like Brown's cows — disorderly

Lippy — cheeky

Little beauty — excellent person

Mad as a meat axe — very angry or psychologically unbalanced

Mates' rates — lower rates based on friendship

Mondayitis — workers' blues at the beginning of the working week

Munted — broken

Murder house — school dental clinic

Ngati Pakeha — New Zealand European

Nippon clipon — Japanese-made extensions to the Auckland Harbour Bridge

No beg pardons — vigorous approach, particularly in sporting situations

North Cape to the Bluff — full coverage of New Zealand

Not much chop — an unimpressive thing or person

Not too foul — good

Not within a bull's roar — not even close

Not worth a brass razoo — worthless

On the bones of your arse — at a low ebb financially

On the knocker — on time

On the pig's back — in a very comfortable aspect

One sheep to the acre — a dim-witted person

Out the back — an outside toilet

Pack a sad — to become morose

Pavs and savs (pavlovas and saveloys) — traditional New Zealand party food

Pay through the nose — excessive price to pay

Pig out — to eat copiously

Piker — someone who opts out

Piss easy — very easy

Piss in someone's pocket — to crawl for favours

Poorman's orange — New Zealand grapefruit

Puckerooed — broken

Pull finger — hurry up

Pull your head in — stop being outspoken

Quite nicely — pleasantly drunk

Rabbit killer — a karate-style blow to the back of the human neck

Ratshit — something in bad condition

Rattle your dags — hurry up ('dags' in this case referring to the dags — dried faeces — hanging on a sheep's backside that rattle when they run)

Ropeable — very angry

Rottenrua — Rotorua, because of its sulphurous smell

Rough as guts — very rough

Rugger bugger — rugby fan

Running around like a blue-arsed fly — dithering

Ruthanasia — Finance Minister Ruth Richardson's heartless welfare cuts policy

Scarce as hens' teeth — rare

Shark and taties — fish and chips

She'll be apples — it'll be alright.

She's Jake — everything's alright

Shit a brick! — bloody hell!

Silly as a piece of string — funny, humorous

Silly as a two-bob watch — extremely silly

Sitting up like Jacky — behaving well

Slackarse — lazy

Spitting the dummy — showing petulance

Squeal like a stuck pig — complain excessively

Stiff cheese — bad luck

Stiff out of luck — unlucky

Swamp foxes — the Thames Valley rugby team

Taiho — wait

Taiho the land court — take it easy

Talking to a brick wall — talking to an unresponsive person

Tall poppy — a Kiwi achiever who arouses 'egalitarian' envy

Tall timber — a rugby term for tall lineout forwards

Taranaki top-dressing — cow dung

The cuts — corporal punishment

The good oil — inside information

The great Kiwi clobbering machine — the way Kiwis tend to stifle individuality

The greatest thing since sliced bread — outstanding

The Shicker Express — the first tram home after six o'clock closing

The whole box and dice — everything

Thugby — uncomplimentary term for rugby football

Tits in a tangle — in trouble or over-emotional

To cark — to die

To charge like a wounded bull — to charge excessive prices

To come a gutser — to come to grief

To get the willies — to get very nervous

To go for the doctor — to run really fast

To go ninety to the dozen — to do something really fast

To go to the pack — to deteriorate

To have a bob each way — hedging your bets

To kick for touch — to avoid confrontation

To rev up — to stimulate

To throw a wobbly — to lose your temper

Toey — fast and agitated

Towie — a tow truck operator

Trap for young players — a danger to inexperienced people

Tukus — expensive male underwear

Two bob each way — hedging your bets

Up-and-under — a high kick in rugby

Up large — excessively

Up the boohai — a remote place

Up the duff — pregnant

Up your nose with a rubber hose — gesture of rejection

Verbal diarrhoea — excessive talking

Weak as weasels — very weak

Weak as weasels' pee — very weak (cup of tea)

Wopwops — a place very much off the beaten track

Wouldn't know shit from clay — a dim-witted person

You can put a ring around that one — you can be certain of that

Zits — acne pimples

Some Viewers May Find These Offensive . . .

New Zealand sex slang

A naughty — sexual intercourse

Bang — sexual intercourse

Black/brown velvet — an offensive term for Maori women as sexual objects

Boat girl — prostitute working on ships

Boiled weiner — erection

Bonking — sexual intercourse

Call girl — prostitute

Carnie — a nubile girl under the lawful age for sexual connection

Cock-happy — a randy male

Crack it — a woman providing sexual intercourse

Dolly — a lesbian prison inmate's fancy woman

Donald Duck — rhyming slang for fuck

Donger — the penis

Double-banger — a woman of intense sexual response

Duffed — pregnant

Dyke — a lesbian

Eat sausage — to engage in fellatio

Fat — an erection

Frenchie — a condom

Frog — a condom

Goolies — testicles

Gripper — a male masturbater

Hard-on — erection

Hide the salami — sexual intercourse

Hooters — female breasts

Huckery moll — sexually promiscuous woman

Humping — sexual intercourse

Jugs — female breasts

Knockers — female breasts

Knocking shop — brothel

Mince — ship-girls' expression for working several boats in port

Mrs — a female prisoner's name for a young lesbian partner

Nookie — sexual intercourse

Parsnip — erection

Poke — sexual intercourse

Pole — erection

Rajah — erection

Rising to the occasion — erection

Root — sexual intercourse

Sausage and eggs — male genitalia

Schoolie — nubile school-age girl

Shaft — sexual intercourse

Shag — sexual intercourse

Shepherd's grummet — a sheep as sexual object

Stiffy — erection

Turn it up — for a woman to allow sexual intercourse

Well hung — well-endowed male

Willie — penis

Namely . . .

New Zealand names

Appropriate business names
Fitness, the chemist
Forsyte, the optometrist
Jim Butcher, the butcher
Petals, the florist
Pullar, the physiotherapist
The mad butcher

Inappropriate business names
Baker's Butchery

Rhyming names
Bevan Bevan
Doris Morris
Gary Barry
Graeme Graham
Harry Barry
Helen Allan
Jenny Penny
Joe Rowe
Martha Arthur
Maurice Morris
William Williams

The Great Oudoors

Signs on toilet doors

Jents
No admittance except on business
Laddies
Laydies
Toilet closed after ours

The Great Indoors

Toilet graffiti

'Shit happens.'
'Poo Bear was here.'
'Wee Willie Winkie hangs out here.'
'Spending a penny? What a way to invest your money.'
'I love Bruce.'
'Do drop Inn.'
'Go for it.'
'Whatever you do at home, don't try it here.'
'Everybody's doing it.'
'Leave the lid up if you like that sort of thing.'
'Whatever gets you through the night.'
'Whatever gets you through the wall.'
'If you can read this perhaps you're a frequenter.'
'Napolean was here. So was Josephine.'

Unmentionables

Undergarment colloquialisms

Underdungers
Tukus
Dungers
Grunds
Grundies
Knickers

Trespassers Will Be Persecuted

Signage of the times

'Staff only. No pubic entry.'
'Do not throw stones at this sign.'
'No public throughfare.'
'Keep out and off the ladder.'
'No swimming aloud.'
'Please don't conserve with the driver.'
'This door may not be open.'
'Trespassers will be persecuted.'
'Pavement rehabilitation.'
'Please slow down and be prepared to shop.'
'Dogs unallowed.'
'Beware off the dog.'
'No junk male.'
'Wimmin only.'
'Stop detour.'
'Mental surface.'
'School bus root.'
'Beware falling debras.'
'Beware of falling fruit.'
'Hi winds.'
'Please swim between the flogs.'
'Extreme car.'
'Diary cows crossing.'
'No admittance please.'
'If you can read this you're not illiterate.'
'Baby on bored.'
'Forget about the dog. Beware of the owner.'
'Beware of the duck.'
'No dogs or children unless on a leash.'

For Those Times When English is Not Enough

Jargon

Pushing the envelope — to challenge the boundaries, although logically it is a primary function of posties
A window of opportunity — an opportunity
Window — an opportunity
Transparent — no information withheld
Transparent window — transparent opportunity
Cascading — information being released
Hardwire — a firm commitment
Level playing field — everyone has the same opportunity
Moving the goalposts — underhanded changing of the rules or parameters
At the end of the day — in conclusion
A line in the sand — a clear demarcation
Pro-active — showing initiative
The big picture — the overview, the totality of a situation
Gaining traction — making progress
Closure — a conclusion, often emotional, being reached
Downsizing — reducing services; closing operations
Up-skilling — learning new skills
Thinking outside the square — thinking laterally
Dumbed down — made less intelligent
Workshopping — attending courses or seminars
Networking — getting to know advantageous people
Mentoring — to be assisted into a role

Retail therapy — wanton shopping to take your mind off more pressing commitments

Pavement rehabilitation — road works

Horizontal violence — bullying in the workplace amongst co-workers

I hear what you're saying — I'm not really interested

I hear where you're coming from — I'm not really interested

Don't go there — Don't evaluate taboo (PC) subjects

Vertically-challenged — short

Differently-abled — not normal

Worst-case scenario — worst possible result

Outcomes — results

Road rage — absurd anger amongst drivers

Self-esteem — self-confidence

Clean stadia — sports grounds free of unfavoured advertising

Weather bomb — a destructive storm

Alcoholically-disadvantaged — drunk

Sartorially-disadvantaged — naked

Stop the World

Distinctive Kiwi placards seen in public places

'All men are created equal — except women.'

'All men are not women.'

'Bob's your uncle — Burt's your aunty.'

'Botham takes it up the Bottom.'

'Bring back Back.'

'Bring back Boock.'

'Bring back Buck.'

'Helen Clark is a big girl.'

'Hi Boss. I've got a medical certificate.'

'Hi Mum, Hi Dad, Hi Uncle Adolf.'

'Kick it to the shithouse, Malcolm.'

'Men cause everything.'

'Muldoon is a bully.'

'Paula. Please ring me after the game.'

'Start the tour.'

'Stop the tour, ban the bomb, kick a cop, punch a pom.'

'Stop the tour.'

'Support the Civil Onion Bill.'

QUOTATIONS

Caught in Two/Too Many Minds

'I've put on five pounds this year. It all went to my head.' — *David Lange*

'Half of the Ngai Tahu Trust Board was out (protesting) with us and the other half was sitting in the stand.' — *Tipene O'Regan in 1981, highlighting the complex divisiveness created by the Springbok tour*

'The Labour Party has never opposed efficiency as far as I'm aware.'— *Sir Roger Douglas*

'It's not two men and a budgie.' — *Pastor Rob Wheeler, Chairman of the National Party, Mt Albert branch, 1986, speaking about the 'ideal' family against the background of Homosexual Law Reform*

'We didn't even know they existed.' — *Colin Reynolds, executive director of New Zealand's 1980s financial darling, Chase Corporation, when it was suggested that his organisation owed its name to US bank, Chase Manhattan*

'Men were all part of the abusing, raping, destructive patriarchy. Women together have an exchange of energy and honesty and intelligence that is undeniably erotic.' — *Marilyn Waring*

'As political halfback behind a beaten pack, he was thoroughly hardened to going down in the face of dangerous rushes and revealed his greatest talent for defence in 1932–35.' — *A political colleague of PM George Forbes*

'I have no intention of buying one of these new CD burners. I'm quite happy with an open fire.' — *Technologically-challenged local body politician*

'Size doesn't matter. Even a minor quake can cause damage.' — *Seismologist*

'The winger was caught in too many minds.' — *Rugby broadcaster, Murray Mexted*

'I can smell the uranium on your breath.' — *David Lange*

'I'd like to kick their balls off every day.' — *A visiting dignitary after kicking the ball off to commence a charity rugby game*

'After officially opening the new bridge, the royal party waved to the large crowd of onlookers before pissing off the bridge.'— *Unfortunate misprint in a local newspaper*

Say Wot U Meen

Dumbed down, or just dumb, statements

'There's no way I'll vote for Winston Churchill.' (Peters)

'Antipasto. That's that Middle Eastern terrorist group isn't it?'

'The cock-less 4s have an outside chance in the rowing.'

'All you have to do is arks.'

'At no time did I never say that.'

'It wasn't me, officer. I have a watertight abili.'

'For goodness sake get on the car-car.'

'Unaccustard as I am to public speaking . . . '

'Without further adoes . . . '

'I'll finish up smairly fartly . . . '

A Stable Diet of Three Veg and Something Dead

Media gaffes and misprints and oddities

'A large bosoming sound signalled the demolition of the old building.'

'The aviary included twits, tom-tits and cock-robins.'

'Ian Bottom was a great all-rounder.'

'Adequate athletic support is the bottom line as far as we're concerned.'

'A 20-carrot gold ring was among the stolen items.'

'At a lively pubic meeting the mayor was forced to field some curly ones.'

'A tot of bum before a big game never went astray.'

'Snubbing the royal party was below the belt. It showed a complete lack of curtsy.'

'Full marks to the local fire brigade,' said Gareth Smith the piggery manager. 'They really saved our bacon.'

'Such behaviour was decidedly abnorman,' the police spokesman said.

'There's still a lot of unclaimed stiff among the debris.'

'Many motorists come across as being very carless at intersections.'

'Ruff Raff is virtually a Kiwi icon.'

'It's up to the referee to decide if a player is playing the man and not the balls.'

'Freshly prepared, nutritious meal with wait service.'

'There's no such word as carnt.'

'It's time we meat up again,' a member of the mayoral party added.

'It was obvious the patient wasn't taking his meditation.'

'The way the bar had adapted to the no-smoking legislation was matchless.'

'The jury found the witless was fabricating evidence.'

'The report was as facial as possible.'

'Pie, peace and puds were still a restaurant stable.'

'A stable diet of three veg and something dead belongs to another area.'

'As well as larger pies, the bakery is now producing smaller goods like pasties, fatties and savouries.'

'It is gratifying that, within the sewing circle, many of the older women are still wonderfully ornate sewers.'

'As far as he was concerned everything was shit-shape prior to the store's opening.'

'The final score was Chelsea 1, Arse nil.'

'A child fare is payable if a child under the age of four occupies a seat at berth.'

'All train prices, turntables and products listed in this brochure are subject to change.'

'In this case the ambulance did end up at the foot of the cliff. Luckily none of the St John's people were seriously injured.'

'The All Blacks played out of their skids.'

'He had a bad attack of the runs on the Pakistan leg of the tour. They were the only runs he got. Very few came off the bat.'

'The greatest thing I could possibly give is my guts.'

'We have hard-wired the ring fence funding.'

'Our policies are transparent. All communication will be cascaded.'

'The Omega 3 was not a trio of SIS-hounded hoodlums, but the name of health-giving oils found in oily fish like mackerel, sardines and errings.'

'Rodney County is a friend of mine. It isn't just an era north of Auckland.'

'It's obvious someone's shifted the foalposts. Its not a level playing field out there.'

'The home side were found wanting in scum and ruck.'

'As the ball struck the up-tight you could sense the mood of the visitors changing.'

'If you pick your nose at home, that's no excuse to pick it in pubic.'

'We have noticed that beast cancer is well documented in this country, but what about the incidence of prostrate cancer?'

'The jury, having considered its verdick, declared the accused not guilty.'

'Following the break-in the shop owners had to call on the services of a carpenter and a cock-smith.'

'Poo Bear is still one of the children's favourite stories.'

'The defendant pleaded guilty to the charge of supplying false pissports.'

'The growth in the number of religious sex is a sign that New Zealanders are not happy with established religions.'

'Urine, women and song. The age-old trilogy — as sacred to some Kiwis as rugby, racing and bear — was in evidence at the week-long celebration.'

'Guy Fawkes night has become so neutered that I reckon a sensitive new age guy is up there on the bonfire.'

'Some New Zealand women have declared they prefer shipping to sex.'

'The loss of many of our most qualified people overseas is just a continuation of the brian drain.'

'WC Fields could be the name of a local septic tank provider, but I'm not in a position to postulate.'

'The defendant avoided a murder charge but was found guilty of mans laughter.'

'Initially the skydiver's parachite wouldn't open.'

'He may be thickset, but he's also just thick,' the disappointed coach announced.

'The new captain was considered to be too tin-skinned to excel in such a role.'

'Thrash' is a possible side-affect of tight-fitting clothes.

'The councillor announced that hencefilth there would be more consultation.'

'Grass Beatles were becoming more than a nuisance in parts of New Zealand.'

'We were clearly out-played,' the visiting coach said. 'It was not a case of throwing in the trowel.'

'"Tobacko", as a word, will eventually disappear from the English language in New Zealand.'

'The Queen Street rot of 1984 was all about too much booze.'

'Although he wasn't of leaving age, he left stool early.'

'He was a touchy-feely sort of parson.'

'After losing the election he felt like dropping out altogether and becoming a trapeze monk.'

'"Man overboard" is technically politically incorrect.'

'The left wing had a clear overlip, but somehow managed to drop the ball.'

'Ship-lifting is rife at this time of year,' the police spokesperson said.

'Sex replacements in rep rugby side. Five new caps.'

'It appears the accident victim fell down the steers.'

'It was a bit like being moroned on a desert island,' one flood victim claimed.

'The man was admitted to hospital with a broken leg and punctured lunge.'

'Such an undertaking is not a priority, the mayor announced. 'It's certainly not on my wish lust.'

'Badminton is an undemanding game. All you need is a racquet, shittlecock and a sense of fair play.'

'Such an undertaking is beyond comprehension,' the undertaker revealed when asked about the disposal of so many bodies.

'There's no reason why this selection shouldn't do really well. The team is bumming with talent.'

'Although the media made strenuous efforts to contact Mr Lindsay, they were informed that he was still on animal leave.'

'Lymphs and Shepherds' is still one of New Zealand's most popular Christmas carols.

'The successful appellants were also entitled to a lum sump payment.'

'Lockjaw is a common symptom of tetanus.'

'Soon New Zealanders will be eating more lice than potatoes.'

'The surveyor's theodolittlewas damaged in the altercation.'

'Sea-girl drop-pings can be very corrosive.'

'To complete the cycle rinse in lukeworm water.'

'The member was still in the loop although there appeared to be a loophole in the system.'

'Exterior touch-ups are a piece of cake,' he reckoned. 'All it takes is a good scrub and a flick of paint.'

'What more could you want for a kiwi get-away-from-it all holiday? Native bush, bird song and limp water.'

'We have a tendency in New Zealand to loinize anyone who wears a black jersey,' she said.

'The titmus test for such a procedure has yet to be refined.'

'A rump sum payment was made in such cases,' the ACC officer announced.

'Its common for casual workers to pack a sucky after New Year's Eve celebrations,' he said.

'The victim was stubbed in the back while standing by the cigarette machine.'

ARCHITECTURE

Of Beehives and Mirror-glass Canyons

In 1832, the initial section of the Waitangi Treaty House was imported from Sydney.

Kemp House, New Zealand's oldest surviving building, was regarded as superior to the wooden houses of Hampstead, England.

In 1841, Governor Hobson laid the foundation stone for St Paul's church in Auckland, the first Gothic Revival building in New Zealand.

Sampson Kempthorne, one of the first members of the Institute of British Architects, came to live in New Zealand in 1842.

Rangiatea church, Otaki, an outstanding Maori church, was built in 1848.

The City of Auckland Building Act of 1856 prohibited the use of wood for building in the central city because of the incidence of fire.

Dunedin's First Church was built between 1868 and 1873.

In the early 1870s, poured concrete, steel beams and cast-iron columns were introduced into New Zealand construction.

Followers of Te Kooti built the Te Tokanganui a Noho marae at Te Kuiti in 1870. It has been rebuilt five times.

In 1871, William Larnach began building his castle on the Otago Peninsula.

WH Clayton was granted the title of Colonial Architect in 1876.

Rua Kenana built a round temple at Maungapohatu, that featured, instead of Maori carvings, painted patterns taken from playing cards.

Gilbert Scott was commissioned to design the Christchurch Cathedral.

A large, brick, T-shaped woolshed was built at Homebush, Canterbury.

Followers of the Maori prophet Te Ua built

a large temple in the shape of a crucifix at Te Tiroa in the King Country.

JBA Acland commissioned architect Frederick Strouts to oversee the building of his large Mt Peel homestead in rural Canterbury.

In 1904, the Government Bathhouse was built at Rotorua.

As a precursor to state housing, the Workers Dwellings Act of 1905 empowered the Minister of Labour to build workers houses. Unfortunately, the architect-designed houses were regarded as 'too swell' for workers and proved difficult to let.

The Dunedin Railway Station, built in 1907, was essentially of the Flemish Renaissance style and designed by New Zealander Gordon Troup.

Parliament Buildings were destroyed by fire in 1907.

The foundation stone of the Auckland Chief Post Office was laid in 1911.

The Californian Mission-style Auckland Grammar School was completed in 1916.

A garden suburb was planned at Papanui, Christchurch, in 1919, made up of 55 roughcast, tile-roofed houses grouped like an English village.

Auckland's great 'picture palace', the Civic, was ready for business in 1929.

Recovery work in Napier and Hastings following the 1931 earthquake left a remarkable art-deco legacy. The earthquake also led to more stringent building codes in case of further earthquakes.

Multi-storeyed New Zealand buildings became increasingly popular with the advent of electric lifts.

Wellington Railway Station was one of the first large buildings constructed after the Great Depression.

More than 10,000 state houses were built in the first three years of the Labour Government's state housing policy.

The Beehive extension to Parliament Buildings took a decade to complete.

Poho o Rawiri, in Gisborne, is thought to be the first meeting house to use steel for its ridge pole.

In 1961, the Futuna Chapel in Karori, Wellington, was completed, using the voluntary labour of priests, assisted by the architect.

When the Auckland City Council's administration building was opened in 1966 it was the tallest building in Auckland at the time.

In 1979, Sir George Grey's restored Mansion House on Kawau Island was opened for public viewing.

The Wellington Town Hall, known as the Michael Fowler Centre, was opened in 1983.

Mirror-glass citadels, the 'pyramids of the yuppies', emerged in the wake of 'Rogernomics'. Cheap and nasty, they represented a mindset that had little to do with architectural beauty or even practical functionality.

Well-built

New Zealand Institute of Architects Awards

NZIA awards made for public buildings

1990 Television Centre for TVNZ, Auckland
1990 Wellington City Council Rental Housing
1990 Old Synagogue Conversion, Auckland
1991 Saint Margaret's Junior School, Christchurch
1991 Department of Health, Wellington
1991 Salvation Army Citadel, Wellington
1991 Municipal Chambers Redevelopment, Dunedin
1993 Extensions to Student Union Building, Victoria University, Wellington
1993 Wellington Library, Civic Centre, Wellington
1993 James Stewart Building, Lincoln University, Christchurch
1994 Bodhinyanarama Meditation Hall and Cloister, Wellington
1994 Eskdale School Hall, Hawke's Bay
1994 Christchurch Railway Station
1994 City Gallery, Wellington
1995 Jackson Bay and Ship Creek Activity Centres, South Westland
1995 Schools of Architecture and Design, Wellington
1996 Order of St John Central Ambulance Station, Auckland
1997 Refurbishment of Parliament Buildings, Wellington
1998 Sky Tower, Auckland
1998 Palmerston North Public Library
1999 Human History Discovery Centre, Auckland Museum
1999 Mathematics and Computer Science Building, University of Canterbury
2000 Christchurch Pier Terminus/New Brighton Library
2000 Westpac Trust Stadium, Wellington
2000 Refurbishment of Auckland War Memorial Museum: Te Papa Whakahiku
2001 New Gallery Building, Auckland
2001 Longbeach School, Auckland

25-year awards

1990 Christchurch Memorial Garden Crematorium
1995 Auckland Synagogue and Community Centre
1996 International House, Student Housing, Auckland
1998 Wanganui War Memorial Hall
1999 Lyttelton Road Tunnel Authority Building, Christchurch
1999 Manchester Unity Building, Christchurch

HOROSCOPES FROM HELL

Outcomes and Incomes

With Mars in your aspect, and the prospect of the seventh house (you are a property owner, right?), becoming conflagrated, don't expect kindness from insurance companies. On the home front, the back might be the best place to be. If you are in a relationship don't expect flavours, unless they reek of the east.

The Ram is a ramshackle lover, so don't expect perfection. The best will in the world won't save your inheritance either. Look beyond the obvious and marry your local optometrist. For the optimistic Ram, the best outlook is a pair of tri-focals, or a three-piece.

You will receive an opportunity that, while it may not be attractive, will bequeath certain advantages or disadvantages — given that the bull is invariably bi-polar. And speaking of polar bears, as bulls often do, or thinking about them at the very least, there could be some interpersonal rutting involved before the opportunity will manifest itself.

Don't be nonplussed by events of the past fortnight. A week in hell is less than a week in heaven. And don't be afraid of purgatory. It's often a good place to dump a load of emotional garbage. Local authorities might stake you out, but as long as your rubbish is well sealed and concealed, all will be revealed.

Someone could come along with an ambiguous offer to lighten your load, or light your bungalow. Do not feel overwhelmed by the whimsicality of the offer, even though you may perceive it as such. As much as you would like to have your way lightened or lit, bear in mind that the powers that be, that is, the Power Board, have the upper hand, and the lower, so be prepared to call your feet into action. Fight or flight is optional quicksand, but it is a path that many of us fear to tread in Hush Puppies, the better to keep the baying dogs of local government at bay.

You have been worrying too much in recent weeks, all to little avail, so perhaps the time is right to throw off the white yolk of mood and go for the red heart of the matter. If you can't change a situation, just remember that the invasion of Poland was inevitable and 9/11 had a certain ring to it. Richard Hadlee's bowling figures against Mongolia were worrying — but only for the Mongolians. So step out, step aside, do the two-step in your own time, and you will find that your bowling figures, 36-24-36, are no less worrying than the time it takes to fly a wide-bodied Boeing into a pyramid.

Saturn has dominated your chart since a few weeks back. Soon it will be satin — and silk — and, if you are that way inclined, cashmere cumberbunds. Or Kashmir. Politics and fashion do mix, as you will find. Throw off the yolk of servitude, cast off the clothes that caste. Nakedness has its own reward — and fines — so flick your pinstripe cares to the wind. Fly in the face of authority, and whatever other body parts that may confront you. Stay positive, but don't take that finger out of the wall socket.

Become real. Actualise and realise. Your outcomes are as critical — and equal — as your income, so it's the side-comes you have to internalise. Hardwire that ring fence until it screams for deliverance. Touch your fellow man — or fellow person — or rather woman person — with all the vehemence and workshopping you can muster. And shop — 'til you drop a cog — or sprog — although childlessness is cool and as random as mentors in the halls of change. Just remember, your house is closely aligned with the mall at this time and that means superfluous purchases are not as ribald or follicly challenged as you are inclined to imagine.

Saturn, as the sign of discipline, is telling you to realign, in terms of the astral

sphincter, so expect a rain of spectral droppings. Try not to walk under flocks of geese; avoid the pigeon-populated fountains and founts of youth outside the latte citadels and flat white facades. Be prepared to be manacled and thrown around the basement floor, but realise that this is just a precursor to winning Lotto and inheriting Tranzrail.

Try not eating. Avoid alcohol. Smoke OPs. Avoid air. Try not to fly, especially on an empty stomach. Avoid thoughts that lead to action. Limit movement of any kind. Blink wisely. Don't build that downloaded bomb — yet. Watch TV with the sound turned down, and the image fuzzed by a total abrogation of electricity.

Something you say may be taken the wrong way. Try singing in public places instead. Embrace karaoke and any other Asian mystic. Kiss the drummer. Rumble with the king of rock. Exhume John Lennon. And remember that Buddy Holly is not dead. He has just passed over — on a new flight to Iowa. Despite a lack of words, the music will speak for itself.

Just when you feel you have the world at your feet, your chiropodist declares that you have two left feet. Waltz right on out of there and take up arms against a sea of flotsam and jetsam. Your flotilla may waver and even capsize, but your arms, fully extended, will weather the storm. Whether your wethers and other offshoots of sheep-slaying will find dry land is all down to a number of fathoms under the sea — unfathomable, a dry argument indeed. Drink more piss.

Your life is all about taking, not giving, so don't forget to not give a shit about the wastrels and minstrels singing in your neck of the woods; your back of beyond; your finger on the pulse; your cock of the roost; your ear of corn be it tin or otherwise. Remember Tom waits for no man. Nor woman, but quite Frankly Sinatra didn't have sin in his name for nothing.

With Mars in your aspect there is no hope. A collision of deathly proportions will see you obliterated and vaporised, before you can undertake that long weekend in Iraq you so richly deserve.

Aries is kind-hearted, but that will not stop you being attacked and left for dead — dead in fact — outside your favourite charity. Get your house in order but then Arians are inveterately tidy anyway.

You will be the subject of suspicion, innuendo and thrown out a window. This is all designed to test the crabs' claws. Hang on in there. Hang on to anything. Express emotion where appropriate.

You have never been more vivacious. Give your favours willingly. Stand on street corners in heliotrope tights — and nothing else. Take the plunge in lycra cutaways. Feel the thrum of quivering flesh in mid-winter minus degrees.

Ever the practical Scorpion, build a house tomorrow before it's too late. Leaky roof syndrome may be looming, but if you don't build a house, something will happen to your children.

That unusual knocking sound you heard in your car's engine is in fact a death rattle. This is unavoidable. Ride it out and hope for the best. Remain positive when all your negatives remain undeveloped. Life is more than just a flash in the pan. (Remember to keep that lid up if you're a non-woman.)

Everything you touch turns to gold. Water turns to petrol. Three loaves and various fishes become fish and chips. Don't hit a gift horse in the mouth, particularly if it's running in the fifth at Ellerslie. You might need to ask it a favour once the Midas touch has gone.

OFFICIAL ABBREVIATIONS

Of CAB and TAB and OSH

ACC — Accident Compensation Corporation

AIDS — Acquired Immune Deficiency Syndrome

AIR — Accident Insurance Regulator

ANZCERTA — Australia New Zealand Closer Economic Relations Trade Agreement

ANZIC — Australian and New Zealand Standard Industrial Classification

ANZUS — Australia, New Zealand and United States security treaty

APEC — Asia Pacific Economic Co-operation

ASEAN — Association of South-East Asian Nations

BDM — Births, Deaths and Marriages

BIPM — Bureau of weights and measures

BRANZ — Building Research Association of New Zealand

CAB — Citizens' Advice Bureau

CCMAU — Crown Company Monitoring Advisory Unit

CER — Australia and New Zealand

Closer Economic Relations

CPI — Consumer Price Index

CSD — Commission on Sustainable Development

CYFS — Department of Child, Youth and Family Services

EAB — External Assessment Bureau

EEO — Equal Employment Opportunities Trust

EEZ — Exclusive Economic Zone

EFTS — Equivalent Full-Time Student

ERMA — Environmental Risk Management Authority

ERO — Education Review Office

ESR — Institute of Environmental Science and Research Ltd

FMD — Foot and Mouth Disease

FRST — Foundation for Research, Science and Technology

FTE — Full-time equivalent

GAAP — Generally Accepted Accounting Practice

GDP — Gross Domestic Product

GNI — Gross National Income

GNS — Institute of Geological and Nuclear Science

GST — Goods and Services Tax

HIV — Human Immunodeficiency Virus

IBAC — Independent Biotechnology Advisory Council

ICAO — International Civil Aviation Organisation

LINZ — Land Information New Zealand

LTSA — Land Transport Safety Authority

MAF — Ministry of Agriculture and Forestry

MED — Ministry of Economic Development

MFAT — Ministry of Foreign Affairs and Trade

MMP — Mixed Member Proportional

MoRST — Ministry of Research, Science and Technology

NIWA — National Institute of Water and Atmospheric Research Ltd

NRWT — Non-resident withholding tax

NZCER — New Zealand Council for Educational Research

NZQA — New Zealand Qualifications Authority

NZSO — New Zealand Symphony Orchestra

NZST — New Zealand standard time

OECD — Organisation of Economic Co-operation and Development

ONZ — Order of New Zealand

OSH — Occupational Safety and Health

PACER — Pacific Agreement on Closer Economic Relations

PAYE — Pay as you earn

PEN NZ — New Zealand Society of Authors

PHARMAC — The Pharmaceutical Management Agency

REAP — Rural Education Activities Programme

RIANZ — Recording Industry Association of New Zealand

SFO — Serious Fraud Office

SIDS — Sudden Infant Death Syndrome

SIS — Security Intelligence Service

SOI — Southern oscillation index

SPARTECA — South Pacific Regional Trade and Economic Co-operation Agreement

STAR — Secondary Tertiary Alignment Resource

TAB — Totalisator Agency Board

TAC — Total Allowable Catch

TACC — Total Allowable Commercial Catch

TEAC — Tertiary Education Advisory Commission

TUANZ — Telecommunications Users' Association of New Zealand

TWI — Trade weighted index

FUNDRAISING

Bull Rides and Burn-outs

**Activities involving an entry fee, with
a cash prize for the winner**

Bed-racing
Black-water rafting
Busking in the mall
Climbing mountains
Come as you are
Egg-and-spoon race
Hair curling on frozen Otago Lakes
Halfback hurling
Home-brew guzzling
Hunger marathons and fasting
Mid-winter swimming in Otago
Most people in a phone booth
Mufti days
Novelty wine tasting
Oyster eating
Pie-throwing
Pigging out on nominated food items
Progressive dinners
Raincoats in summer
Sheep racing
Skydiving
Sleep deprivation
Stone skimming
Trick or treat
Tug-of-war
Underwear days

Wearable art
Wearable food
Wearable garbage
White-water rafting

Activities involving a product to sell

All-day breakfasts, with no breaks for
    meals
Cake stalls
Car-boot sales
Christmas tree sales
Firewood sales
Garage sales
Golf balls retrieved from golf course
water traps
Novelty sausage sizzles — utilising hot
    pavements, car engines and corrugated
    iron roofs
Sausage sizzles
Selling garages

Raffle Items

Bottles of Hokonui
Clamped cars
Ex-All Blacks

Home-made Chardonnay
Home-made chilli goop
Pukeko soup
Sides of beef
Spiked cakes

Celebrity Auction items

Colin Meads' empties
Famous underwear
Helen Clark's address book
Sir Edmund Hillary's old newspapers

Awards involving an entry fee, with a cash prize for the winner

Outstanding body scars
The closest-set eyes
The flattest feet
The knobbliest knees
The least amount of head hair
The longest toenails
The most head hair
The most outlandish haircut or style
The most protruding ears
The most unobtrusive buttocks
The slackest chin
The widest girth

Dangerous activities involving an entry fee and a cash prize for the survivor

Dressing up as a beggar
Fire eating
Home-made bungy jumps
Lucky dips in the Huka Falls
Raffling off the foreshore
Selling umbrellas in Wellington

Bizarre activities

Bogus religious appeals in pubs
Charging patrons to gain entrance to
    public toilets
Kidnapping cattle, with a ransom fee
Lingerie evenings for men
Nappy-changing races
Providing security at Sunday school
    picnics
Tupperware parties in the public bar
Underwater rafting

Activities involving a service for a fee

Bob-a-job
Building demolition
Bull rides
Burn-outs in Queen Street
Car-cleaning on motorway off-ramp
Donkey rides
Doughnuts in Courtney Place
Mazda 323 rides
Painting houses

REALLY IMPORTANT TRIVIA

The Highest and the Flightless

The moa was a flightless bird found only in New Zealand until 1400–1500 AD, when it became extinct. The largest moa was 3.5 metres in height, the largest bird that ever lived.

The Maori had no word for themselves as a race, calling themselves 'maori' or 'ordinary' people, as opposed to foreigners. British settlers, after 1835, began calling them 'Maoris'.

When the old-age pension was introduced in New Zealand in 1898, it was the first of its kind in the world.

In World War II, New Zealand had the highest percentage of men in arms, the greatest percentage posted overseas, and highest percentage killed, of all the Allied nations.

New Zealand's first national flag was that of the 'Independent Tribes of New Zealand', in 1834.

The International Date Line passes about 160 kilometres east of Gisborne.

The average weekly wage for New Zealanders in 1906 was: males: one pound, 16 shillings and fivepence; females: 16 shillings and threepence.

Lake Taupo was formed about 130 AD.

Christchurch is built on the old bed of the Waimakariri River.

Five New Zealand Prime Ministers have died in office: John Balance (1893), Richard John Seddon (1906), William Ferguson Massey (1925), Michael Joseph Savage (1940), and Norman Eric Kirk (1974).

The *Edmonds Cookery Book* is the biggest-selling New Zealand book.

In the 1920s, Lloyd Mandeno invented the single-wire earth-return power reticulation system, which enabled electric power to be distributed economically to remote areas.

Shooting is the oldest officially recognised sport in New Zealand.

The New Zealand kotukutuku or tree fuchsia is the largest fuchsia in the world.

The world's largest forget-me-not is found in the Chatham Islands.

The smallest small business in New Zealand is a hostess agency that operates from an Auckland phone box.

Bibliography

Bromby, Robin. *Rails that Built a Nation*, Grantham House, Wellington, 2003.

Burton, David. *The New Zealand Cheese Book*, Reed Methuen, Auckland, 1988.

Cooper, Michael. *Wine Atlas of New Zealand*, Hodder Moa Beckett, Auckland, 2002.

Coppell, WG. *Sportspeak: an Encyclopedia of Sport*, Reed Reference of Australia, Port Melbourne, 1995.

Crimp, Daryl. *Hook, Line and Sinker*, HarperCollins, Auckland, 2003.

Crimp, Daryl. *The Wildfoods Cookbook*, Reed, Auckland, 2003.

Cryer, Max. *Curious Kiwi Words*, HarperCollins, Auckland, 2002.

Cryer, Max. *Day by Day*, Hodder Moa Beckett, Auckland, 1998.

Dix, John. *Stranded in Paradise*, Paradise Publications, Wellington, 1988.

Eames, Penny. *Fund-raising*, Random House, Auckland, 1995.

Eastaway, Rob. *What is a Googly?*, Robson Books, London, 1999.

Ell, Gordon. *An A–Z of Kiwi Fact and Folklore*, New Holland, Auckland, 2003.

Elliott, Matt. *Kiwi Jokers*, HarperCollins, Auckland, 1997.

Fielder, Alexander, Finnegan, Patrick & Lee, Tony. *Racing with Pacific*, Pacific Radio, Auckland, 2000.

Fraser, Bryce (editor). *New Zealand Book of Events*, Reed Methuen Publishing Ltd, Auckland, 1986.

Froude, Tony. *Reel Entertainment*, self-published, Paraparaumu, 2002.

Gossett, Robyn. *New Zealand Mysteries*, The Bush Press of New Zealand, Auckland, 1996.

Harris, Diana. *The Kiwi Fact Book*, Golden Press Pty Ltd, Auckland, 1989.

Hassall, Peter. *The New Zealand Files: UFOs in New Zealand*, David Bateman, Auckland, 1998.

Holden, Philip. *The Golden Years of Hunting in New Zealand*, Hodder & Stoughton, Auckland, 1983.

Howitt, Bob. *Rugby Greats*, Hodder Moa Beckett, Auckland, 2004.

Hutchins, Graham. *Rugby Shorts*, Celebrity Books, Auckland, 2001.

Ivory, Arthur EE. *SMS: Short Messaging Service Texting Dictionary*, Pacific index of abbreviations, Christchurch, 2001.

Jackson, Keith & McRobie, Alan. *Historical Dictionary of New Zealand*, Addison, Wesley, Longman New Zealand Ltd, Auckland, 1996.

Jackson, Philip. *Fighting Political Correctness*, Bounce Back, Auckland, 1996.

King, Michael. *The Penguin History of New Zealand*, Penguin, Auckland, 2003.

Knight, Lindsay. *The Shield*, Celebrity Books, Auckland, 2002.

McCrystal, John. *100 Years of Motoring in New Zealand*, Hodder Moa Beckett, Auckland, 2003.

McGill, David. *Ghost Towns of New Zealand*, Reed, Wellington, 1980.

McGill, David. *David McGill's Complete Kiwi Slang Dictionary*, Reed, Auckland, 1998.

McLachlan, Gordon (editor-in-chief). *New Zealand Encyclopedia* (Third Edition), David Bateman Ltd, Auckland, 1992.

McLauchlan, Gordon. *A Short History of New Zealand*, Penguin, Auckland, 2004.

McLintock, AH (Editor). *An Encyclopedia of New Zealand*, RE Owen,

Government Printer, Wellington, 1966.

Miller, Geoff. *The Reed Book of All Black Records, 1883–2003,* Reed, Auckland, 2003.

New Road Atlas of New Zealand, Beckett Publishing in association with Department of Survey & Land Information, Auckland, 1991.

New Zealand Herald Book of the Century, W & H Publications, Auckland, 1998.

Orsman, Harry. *A Dictionary of Modern New Zealand Slang,* Oxford University Press, Auckland, 1999.

Orsman, Harry. *Heinemann New Zealand Dictionary*, Heinemann, Auckland, 1989.

Palenski, Ron. *Century in Black,* Hodder Moa Beckett, Auckland, 2003.

Palenski, Ron. *Kiwi Milestones,* Hodder Moa Beckett, Auckland, 2004.

Reed, AW. *Two Hundred Years of New Zealand History,* AH and AW Reed Ltd, Wellington, 1979.

Rice, Geoffrey W (editor). *The Oxford History of New Zealand* (Second Edition), Oxford University Press, Auckland, 1992.

Romanos, Joseph. *New Zealand Sporting Records and Lists,* Hodder Moa Beckett, Auckland, 2001.

Salmon, JT. *Native New Zealand Flowering Plants,* Reed, Auckland, 1999.

Sibson, Richard B. *Birds at Risk,* Reed, Auckland, 1982.

Staff, Brian & Ashley, Sheran. *For the Record – A History of the Recording Industry in New Zealand,* David Bateman, Auckland, 2002.

Statistics New Zealand/David Bateman. *New Zealand Official Yearbooks,* Wellington.

Stewart, Graham. *When Trams were Trumps,* Grantham House, Wellington, 1985.

Stewart, Keith. *The Complete Guide to New Zealand Beer,* Craig Potton, Nelson, 2002.

Stratford, Stephen. *The Dirty Decade,* Tandem Press, Auckland, 2002.

Wilson, John. *AA Book of New Zealand Historic Places,* Lansdowne Rigby, Auckland, 1984.

Young, Sherwood. *Guilty on the Gallows,* Grantham House, Wellington, 1998.